THE FOREIGN POLICIES OF CARIBBEAN AND CENTRAL AMERICAN COUNTRIES

Selections from
PROSPEL's 1986 Anuario
LAS POLITICAS EXTERIORES DE
AMERICA LATINA Y EL CARIBE:
CONTINUIDAD EN LA CRISIS
edited by Heraldo Muñoz

Edited by Jane G. Marchi
with a Foreword by
Jaime Suchlicki

Published by the
Institute of Interamerican Studies
at the
Graduate School of International Studies
University of Miami

ISBN: 0-935501-22-3

THE GRADUATE SCHOOL OF INTERNATIONAL STUDIES

THE GRADUATE SCHOOL OF INTERNATIONAL STUDIES at the University of Miami was established with responsibility for (1) coordinating and developing work in the international field among various schools and departments of the University; (2) conducting interdisciplinary graduate courses in international affairs and organizing and administering interdisciplinary studies programs leading to a number of graduate degrees; and (3) conducting interdisciplinary research in international affairs. Fields of special academic and research emphasis are Latin American and Inter-American affairs; the Soviet Union and Eastern Europe and their interactions with U.S. interests; and the Middle East.

INSTITUTE OF INTERAMERICAN STUDIES

THE INSTITUTE OF INTERAMERICAN STUDIES coordinates studies at the Graduate level at the University of Miami. Graduate degrees offered include the MA, the Ph.D. and the Doctor of Arts in Interamerican Studies, interdisciplinary degrees combining a concentration on the traditional disciplines with an in-depth study of contemporary Latin American problems. The principal focus of the Institute's research and teaching activities is on U.S.-Latin American relations, U.S. foreign policy toward Latin America, and Latin American policies. The Institute publishes books monographs and occasional papers as well as two quarterlies, the prestigious *Journal of Interamerican Studies and World Affairs,* and *Contents of periodicals on Latin America,* a bibliographical aid that reproduces the tables of contents of over 100 journals and magazines dealing with Latin America. Public lectures and seminars are periodically held and the Institute staff responds often to requests from television, radio, newspapers and magazines for comment on international events.

THE FOREIGN POLICIES OF CARIBBEAN AND CENTRAL AMERICAN COUNTRIES

FOREWORD

In 1988, DURING A VISIT of Heraldo Muñoz to the Institute of Interamerican Studies, GSIS, of the University of Miami, we first discussed the possibility of bringing to a North American readership an English translation of PROSPEL's *Anuario* of Latin American foreign policies: LAS POLITICAS EXTERIORES LATINO-AMERICANAS Y EL CARIBE: CONTINUIDAD EN LA CRISIS.

In our innocence we vastly underestimated the time and expense that would be involved in translating and editing this very complete collection of 28 articles with accompanying appendices. Thus, to accomodate our limited resources, it was necessary to set limits to the projects. We chose to concentrate on a given region: foreign policies of those countries that are located in Central America and the Caribbean. This is how Latin American analysts and scholars viewed the situation of these respective countries in 1986. Even though it has taken so long to translate and produce these essays, we feel that they still contain valid information and analyses about the complexities of the foreign policies of these countries.

This collection has been directed and edited by Jane Marchi, Managing Editor of the JOURNAL OF INTERAMERICAN STUDIES AND WORLD AFFAIRS, with the able assistance of Louise Strauss, who also served to coordinate the team of translators. Among the latter, we are most indebted to María Teresa Bancalaria, Adriana Campo, Mary D'Leon, Jenny Edelstein, Lissette Fernández, Manuel Fernández, Miguel Fernández, Miguel A. González, Frank Mora, Sara Sánchez, and — above all — Louise Strauss.

A special word of thanks must go to the Organization of American States (OAS) which assisted with financial aid for this project.

Jaime Suchlicki
Director, Institute of Interamerican Studies
Summer 1990

PROLOGUE

THIS *ANUARIO* of the *Programa de Seguimiento de las Políticas Exteriores Latinoamericanas* (PROSPEL) is the third in a series which began in 1985, analyzing the 1984 international relations of the countries of Latin America and the Caribbean. The present volume continues this series, examining — for 1986 — the foreign policies of individual countries as well as major international concerns of the region.

As we have previously announced, the PROSPEL program of CERC, *Academia de Humanismo Cristiano*, was created to fill a vacuum, academic as well as practical, in relation to the international activities of the countries of Latin America and the Caribbean. Thus, we wanted to respond to the needs of three distinct types of public: (1) the specialized intellectual community, (2) the Latin American government ministries (or others interested in our region), and (3) that part of the media which is concerned with international affairs. Our future goal is to progress towards a comparative analysis of Latin American foreign policies, for which the *Anuarios* (yearbooks) will serve as the foundation on which to build.

In a little more than three years, the work of PROSPEL has been sufficiently productive to encourage us to continue on the path so recently begun. Positive comments on the *Anuarios* from Heads of State, government ministers and Latin American diplomatic personnel in general, from newspapers and magazines in Europe and America, as well as from many international colleagues, have been particularly encouraging. Moreover, we have been gratified that our work has tended to stimulate development throughout the region of other projects and initiatives in the study of Latin American and Caribbean foreign policy.

This has been possible because of the support of the Ford Foundation, the collaboration of associate researchers and consultants, and the efficiency of the Grupo Editor Latinoamericano in publishing the Yearbook. We are grateful to all of them.

Heraldo Muñoz
Santiago de Chile
January 1987

INTRODUCTION

FOREIGN RELATIONS OF LATIN AMERICA AND THE CARIBBEAN IN 1986: CONTINUITY IN CRISIS

by HERALDO MUÑOZ

FOR SEVERAL YEARS, the countries of Latin America and the Caribbean have been faced with serious external problems. In fact, despite the efforts of many governments in the region to resolve them, these problems have been getting worse or do not show any clear signs of alleviating. Among the most prominent are the region's foreign debt crisis and the Central American conflict. On the other hand, 1986 was distinguished by the growing importance of the subject of the narcotraffic in the foreign relations of the various Latin American countries, and by the appearance of the Argentine-Brazilian cooperation/integration accord, an initiative which has stimulated both interest and hope in a region overwhelmed by the most profound economic crisis of any in the present century.

As indicated in the *Anuario*'s chapter on foreign debt, it was only a short time ago that it was commonplace to say that "Latin America confronts its worst crisis since 1930." However, in the face of the persistence of the tendency to recession, this diagnosis has been replaced by another even more negative: according to the Interamerican Development Bank, the Latin American recession is already worse, and longer, than the Great Depression which started in 1929 and began to be overcome in 1933. Despite the

Heraldo Muñoz received his Ph.D. from the University of Denver and currently serves as Director of PROSPEL-CERC in Santiago de Chile.

adjustment policies which the majority of governments in the region have adopted to deal with the crisis, the Latin American countries — with only few exceptions, such as Brazil — have registered, in 1986, falls in production, employment, imports and investments, and, in consequence, falls in per capita income and the standard of living of everyone. The basic external cause of this situation continues to be the foreign debt.

In 1986, regional foreign debt grew at a moderate rate of about 2.4%, reaching $382 billion dollars and setting a record for Latin America and the Caribbean. On the other hand, the region sent about $30 billion abroad as interest payments; in the 1982-1986 period overall transfers resulted in an exodus of $132 billion.

The drop in international interest rates for 1986 was more than compensated for by a new deterioration in the terms of exchange on the order of −8.7%. The drop in the price of oil produced some contradictory effects, bringing relief to the importing countries but having a disastrous effect on the exporting countries, like Venezuela, Mexico, and Trinidad/Tobago — and even including Cuba, which had been re-exporting a quarter of the petroleum it received from the Soviet Union, thereby earning about $500 million annually.[1]

In more specific areas, nations in the Caribbean were affected by a drop in prices of primary products, such as bauxite and sugar, which latter Caribbean product *par excellence* was affected by a reduction in the US sugar quota. In his chapter on the general situation in the Caribbean, Jorge Heine maintains that, in the post-plantation period, the general adverse external environment has exacerbated structural problems of the Caribbean economies, which stem from reliance on quotas and mechanisms of preferential access to the markets of the developed countries rather than on the competitiveness of their products.

For Latin America and the Caribbean, the external debt and unequal terms of exchange continued to receive top priority in foreign relations. In 1986, the Latin American countries disparaged the Baker Plan as being ineffective to deal with the region's debt crisis; several governments tended to favor radicalizing the position on debt repayment — Brazil, Peru, and Jamaica among them. At the same time, the region felt that the orthodox adjustment strategy, promoted by the International Monetary Fund (IMF), had been exhausted and searched for solutions which would stimulate the growth of Latin American economies.

During the year, various leaders in the region maintained that the very survival of stable and democratic regimes was endangered by the ongoing foreign debt debt problem. The debt has thus come to assume a high priority on the security agenda of Latin American and Caribbean countries, particularly those — such as Argentina, Brazil, Uruguay, Guatemala, Peru and others — which have only recently returned to democracy. In this regard, a variety of ideas and proposals intended to strengthen the bonds between the region's democratic governments were circulated to encourage democratic development in the hemisphere. So, for example, in November 1986 a *Consejo de Jefes de Estado Libremente Elegidos* (Council of Freely Elected Heads of State) was organized, consisting of leaders then in power, like Prime Minister of Barbados Erroll Barrow, the presidents of Argentina (Raúl Alfonsín) and Guatemala (Vinicio Cerezo), and former heads of state, like Jimmy Carter, Osvaldo Hurtado, Fernando Belaúnde Terry, Rafael Caldera, Pierre Trudeau, Daniel Oduber and others.

On another level, the Central American conflict continued to concern most of the countries on the continent who did not want to see themselves dragged into a conflict of even greater magnitude on the isthmus which would heighten the rationale of East-West confrontation. The United States continued to increase tension in the area through its support of the Nicaraguan *contras* and an attitude of increasing hostility towards the Sandinista government in Nicaragua. In 1986, the Reagan Administration again obtained approval from the US Congress for $100 million for the anti-Sandinistas and continued its "war of attrition" against Managua — without ruling out the possibility of invasion — which became extremely onerous for the Sandinistas but was of relatively low cost for Washington. It is worth mentioning that the "Irangate" scandal — i.e., acknowledgement, by the end of 1986, of the White House sale of arms to Iran in return for freeing US hostages and the illegal transfer of the proceeds to the Nicaraguan *contras* —helped make the anti-Sandinista cause considerably more difficult in a Democrat-controlled Congress and, eventually, contributed to the erosion of the Central American policy of the Reagan Administration.

Despite these inadequacies and frustrations, in 1986 the Latin American nations continued to support actions of the Contadora Group — created in 1983 and strengthened in 1985 by establishment of the South American Support Group — as the regional instrument for reaching peace in Central America through negotiated settlement.

The first draft of the Contadora peace plan emerged in September 1984 and was immediately accepted by Nicaragua, although Costa Rica, El Salvador, and Honduras — strongly encouraged by Washington — felt it needed various revisions. A new version was drafted by the end of 1985 and this time Nicaragua refused to sign unless the United States agreed to a special protocol promising to end its policy of aggression toward Managua. On 7 June 1986, the last draft of the treaty was presented but was not signed due to "subjects pending:" arms control and military maneuvers by outsiders. This time, Nicaragua decided to accept and sign the draft, but El Salvador and Costa Rica criticized various "omissions" in this last version.

After the Panama meeting disintegrated in June, Costa Rica and El Salvador promised to draw up their own version of a peace treaty without the "fraternal sponsorship" of Contadora, and, at the same time, they tried to organize an anti-Nicaragua coalition with the addition of Honduras and Guatemala. However, Guatemala disapproved of a peace treaty detached from Contadora and rejected the proposal to establish an anti-Sandinista alliance. The year ended with a new meeting of the foreign ministers of the Contadora Support Group (on 17-18 December in Rio de Janeiro) at which they reaffirmed their desire to maintain efforts to bring about peace in Central America, and — even more interesting — they agreed on the convenience of using Contadora to discuss other subjects of Latin American interest. As a result, by the end of 1986, the situation in Central America seemed to have reached an impasse: on the one hand, the United States continued its war of attrition against Nicaragua, and, on the other, there had been only limited progress toward a negotiated solution, such as that proposed by Contadora.

Beyond the Central American issue, Washington began to view Latin America as the principal outside source of drugs for US drug consumers. In 1986 the Reagan Administration began defining the narcotraffic as a "a problem of national security" and called for drastic measures of military-political repression in the producing countries: Mexico, Colombia, Bolivia and others. Consequently, over the past year the subject of narcotraffic has risen to the top of the foreign policy agenda of many Latin American countries.

The White House again viewed the subject through an East-West prism and began to use the term *narcoguerrilla* to disqualify various insurrectionary movements in the region, even the government of Nicaragua, by linking them to the international drug traffic. For Latin America, on the other hand, the drug issue served only to broaden and diversify the inter-American relations agenda, for which the priorities remained finding solutions to the problems of foreign debt and developing of democracy.

Finally, an encouraging note in the 1986 foreign relations of Latin America and the Caribbean was the agreement signed in July by President Sarney (Brazil) and President Alfonsín (Argentina) to establish an ambitious "Program of Integration and Cooperation" between their two countries. The program — which includes 12 protocols covering such subjects as capital goods,[2] trade, binational companies, biotechnology, nuclear cooperation, and aeronautic construction — emphasizes their intention to "consolidate democracy as a way of life and a way of government." In fact, it declares that the basic requirement for third parties to participate is that they be countries with a democratic government. Uruguay has been incorporated into the arrangement since meeting this requirement. The Argentine-Brazilian accord, which has been viewed with interest by countries such as Venezuela and Mexico, offers a new opportunity for regional integration and cooperation at a critical point of a crisis which makes the search for coordinated solutions more urgent than ever.

NOTES

1. On this subject, see chapters in this volume by Jorge Heine on "The International Relations of the Caribbean in 1985-86" and of Boris Yopo on "The Foreign Policy of Cuba."

2. The protocol on capital goods aims to reach a reciprocal exchange in this sector of $300 million annually, with an increase of 30% in the first 4 years. In this area, the total volume of bilateral trade would double to achieve a balance in mutual exchange.

had qualms about a problem of Panama's security, and called for drastic measures of military pressure on the producing countries: Mexico, Colombia, Bolivia and others. Consequently, over the past year the subject of narcotics has risen to the top of the foreign policy agenda of many Latin American countries.

The White House maintains... views the subject through... With a pragmatism that has caused them to argue fully... various insurrectionary movements in the region, even the government of Nicaragua, by linking them to the international drug traffic. For Latin America on the other hand, the drug war served only to broaden and diversify the Inter-American relations, goals for which the priorities remained futile solutions to the problems of foreign debt and the shaping of democracy.

Finally, an encouraging note, in the 1990 region technology of Latin America and the Caribbean was the agreement signed in July by President Carlos Braz... and President Alfonso Augusto to establish an ambitious "Program of Integration and Cooperation" between their two countries. The program — which includes 12 protocols covering such subjects as capital goods, trade, finance, oil companies, biotechnology, nuclear cooperation, and automatic production — emphasizes their intention to consolidate democracy as a way of life and a way of government. In fact, it declares that the basic agreement for third parties to participate is that they be countries with a democratic government. Uruguay has been incorporated into the arrangement, assuming its equipment. The Argentine-Brazilian accord, which has been viewed with interest by countries such as Venezuela and Mexico offers a way/opportunity for regional integration and cooperation at a critical point of a crisis which makes the search for economic and... more urgent than ever.

NOTES

MEXICO: A DEFENSIVE FOREIGN POLICY

by LORENZO MEYER

IN THE MIDST OF A CRISIS…AN EARTHQUAKE

IN OCTOBER OF 1985, the president of Mexico, Miguel de la Madrid, was scheduled to make a trip — planned some time in advance — to Japan, a country with whom Mexico has increasingly engaged in trade and financial transactions, and whose direct investments in Mexico continue to climb. Nevertheless, the trip was canceled and no one in Japan took it amiss; the whole world knows that, on 19-20 September 1985, Mexico City — one of the largest urban concentrations in the world — fell victim to an earthquake of such magnitude that it caused enormous physical damage to the center of the city, the death of thousands of persons (a complete list of victims still does not exist), and affected many cities and towns in the western part of the country.

The state of emergency still lingers in the Mexican capital — the tragic consequences still visible a year later — and directly affects a half million people who have lost their homes; it also destroyed or seriously damaged a fifth of the hospital installations, as well as numerous schools and public buildings, and caused the source of many jobs to disappear. Loss of life, buildings, and livelihood, however, was not the only damage caused by the quake: there were also political consequences, although of lesser impact. In effect, the action of the authorities in the work of rescue, construction and supply of shelters, and reconstruction of housing was perceived as slow and inefficient by a good part of the general

---

Lorenzo Meyer is a political scientist and researcher at El Colegio de Mexico, in Mexico City.

public, which had negative repercussions on the already tense relationship between the governors and the governed. Roots of this tense relationship derive from the economic crisis which overtook Mexico at the end of 1982 and which has never been overcome.

As news of the tragedy in the Mexican capital was broadcast to the world, various foreign governments and private organizations offered their help to Mexican authorities. At first, the Mexican government discouraged this help, but soon modified this position as the magnitude of the disaster became apparent. By the first of October, Mexico had already received concrete assistance from 54 countries and seven international organizations. The Secretary of the Controller-General of the Federation created a control mechanism to guarantee management of the inflow of aid. Nevertheless, a large part of this aid was channeled through private Mexican organizations (the Catholic Church, the Red Cross, etc.) because the donors saw these as the best vehicles for making sure their contributions reached those in greatest need, thus circumventing bureaucracy and corruption — a perception which caused great irritation in high official circles.

The foreign aid which Mexico received during the months following the September 1985 earthquake covered only a small part of the total cost of reconstruction. Rebuilding and repairing the damage of the earthquake to the Mexican capital, as well as to the other cities affected, has been calculated at $4 million.

THE DEBT

THE EARTHQUAKE OF 1985 aggravated an already difficult economic situation. Since 1982, the vulnerability of Mexico's political system, internal as well as external, has been heightened by excessive debts to international banks. By the end of 1985, this indebtedness had risen (to $96 billion), and service on the debt — interest plus payment upon principal — had risen to $13.2 billion: that is to say, to 61% of export income, or the equivalent of more than 6% of the Gross Domestic Product (GDP). The 1982 agreement which Mexico had obtained from the International Monetary Fund (IMF) and the rest of the international banking community mandated, among other things, a drastic, sustained reduction in public sector expenditure. Obviously, the needs of reconstruction conflicted with the agreement to reduce government expenses, yet the latter commitment was maintained. At the end of 1985, Mexico sought, and obtained, from its creditors deferral of its payment (of almost $1 billion) which was due at that time. Nevertheless, even this relief turned out to be insufficient; during 1985 and almost all of 1986, Mexico received no new money and each time the disjunction of the country became more clear as it tried to arrange a new, larger loan (estimates fluctuated between $5-20 billion) or to declare a moratorium.

Up until 1970, Mexico's public foreign debt amounted to about $3.8 billion, and little importance was given to the total. In those years, Mexico's debate on the role of foreign capital focused more on direct investment by companies, not on loans. Nevertheless, due to deterioration in the balance of payments during the 1970s and to poor structural functioning in the industrial sector, the government turned to external debt as a way to maintain the rhythm of its historic growth of GDP — which had averaged 6% per year ever since 1940 — and thus avoid paying the political costs of tariffs and fiscal reforms. In 1976, at the end of the Echeverría administration, the debt reached $19.6 billion dollars. When his successor, José López Portillo, left office in December 1982, Mexico's public debt had climbed to almost $58.9 billion dollars and was still climbing. By the end of 1986, it was $100 billion dollars. The irony of this last stage of indebtedness is that loans were contracted even though they were not needed because the price of Mexico's chief export, petroleum, was on the increase. The debt was justified as a means to accelerate the growth rate even more, and to make Mexico — in the words of its government — a "middle power."

In effect, the speed with which Mexico's external debt grew after 1977 was directly related to a program of accelerated expansion of production of petroleum and its derivatives. The goal was to take advantage of high world prices for crude oil to finance a qualitative leap in Mexico's development process. Therefore, it was decided to raise production to almost 3 million barrels per day, half of which would be for export. This wealth, more potential than real, served to guarantee the galloping debt. Petrodollars were abundant then, and large and small banks in the United

States, Europe, and Japan made loans to the Mexican Government and to certain large private enterprises without paying much attention to the projects in which these resources were invested. In the final analysis, an important part of this capital was wasted, due either to investments which were poorly planned or uncompleted, or to the capital flight which resulted from over-evaluation of the peso.

The problem of external debt reached crisis proportions in 1981 with the fall in the price of petroleum. Already by 1982, Mexico did not have sufficient funds to service the debt and, in fact, declared a short moratorium while it renegotiated its loans. The Mexican crisis carried international repercussions, since it provided the occasion for the international financial community to realize that all of Latin America was in danger of bankruptcy. Subsequently, Mexico fell into a vicious cycle with its creditors: seeking new loans to pay for old, in the hope (1) that the petroleum market would improve — which has not happened yet — and (2) that its non-petroleum exports would increase as the result of a painful policy of "industrial reconversion," which is hardly in its initial stage.

At the end of 1985, Saudi Arabia increased its oil production, thereby provoking an even greater fall in the price of crude oil, in order to force other producers either to leave the market or to accept a situation in which prices would be set by the world's leading exporter of petroleum. This action aggravated the Mexican crisis even more because, by mid-1986, the price of petroleum had fallen to less than $10 per barrel — very near to Mexico's cost of production, estimated at an average of $7 per barrel. At the end of the period examined here, the petroleum market continued to be uncertain and Mexico's losses had become enormous, since not only the price, but also the volume, of petroleum sales abroad had fallen. The goal of an average 1.5 million barrels per day was not reached due to lack of demand and, in some months, didn't even reach a million. In summary, the 1986 income from petroleum exports was about $8 billion, precisely half the income earned four years previously.

In 1985, the loss of money reserves by the Bank of Mexico was the greatest in Latin America (more than $2 billion dollars). During the first half of 1986, the Secretary of Hacienda (Treasury), Jesús

Silva Herzog, and his advisers engaged in thorny negotiations with the IMF and a committee of international banks (who represented the approximately 500 banking institutions which held Mexican debt paper) in the hope of obtaining a lower rate of interest, a discharge of some of the capital owed, and a longer term to repay. In the end, they got nothing.

The tension generated by the intransigence of the creditors, as well as differences among Mexico's economic advisers, caused Jesús Silva Herzog to tender his resignation to the Secretary of Hacienda, and to be replaced by Gustavo Petricioli, who took it upon himself to reopen negotiations with the creditors. By the end of September 1986, Mexico, the International Monetary Fund, and the World Bank at last reached an agreement whereby the international organizations and private international banks would provide Mexico with up to $13.7 billion dollars over the next two years, but without any substantial reduction in interest rate nor decrease in the amount of capital owed, although they did agree to extend the due date and the grace period for almost half the debt.

Thus Mexico succeeded in negotiating its first important foreign credit in 20 months. Obtaining new resources was announced by the Mexican government, the IMF, the World Bank, and the US government as a victory for all, since, it was said, Mexico would continue to pay and, at the same time, would be able to grow in 1987 and 1988 — important election years in Mexico — at an annual rate of 3%, which, if less than its historical growth rate, at least would contrast favorably with the situation in 1986, which witnessed negative growth in the GDP (-3.5%) and inflation of more than 100%.

Critics of the new agreement between Mexico, the financial organizations, and international banks, consider that the loans, which begin in 1987, will offer only a respite that will not resolve, and perhaps may aggravate, the basic problem. In fact, the new loans will permit a lessening of social and political tension at a time of presidential succession (a process which will doubtless bring victory to the candidate of the government party, which has not lost an election since 1929). It will be difficult, however, and perhaps impossible, for Mexican exports to grow sufficiently by 1989 to be able to service the debt, which will amount to some

$110 billion by then, and also to provide the currency needed to import products at the rate required to maintain the necessary economic growth.

Finally, the September 1986 accord signed by Mexico and its creditors was considered to have set in motion in Latin America the so-called "Baker Plan," i.e., the plan presented in 1985 by US Secretary of the Treasury James Baker to resolve the problems of indebted Third World countries without resort to a moratorium. As will be recalled, the plan requires that new loans be granted to Third World economies in crisis only if they (1) reject a moratorium, (2) liberalize their foreign trade, (3) lower government expenditures, and, in general, (4) reduce the role of the state in the economy and return to the private sector — national and foreign — the initiative in the process of development and economic growth.

In anticipation of this renegotiation of the foreign debt, the Mexican government had paved the way by a measure destined to have fundamental importance for the future of the country: Mexico's adherence to the General Agreement on Tariffs and Trade (GATT). Mexico's entry into the GATT, during the second half of 1986, represents a break with its historical model of economic development. Indeed, from World War II to the beginning of the 1980s, Mexico's basic economic policy was to industrialize through import-substitution, a policy generated and sustained by a complex system of subsidies, plus tariff and administrative protection for national industry. The result was an economic model noted for its autarchy and dependence of the private sector upon the protection of the state, which permitted large Mexican enterprises to develop without foreign competition. Mexico's entry into the GATT, in 1986, signified the beginning of a painful process of industrial reconversion which will surely destroy numerous inefficient industries — large and small — whose long-term success is no longer certain. As of 1986, the nature of Mexican exports continues being that of producer of raw materials and not of manufactures: crude oil and natural gas represented 42% of the exports; whereas agriculture and forest products contributed 12%, and metallic products, machinery and equipment accounted for 16%.

Also, the 1986 debt renegotiation was preceded by the elimination of many subsidies to transportation, to public consumption through sale of state-owned businesses to the private sector (it was even announced that part of the petrochemical industry, exclusively in state hands until then, would be open to private capital), and by a call for direct foreign investment. In essence, in 1986 Mexico adopted a liberal model with which to face to its economic future. All the above, however, did not prevent doubts about the future of the Mexican economy from persuading certain international banks to sell Mexican debt paper at 60% of its face value, i.e., below the quotes for similar paper representing the debt of Argentina or Brazil.

A VERY UNILATERAL BILATERALISM

DURING THE YEAR COVERED by this analysis, the bilateral relationship which traditionally absorbs the largest amount of attention and energy in Mexico — its relationship with the United States — continued to have many problems, generated mostly by the domestic economic crisis and the unilateral approach the United States uses in its foreign relations, including those with its Mexican neighbor.

By the end of 1986, Mexican-US relations appeared to embark upon a downward spiral, a state of affairs not experienced since 1940 when the Mexican Revolution ended. One cause of this constantly deteriorating political relationship derives from the fact that the US government (particularly specialists on Mexican affairs at US universities, as well as members of the media in that country) concluded that the Mexican political system — the most stable in Latin America — had become too inflexible and, for that reason, was no longer able to respond to the real needs of Mexico nor to guarantee its future stability.

There can be no doubt that, for some time now, the main US interest in Mexico has been political rather than economic: i.e., the maintenance of social peace and internal order in its southern neighbor, without which control of the more than 3,000-kilometer border between the two countries could become a grave problem for the government in Washington. For this reason, in 1985-1986, various interest groups in the United States kept up their criticism of, or increased their pressure on, the Mexican political system to abandon its authoritarianism and initiate the difficult, but necessary, transition to a more pluralistic, democratic political model. This pressure was met with great resistance by the Mexican political elite, who responded by trying to arouse a latent nationalism.

The 1985-86 federal elections for the legislature and various local elections — in particular those that took place in Sonora and Chihuahua — received adverse publicity in the United States and the rest of the world, based on the allegation that the government party won through the use of fraud. Although the US government never issued any official statement on the matter, since this was exclusively an internal affair of Mexico, there is little doubt that it shared this suspicion. In 1986, Senator Jesse Helms presided over hearings of the US Senate Subcommittee on Hemispheric Affairs, at which was brought up, among other things, the subject of fraud within the Mexican system. This accusation was sharply repudiated by spokesmen for the Mexican government, for whom the Mexican Revolution of 1910-20 and its achievements make political democracy consonant with the uninterrupted control of national politics by the same party from 1929 to the present. In spite of this, the US press publicized various analyses of the Mexican political process by US intelligence agencies which recommended political reform to end the monopoly of the Institutional Revolutionary Party (*Partido Revolucionario Institucional* or PRI) peacefully, thus clearing the way for a true party process capable of restraining the Mexican presidency — which is no longer useful to the US national interest and creates more problems than it resolves.

This US interest in perfecting Mexican democracy cannot be clearly understood without highlighting the fact that the main opposition party in 1986, and the one which would benefit most by a change in rules of the Mexican political game — the National Action Party (*Partido de Acción Nacional* or PAN) — was a conservative force which, at bottom, shared the dominant values of the current US government.

In 1986, it was estimated that 37 million inhabitants of the United States were either habitual or occasional users of marijuana and other recreational drugs. In that year, the war on drugs became a high priority on the domestic US political agenda. This, added to the fact that, according to information in the hands of Washington, Mexico was the single greatest source of drugs consumed in the United States, caused the media, as well as various members of the Congress and of the executive branch, to criticize the supposed inefficiency and corruption of Mexican authorities in the fight against the narcotraffic both openly and systematically. In the United States, the press reported links to the narcotraffic by officials high in the Mexican government, mentioning, among others, General Juan Arévalo Gardoqui, Secretary of Defense, and José Antonio Zorilla former director of the *Policía Federal de Seguridad*. US television also mentioned, although without providing any clear evidence or proof, the names of family members of Mexican politicians who were suspected of ties with the drug world, among them Edmundo de la Madrid, cousin of the president and son of General Arévalo. This whole attitude toward Mexico came to a climax in October (1986) when the US Congress passed an anti-drug law which, among various considerations, criticized the Mexican government for inefficiency and, moreover, provided for the application of economic sanctions to those countries which had not pursued the war on drugs to the satisfaction of the US government.

Mexico, on the other hand, felt that the main reason for the existence of a complex network of drug dealers capable of bribing a goodly number of police and officials owed much less to the corruption or lack of diligence of the Mexican government — which has assigned 25,000 soldiers and thousands of police to its anti-drug campaign — and much more to the attractions of the powerful US drug market, with an (estimated) value of roughly $110 billion a year. It was clear to Mexico that as long as the consumption of drugs and tranquilizers went uncontrolled within the United States, poor countries (like Mexico, Colombia, and Bolivia) would be unable to free themselves in any meaningful way from the unwanted presence of drug trafficking rings, organized and well-armed.

In the same month (October 1986), the US Congress also passed a controversial immigration control law which included, among other things, amnesty for undocumented foreign residents who could prove that they had lived continuously in the United

States since 1982, as well as provided legal means to remain for those who worked in agricultural activities which required their presence. On the other hand, the law imposed sanctions on those employers who hire illegal workers. In both the United States and Mexico, the law was perceived as a way to limit entry by undocumented Mexican workers, who, without doubt, constitute the largest number (2-3 million) of illegal migrants into the United States. The latter work for substandard salaries under substandard working conditions, and, although they pay taxes, receive few, if any, of the services provided by the US Social Security system. In both the United States and Mexico, there has been speculation as to the effects this law will finally have, such as the increase in resources (50%) which will be needed by the US Border Patrol to stem the flow of undocumented Mexicans across the border. In any event, it is estimated that, despite the new law, so long as demand for their services exists in the United States, the phenomenon of undocumented migrant workers will not disappear.

These and other difficulties in the bilateral relationship were directly reflected in two areas: presidential meetings and notes of protest. In 1986 the presidents of Mexico and the United States met twice: first in Tijuana (January) and again in Washington (August). The unusual frequency of these meetings between Miguel de la Madrid and Ronald Reagan was due to the need to lessen the tension between the two countries. The meetings produced joint declarations in which positive aspects of relations between the two countries were highlighted, particularly the efforts of Mexico to deal with its economic crisis and to wage war on the narcotraffic. Nevertheless, the tense atmosphere between the two countries changed little, and the effect of the summit meetings proved ephemeral.

US-Mexican differences had built up gradually and tended to remain in place throughout 1986. During the latter half of the year, President Reagan finally obtained approval from the US Congress for $100 million in aid for the Nicaraguan *contras*. Prior to this move, Mexico was already on record denouncing this policy as a flagrant, unacceptable violation of the most important of inter-American principles: that of non-intervention.

In May 1986, Mexico sent a note to the White House to protest the testimony of US government officials before the above-mentioned Congressional hearings as constituting unacceptable interference in its internal affairs. The obvious reference of the note was to the testimony of William von Raab, who had criticized Mexico for inefficiency in pursuit of its antinarcotic policy. Later (October 1986), Mexico sent two more notes: one protesting the announcement of a tax of 11.7 cents per barrel of imported petroleum — a decision which, if carried out, would affect Mexico's most important export — and another protesting the threats and pressure on Mexico contained in the antidrug law. On its side, the United States sent a formal protest to Mexico regarding the torture of Víctor Cortés, an agent with the US Drug Enforcement Agency (DEA) by the Guadalajara police. Finally, the Mexican Congress was also active in the sending of notes to their counterparts in the United States protesting those actions and attitudes of US legislators which compromised the interests and dignity of Mexico. In practice, little came of any of these protests.

In spite of the accumulated friction, resentment, and mutual distrust between the US and Mexican governments, finance officials in Washington supported Mexico's request for a new loan (September 1986) from the International Monetary Fund, the World Bank, and private international banks. The need to avoid a Mexican moratorium, which might provoke a chain reaction throughout Latin America, ensured that the US government would, in this case, agree completely with the Mexican position and not employ any economic pressure against Mexico which would, in the long run, have been counterproductive for the United States and its industrialized allies.

Finally, it should be noted that Mexico withdrew its ambassador — Porfirio Muñoz Ledo — from the United Nations, an envoy who had distinguished himself there by insisting upon supporting resolutions irritating to the United States, such as those concerning Namibia and the Middle East. His replacement, Mario Mora Palencia — like Muñoz Ledo, a distinguished member of the political elite — opted for a more conservative attitude and lower visibility, thus lessening the friction between Mexico and the United States in this area.

CENTRAL AMERICA, CONTADORA, AND A STREET WITHOUT AN EXIT

DURING THE TIME FRAME under discussion, the official Mexican position toward the increasingly complicated Central American problem — especially the struggle between the Reagan administration and the Sandinista government of Nicaragua — remained the same as in the immediate past: i.e., that the only viable solution to the crisis is to respect national sovereignty and negotiate the regional conflict by means of the proposal of the so-called "Contadora Group," of which Mexico is a member together with Venezuela, Colombia, and Panama. This proposal is the outcome of a treaty (*Acta de Paz de Contadora*) which the Contadora countries have presented to the governments of Central America for ratification and approval.

In November 1985, Nicaragua rejected the *Acta de Contadora* — a previous version of which had already been rejected by the anti-Sandinista governments of Central America — on the grounds that its provisos regarding military maneuvers and reduction of arms would undermine Nicaraguan military security unless the United States would first agree to normalize its relations with Nicaragua. Shortly thereafter, Honduras rejected a Mexico-sponsored resolution which had been presented — in the name of the Contadora Group — to the General Assembly of the United Nations (UN), and which urged the governments of the region to negotiate under the conditions set forth in the Act. The Contadora Group failed to overcome this impasse through mediation during 1986. Mexico was also unsuccessful in restoring direct negotiations between the United States and Nicaragua, which had previously been opened in the Mexican port of Manzanillo, since the US government adamantly refused to participate.

By the end of 1986, it was obvious that President Reagan had decided to step up pressure on the Nicaraguan government by means of (1) military aid, both overt and covert, to the *contras* and by (2) an economic boycott of the Sandinistas. The declared goal of the White House was not to negotiate terms by which Nicaragua's revolutionary regime could satisfy US interests, but to destroy *sandinismo* gradually, by economic, military, and political means. In the face of the US desire to put an end to *sandinismo*

— allegedly an instrument of Soviet policy in the area — there was little that Mexico and Contadora could do, in practice, to obtain a negotiated peace between such bitter enemies. Nevertheless, and despite the ineffectiveness of its position, Mexico continued to reject, in principle, the interventionist policy of the United States — or any other country — in the internal affairs of any Central American nation. In reality, Mexico had no other choice, given the fact that non-intervention is the central principle by which it defends its own national interest *vis-a-vis* the United States.

GUATEMALA, THE FORGOTTEN NEIGHBOR

TRADITIONALLY, MEXICO'S RELATIONS with its neighbor to the south, Guatemala, have been a problem. The distrust between them increased when the Guatemalan military government instituted a policy to eliminate the armed opposition of the Left, which provoked a wave of refugees (mostly indigenous peasants) to cross the border into Mexico — who were then pursued by incursions of the Guatemalan army on the grounds that the refugees gave cover to the guerrillas whom they were fighting. This pressure from Guatemala led Mexico to transfer, by force, a goodly number of the refugees to zones further away from the border.

The election victory of a civilian — Vinicio Cerezo — to the presidency of Guatemala paved the way for some amelioration in Mexican-Guatemalan relations. Miguel de la Madrid and Cerezo met several times to discuss economic cooperation between their two countries and to resolve the problem of the approximately 40,000 Guatemalan refugees who still remain in Mexico. It was agreed that the return of the Guatemalans who still remain in temporary asylum in Mexico will be gradual and entirely voluntary. It remains to be seen how this political accord is put into practice.

It is important to Mexico that a definitive solution to the problem of political violence in Guatemala be found to enable it both to resolve the refugee problem and to re-establish control over the border. It is equally important to encourage Guatemala to maintain its distance from a position of open hostility toward Nicaragua — such as that of three other Central American countries (El Salvador, Honduras, and Costa Rica) — for if Guatemala were to add to the anti-*sandinismo* in the region, achievement of Contadora's negotiated solution would be just that more difficult.

SUMMARY

BETWEEN OCTOBER 1985 AND October 1986, the foreign policy of Mexico was, at bottom, the policy of a country weakened, internally and externally, by an economic crisis that had gone on for four years and which had begun to have political consequences. Externally, this weakness was magnified, because it coincided with a particularly aggressive phase by the hegemonic power in the area, the United States.

As a result, Mexico's international activity became somewhat defensive during this time, although there were positive aspects as well. For example, in mid-1986, in anticipation of the second US-Soviet summit meeting in Iceland, the heads of state of Argentina, India, Greece, Sweden, and the former head of state of Tanzania met in Mexico to draw up a disarmament proposal to be presented to the United States and Russia. This call by the "Group of the Six," in Ixtapa-Zihuatanejo, was well received by the Soviet Union but publicly rejected by the United States. Subsequently, at the end of 1986, Mexico's Ministry of Foreign Affairs revived a proposal for economic and political cooperation among the countries of Latin America, particularly with Argentina and Brazil.

In any event, Mexico's effort, through Contadora, to alleviate the enormous tensions in Central America produced practically no positive effect since the United States viewed its confrontation with Nicaragua as non-negotiable in the context of the East-West global conflict. Nevertheless, Mexico persisted in maintaining Contadora's presence — despite the skepticism with which it is viewed by many within the country — both as an expression of its desire to nurture the principle of non-intervention and as offering the only means by which — should circumstances change — a peaceful resolution of the conflict could immediately be effected. However, by the end of 1986, there appeared no end in sight.

REFERENCES

Centro de Investigación y Docencia Económica (CIDE) (1986) Carta de Política Exterior Mexicana, Year VI, No. 1 (January-March).

______ (1985) Carta de Política Exterior Mexicana, Year V, No. 4 (October-December).

Excelsior (Mexico) (1985-86) Various issues.

(La) Jornada (Mexico) (1985-86) Various issues.

(The) New York Times (United States) (1985-86) Various issues.

Revista Mexicana de Política Exterior. (1986) Issues of January-March and April-June. Mexico City, Mexico: Mexican Ministry of Foreign Relations, Matías Romero Institute for Diplomatic Studies.

______ (1985) Issues of October-December. Mexico City, Mexico: Mexican Ministry of Foreign Relations, Matías Romero Institute of Diplomatic Studies.

SZEKELY, G. (ed.) (1987) Mexico-United States, 1985. Mexico, DF: El Colegio de Mexico.

Washington Post (United States) (1985-86) Various issues.

EL SALVADOR: LITTLE ROOM FOR MANEUVER IN FOREIGN POLICY

by CRISTINA EGUIZABAL

IT HAS OFTEN BEEN SAID that the Central American countries have usually been the "objects" of foreign policy but seldom actors themselves (in the political, not legal, sense) in international affairs. This statement contains much truth since, due to their geographic proximity to the United States, they have always been a part of US security considerations. From a more general perspective, their location between the two oceans, the presence of the Panama Canal, the small size and vulnerability of these nation-states so close to a great power have made them "factors to be considered" by the world powers. Nevertheless, it is not enough to refer to the "passivity" of these countries on the international scene because it does not explain much. It is more useful to ask how this passivity has varied in the past: has it been greater or smaller according to the international situation? according to the governments in power? or according to the countries or regions with which it has been involved?. Even more salient, contradictory though it appears in the light of the current Central American political situation, the room for maneuver which existed in the past has now disappeared. In this respect, the Salvadoran case is highly significant.

It is in its relations with the United States that El Salvador has traditionally displayed a posture of increased passivity and diminished autonomy; this has so much been the case that the

Cristina Eguizábal is a political scientist and coordinator of the Foreign Policy Project for Confederación Universitaria Centroamericana (CSUCA) in San José, Costa Rica.

very concept of "autonomy" is inadequate in this context. However, if we set aside the notion of autonomy and substitute the less ambitious one of "maneuver," and if we use instead the variable "room for maneuver" within the set of options open to a government facing a given problem, the problem of more or less autonomy becomes not so central as the possibilities open to that government by which it may increase its options as well as its ability and will to do so.

Usually the US administration in power been able to exercise a sort of "veto power" over El Salvador's policies. Up until the 1970s, El Salvador's foreign policy, in relation to other countries, was very limited, and although it diversified its relations to some extent, its limited ability to take action within the international system and its obedience to Washington soothed the latter's peace of mind regarding the loyalty of this Central American ally. El Salvador never gave the US government any cause for alarm regarding its alliance with the West (despite US concern over some of its domestic policies), although Salvadoran elites did challenge the United States on the issue of human rights, so important to the Latin American policy of the Carter Administration, which led indirectly to the present crisis.[1]

In the years that followed the resistance, of the General Molina government, to US pressure to demonstrate greater respect for human rights within the country, even at the price of a substantial reduction in the military aid it received from Washington, everyone knew that the regime was deteriorating politically until the situation degenerated into civil war. It was then that the new Republican administration in the United States defined the internal war as a problem of East-West rivalry which, according to its strategists, involved the security interests of the West, and intervention into the internal affairs of this Central American country became total and direct, though not indiscriminate, as we shall soon see, in regards to its foreign policy.

Our analysis begins with the following hypotheses:

1. The margins for maneuver of foreign policy open to the Central American countries generally, and to, in this case, El Salvador in particular, are determined (a) by their situation as small countries located on the periphery of a great power, and (b) by the type of domestic policies instilled by

the country's elites and the degree of internal support they command.

2. The efficacy of that foreign policy is going to depend as much on what its place is on the domestic agenda as on the means available to carry out its objectives.

3. The range of options available to design and carry out an international policy is going to vary according to the area to which it is directed (neighboring, regional, world, or hegemonic) and to the type of proposition (issue) being dealt with and under what circumstances (normal or ones of crisis).

I. DETERMINANTS OF SALVADORAN FOREIGN POLICY WITHIN THE CHRISTIAN DEMOCRATIC FRAMEWORK

Difficulties of Domestic Legitimacy for the Duarte Regime

AN IMPORTANT TURNING point for El Salvador's historical development took place on 15 October 1979. It marks the moment when the present form of government was established, primarily as a response to the public criticism of the previous type of rule, characterized by a strength and degree of organization unusual in Salvadoran history.

In the 7 years that have transpired since then, the ruling classses, pressured by the US government, joined together and succeeded in establishing, not without great difficulty, a limited consensus and a regime capable of keeping the opposition forces in check. In its favor, this regime has earned more international respect than most of its predecessors during the preceding 15 years.

Difficulties arose from the variety of plans, often contradictory, as to the best way to handle criticisms of the regime. These range from proposals that are definitely warlike, by sectors of the traditional Right, to those with a strong political component by groups in the political Center. All revolve around the issue which constitutes the center of debate among the productive sectors, such as: the advantages and disadvantages of agrarian reform, and of economic activity by the government, *via* nationalization of banks and foreign trade. The compromise which has been reached was made possible because the government of President Reagan placed all its weight on the side of the reform project which served as the platform of the Christian Democratic Party (*Partido Demócrata Cristiano* or PDC).

Simply stated, in the area of political economy, the reforms and nationalizations were maintained as a symbol, at the least, of the regime's compromise with the majority sectors; in the political military area, it agreed to contain, or defeat, the insurgent forces. Finally, in the political area alone, the goal was to consolidate the forms of representative democracy as a means to establish domestic and international legitimacy.

Despite rumors of a *coup d'etat* which continually circulated throughout the Salvadoran capital, the ruling groups reached a limited agreement regarding the proposals for political reform sponsored by the Duarte government, consonant with the US view. In the economic area, due to the irreversibility of the first phase of agrarian reform and the nationalization of banks, these appeared certain of acceptance. The same could not be said for state control of foreign trade, nor of the degree to which the state should be able to intervene in the economy.

This became apparent when the Salvadoran Association of Coffee Producers (*Asociación Salvadoreña de Cafetaleros* or ASCAFE) brought a complaint before the Supreme Court of Justice charging that Decree No. 75, which created the National Institute of Coffee (*Instituto Nacional del Cafe* or INCAFE) on 25 May 1985, was unconstitutional. The strength of the groups interested in re-privatizing coffee grown for export could be measured by the fact that the Court had not yet issued a decision, in any substantive sense. Besides which, for reasons of form, not only did it postpone its decision, but the Attorney General of the Republic, based on ASCAFE's allegations that funds were mismanaged, ordered the Court of Accounts to open an audit of INCAFE in September 1986.

The second point of disagreement leapt into prominence when the Christian Democratic government announced the means by which it planned to implement its political economy program. On 22 January 1986, President Duarte made public, over a national network, his vigorous pursuit of the "Plan for Economic Stabilization and Revitalization." In spite of his strong presentation of the new plans, the announcement provoked a general outcry. As expected, the Right took the opportunity to denounce the restrictions inherent in the state's over-regulation of production, emphasizing, in their attacks, the negative and interventionist aspects of the plan.

Labor groups, including those worker and peasant unions affiliated with the PDC, denounced the increase in the cost of living which the rise in government-established prices implied. In the long run, their opposition could prove more dangerous than that of the ruling groups. In fact, the survival of the PDC Plan could only be guaranteed if it succeeded in building a base of popular support to back its reform policies. Actually, its main support came from Washington, despite its avowed intention to create mass organizations composed of those areas of the public who would benefit most from specific government guaranties, while organizations supposedly tied to the insurgency remained harassed by those same authorities.[2] Support from the US government could not continue indefinitely; sooner or later the US taxpayers would make their protests heard.

The Christian Democrat administration was very conscious of this. This was so much the case that, faced with popular dissension (made evident by the increase in labor disputes in the public sector as well as in the private one), Antonio Morales Ehrlich, Mayor of San Salvador, suddenly announced, upon leaving a meeting with *campesino* organizations to discuss the plan for development and consolidation of agrarian reform (and of whose Advisory Council he was the Executive Secretary), that the plan's second stage, the only one not yet in operation, would begin in December 1986.[3]

Another policy of the Christian Democrats which came under fire from a variety of groups was the administration position on dialogue with the insurgency. Right-wing groups continued to oppose every proposal to negotiate. Nevertheless, it was interesting that apropos the possibility of a third round of conversations between the government and the two front groups (FDR/FMLN or *Frente Democrático Revolucionario/Frente Faribundo Martí de Liberación Nacional*), the various political representatives did not speak with one voice. Some had already begun to change their positions with respect to who should participate in the dialogue, as well as with respect to their institutional role.[4]

In spite of pressure from the general public favoring dialogue with the guerrillas, including those organizations basically in sympathy with the regime, between June and September they were unable to reach any agreement with the FDR-FMLN nor to arrive at any understanding on questions of security, on the participation of other groups in the dialogue process (sought by the major labor unions), nor even on what topics to place on the agenda for discussion.

Faced with the declining prestige of the government which, for reasons beyond their control, was bound to their own, the Armed Forces embarked upon a propaganda campaign towards the end of 1986, aimed at the country's productive sectors (both managers and workers), regarding a plan called "United to Rebuild." The new counter-insurgency strategy was put into practice so that the military, without having to take over control of the state, could strengthen the government's political leadership whose prestige had eroded during the present administration.

As often occurs in cases of national emergency, the earthquake that hit El Salvador toward the end of the year only sharpened the hostility of those sectors already critical of the government. President Duarte placed the administration of foreign aid in the hands of private enterprise in a public effort to invite the support of this critical group.[5] Those most affected by the earthquake, the general public, were politically immobilized by the catastrophe, at least during the first weeks that followed.

The Importance of Foreign Policy in the Overall Policy of the Christian Democrats

It is obvious, as mentioned above, that the place of foreign policy was as important as that of domestic policy on the national agenda. First, domestic survival was directly related to its "extraction ability" at the international level. Second, its strength was also related to the interests of at least two international actors who were directly involved in the Salvadoran political process: the United States government and the Christian Democratic International.

By "extraction ability," we allude to the ability to extract resources from the international system, political resources, like prestige and legitimacy, as much as material resources, like economic and military aid.

The prestige and legitimacy which the Christian Democrat administration lacked before other domestic political actors were strengthened each time President Duarte successfully carried off some effort in the international field. Highly important were his presidential visits to the United States and recognition of his regime's labor reforms, which many interested observers in the United States viewed as successful. For a variety of reasons — the kidnapping of his daughter at the beginning of the year and, more recently, the state of emergency declared after the earthquake destroyed the capital — the Salvadoran President had to cancel two visits to various US cities which could have helped restore his image.

It was no secret that the government's war against its armed opposition was being financed by foreign resources, primarily from the United States. The foreign debt rose to some $ 2,300 million dollars. The United States financed close to 60% of the national budget and almost 15% of the gross national product (GNP). The desperate situation created by the earthquake forced the government to seek more international aid. According to the president himself, reconstruction would require at least $500 million, perhaps even $2,000 million.[6]

The major Salvadoran sectors need to obtain resources from the international system to carry on the war as much as to rebuild the country. As long as the Christian Democratic political agenda remained acceptable to the Reagan administration, the government was the best guarantee for obtaining those resources which the US government justified on the grounds of its national security. They knew this and it was the only reason they accepted Duarte's *comunitarismo*.

Washington was interested in the Salvadoran government improving its image and acquiring greater legitimacy on the international scene. In the sense that the national security of the superpower required prevention of an insurgents' victory in El Salvador (a second Nicaragua or a third Cuba), and that the international political situation made it extremely costly to support dictatorial regimes openly, it was vital that the Salvadoran Christian Democracy appear to be a centrist regime building democracy. At the same time, that incorporated the Christian Democrat International into US strategy and converted it, willy-nilly, into an ally.

Once limited to the European post-war political scene, parties adhering to a Christian Democratic ideology gave themselves to the task of cooperating in the organization of new parties who shared their ideology in societies outside of Europe, mainly among the Latin Americans due, among other things, to their long Catholic tradition. For this reason, from the end of the 1950s, Christian Democratic parties began to appear in various Latin American countries. The most important were those of Chile and Venezuela which, once they consolidated, helped to strengthen others, like the Salvadoran one.

In the beginning, El Salvador's PDC established its first international ties with the PDC in Chile. Large numbers of young people were politically trained in Santiago. Later on, with the change in the Chilean political regime and the simultaneous strengthening of COPEI (*Comité de Organización Política Electoral Independiente*), Salvadoran ties with Venezuela grew closer. When Napoleón Duarte had to go into exile after the 1972 presidential elections, he took up residence in Caracas, which brought the two parties even closer.

Some Characteristics of Foreign Policy Implementation under the Duarte Administration

The Foreign Ministry, as well as the president, defined the country's situation as one of defending itself from Soviet aggression,

> characterized the intervention, at times direct and at times indirect, in our internal affairs ... through Cuba and Nicaragua, by providing support, both political and material, to those fraudulent armed groups that operate in the country.

In the international arena these groups have displayed

> a constant and well-structured diplomatic and political campaign ... whose objectives are to minimize and undercut the achievements of the democratic process and, consequently,

to obtain both political support and funds to pursue their violent, irrational struggle.[7]

For this reason, official rhetoric set forth the following as basic goals of Salvadoran foreign policy: *First*, "to maintain and increase economic and political links and cooperation with the international community." *Second*, "to neutralize the misinformation and defamation campaign which the insurgent armed groups carry on outside the country." *Third*, within the region, the Salvadoran government declared "the need to promote and strengthen pluralistic democracy, attain peace, and seek cooperation and integration within Central America."[8]

The style of the Duarte Government, emphasizing presidential leadership and centralization, reinforced the tendency, common in Latin America, for the president to dominate foreign policy. The means chosen for this approach consisted of presidential trips, the "diplomacy of direct contact," since, in the words of the president:

> the presence of a head of state in the countries visited has a greater impact on the communications media, and on public opinion in general, that creates the spaced necessary to project and explain the true situation in El Salvador and to counteract, in this way, the orchestrated campaign of disinformation that has been developed outside of El Salvador by the armed opposition and its international allies.[9]

Given the precariousness of its income, and in spite of the importance accorded this external projection (the budget of the Ministry of Foreign Relations was lower than any other secretary of the state), besides utilizing the usual means of communication between governments, the Salvadoran government used the international links afforded by its Christian Democrat affiliation efficiently, particularly those with Christian Democratic governments in Europe. On the other hand, membership in the party was practically universal among officials in El Salvador's foreign service, since they essentially gained their experience in international affairs during their years of party training.

II. FOREIGN POLICY AGENDA OF THE DUARTE ADMINISTRATION

The Various Problems

FOR ANALYTICAL PURPOSES, as indicated in the introduction, the external framework of El Salvador's foreign relations have been divided into sub-categories on the basis of the type of relations and problems which have occurred in a bilateral relationship and which form part of each sub-category:

(1) the *contiguous* context refers to that composed of its immediate neighbors and implies there may be a greater number of links with these countries and, as a result, they may share a greater number of the same items on their respective agendas;

(2) the *regional* context comprised not only those Central American countries *not* on El Salvador's borders but all other Latin American countries as well;

(3) the *global* context covers all countries which have bilateral relationships with El Salvador but with whom those links are minimal; and finally,

(4) the *hegemonic* context refers to the network of links between El Salvador and the United States, the dominant power.

Besides considering the issues according to their sub-category, it may be useful to take into account whether or not a country was linked to the regional crisis, using the US definition of the crisis. In the first instance, obviously, the hypothetical approval of Washington will be greater than in the second.

Relations With the Hegemonic Power

Because the survival of the Duarte government depended, very directly, on the economic and political support which it received from Washington, when it came to making decisions, it had almost no room for maneuver *vis-à-vis* the United States. This was true in every area; nevertheless, we believe that certain priorities were established on the bilateral agenda: there were issues on which

Salvadoran alignment was total, and others which were open to a range of options, limited, but real just the same.

Let us view this in more solid fashion through analysis of the major issues.

A. On Resolving the Conflict in El Salvador

In spite of constant references to the fatal consequences of a purely military solution, as advocated by President Reagan, compared to the benefits of a negotiated solution, it was impossible to envision any kind of solution that would not contain some elements of both. In methodological terms, resolution of the Salvadoran conflict had to be seen as a continuum in which a military solution rested at one end and a political negotiation at the other, with any firm solution — composed as much of military elements as of political ones — located at some point along the continuum. The interested parties would have had to agree on what was negotiable and what was not regarding the problem itself and their own differences of opinion about it.

As for the United States, though the different sectors belonging to the "establishment" involved in the Salvadoran question shared a general view of the situation, i.e., the unacceptability of a guerrilla victory, they differed over priorities and concrete solutions to specific problems.

For example, within the Executive branch, different departments were trying to resolve the problem of conflict between the increasing cost of keeping the armed forces in control of the military situation, consolidating the civil regime, strengthening the machinery of representative democracy, and maintaining an important part of the population outside the political community. From this situation stemmed the ambiguous attitude of the United States towards the professionalism and honesty of the Salvadoran military, its direct, practically open, intervention on behalf of the Christian Democratic candidate during the last presidential election, its support of Duarte's requests that the political parties which make up the FDR participate within the prevailing constitutional framework, and its vascillation over the possibility of dialogue with the guerrillas.

However, the greatest conflict was between the US Congress, closer to the concerns of electorate, and the Executive, which was primarily concerned with questions of national security, apropos how much weight should be given to El Salvador's record on human rights as a condition for granting economic and military aid. The constituency of those religious and human rights groups concerned about civil rights abuse within in El Salvador was sufficiently important that, on several occasions, President Duarte had to journey to the United States to convince the US Congress to grant military aid to his country.

B. On the Political Economy

Everyone knows that US experts helped to draw up the agrarian reform law and neither was it a secret that, through the recommendations of the International Monetary Fund (IMF) and the World Bank, the US government is able to control, indirectly, the economic policies of those countries who have problems making payments on their foreign debt.

Now then, there are also a number of economic questions which create problems for US policies: how to reconcile the needs of a new strategy for development and a sound economic effort with a war situation? how to make El Salvador's private sector accept reforms which it feels are prejudicial to its interests? how to provide incentives for private investment, both domestic and foreign, within a context of increasing state intervention and permanent insecurity.

At the time, Washington's priorities consisted of maintaining both agrarian reform and nationalization, despite opposition from the nation's agricultural and industrial sectors, and of instituting certain measures designed to decrease the budget deficit, mostly to soothe its opponents in the US Congress who were horrified at being asked to finance both constant increases in the Salvadoran budget and, at the same time, the US own budget deficit. It was no accident that the second package of economic measures announced by the Duarte government — on the eve of his scheduled tour of the United States and a few days before an earthquake destroyed San Salvador — was opposed by a majority of the public. (Due to this disaster, the visit was cancelled and later re-scheduled so he could solicit aid to rebuild). Neither were the Salvadoran coffee-producers ingenuous when, as part of their opposition to INCAFE, they made a direct, public appeal to President Reagan to support their cause.[10]

C. El Salvador's Foreign Policy toward the Regional Crisis

Regarding the efforts made by the Contadora Group and its member countries, the position of President Duarte's government was very similar to that of the United States: a support that was, in fact, both skewed and rhetorical. Both countries viewed the Sandinista regime as the cause of regional destabilization and the Contadora Group as incapable of resolving the situation.

On 16 January 1986, while attending Vinicio Cerezo's inauguration, El Salvador Foreign Minister Rodolfo Castillo Claramount signed, together with the other Central American foreign ministers, the Declaration of Guatemala endorsing the Caraballeda Message, in which the Contadora Group countries urged Central Americans to pursue the path of negotiating a solution to the crisis. In April 1986, while in Panama where Contadora Act negotiations were being concluded, Castillo Claramount declared that the Salvadoran government was willing to sign the Act but emphasized that, once again, Nicaragua had been an obstacle to accepting the document. In May, during his tour of those countries who are part of the Support Group, Duarte renewed his support of Contadora.

All that, however, did not stop the Salvadoran Ministry from announcing a few weeks later in early June, after the Sandinista government had accepted the Act, that Contadora's mediation function had ended, in the sense that the document presented at the Panama meeting did not satisfy the aspirations for peace in the region. Putting this strongly, the foreign minister said that:

> The tutelage of the Contadora Group has ended and we Central Americans are assuming responsibility in the search for peace in our region and among our people. ... There is no more tutelage, no more maneuvers ... We are going to decide what meetings to have and when and where we want to have them.[11]

Even before his address to the Assembly, the foreign minister had stated that his "thesis" would be "the vacuum in Central America," characterized by "the absence of forums and machinery of its own which would enable factors of tension in the region to be overcome."[12]

According to official statements by the foreign minister and President Duarte himself, the Latin American mediation process arose as an attempt to avoid the likelihood of a generalized military conflict, but later the efforts of the Group, with respect to the Act itself, basically referred to the problem of access to political power. On behalf of this reading — the Contadora Act as the only guarantee of the processes of representative democracy compatible with its aims — the Christian Democrat government supported unreservedly the efforts of the Group in the sense that, on one hand, this definition excluded the Nicaraguan government which did not admit its exclusion, and on the other, the Salvadoran government, in accepting it, justified itself to the international community, particularly the Latin American one.[13] The Peace Act itself was extremely complex and implied very broad obligations, particularly in those areas relating to the national security of the countries involved, so that the Salvadoran position towards the Act was revealed, in practice, as one that basically contravened the proposals of the Contadora and Support Groups, whether those dealt with mediation or security alone.

More specifically related to Nicaragua, President Duarte announced a peace plan for Central America at a press conference with foreign correspondents held in San Salvador. Of the Salvadoran leader's proposals, two were already on the table having been introduced by President Cerezo of Guatemala: (1) a meeting of Central American presidents and (2) establishing a regional parliament. The third was an offer made to President Ortega proposing that two dialogues take place simultaneously: one between the Nicaraguan government and anti-Sandinista political-military groups, and the other between the Salvadoran government and the FDR/FMLN — thus echoing a similar proposal made by the White House some months earlier.

El Salvador's Policy towards, and Relations with, its Immediate Neighbors

Despite Washington's efforts on behalf of its regional strategy, relations between Honduras and El Salvador remained strained even after both countries signed the General Peace Treaty in Lima (30 October 1980), and it was later ratified by both congresses.

The very interdependence created by their common border and by many ties existing for decades made their problems more complex. This was even more the case when old disputes and misunderstandings (which had led to the armed conflict in 1969) and were never worked out were superseded by new frictions generated by the civil war in El Salvador and regional tension.

Honduras and El Salvador share a common border of 340 kilometers, of which 225 are defined and relatively well-demarcated. Boundary disputes constantly arise over the demarcation of the remaining 115 kilometers and over the Gulf of Fonseca. Land areas that have not been marked off, the so-called *bolsones*, amount to 419 square kilometers, which represents 2% of present Salvadoran, and 0.37% of Honduran, territory. Among the islands under dispute in the Gulf of Fonseca, the main one — the Island of Meanguera — has a surface area that is barely 15.8 kilometers square and has been the one most sought after by Honduras for its strategic value, based on its location.

For any Salvadoran government the boundary disputes have been, and continue to be, a problem. Because of its small size, El Salvador cannot allow itself to lose any of it, much less to a neighbor which it views as "big." The territorial disputes were a particularly critical issue for the Duarte government because, on the one hand, a good part of the *bolsones* were under the control of the FMLN-FDR, which made any kind of negotiation with Honduras difficult, and, on the other hand, as happened on other occasions, Right-wing political sectors were able to manipulate feelings of nationalism, shared by a majority of the population, in favor of their own interests which, at the time, were opposed to the Duarte Government, which they alleged to be under too much foreign influence.

The 1980 Peace Treaty renewed diplomatic and consular ties and re-established the circulation of people and goods on the same terms that had existed before the war. From the US standpoint, the most important postwar development was that machinery for cooperation between the armed forces of both countries was established, enabling US military advisers to train thousands of Salvadoran soldiers on Honduran soil. Nevertheless, tension between the two continued to manifest itself, which the Honduran army ended by forbidding any more training of Salvadoran soldiers.

As for the question of demarcating the national boundaries, the Peace Treaty had also stipulated that if complete agreement had not been reached within 5 years of its signing, both countries would agree to submit themselves to the jurisdiction of the International Court of Justice at The Hague. This is what happened and, in accord with the agreement, both countries entered into negotiations to reach agreement on questions of procedure in order to present their dispute together. As a result of those discussions, El Salvador and Honduras signed an agreement (on 24 May 1986) during the summit meeting of Central American leaders held in Esquipulas (Guatemala), in which both countries agreed to accept the decision of the International Court.

The issue of migration has always been part of the bilateral agenda: until 1969, emigration to Honduras had served as an escape valve to relieve the problem of overpopulation in El Salvador, aggravated by its poor distribution of land. In 1965, in order to regulate the migratory flow from El Salvador which had begun to worry Honduras, the two countries, under the auspices of Central American integration mechanisms, signed a Migration Treaty that dealt specifically dealt with the problem of undocumented persons. When Honduras refused to renew this Treaty, massive expulsions of Salvadorans with irregular status followed and were the major reasons behind the 1969 war.

Fifteen years later, the issue of Salvadorans in Honduras arose again but in a different way. In 1986 refugees crossed the border to flee the war, and the majority settled near the border in hopes of returning soon. The proximity of the camps to the joint border and the absence of defined boundaries in many areas contributed to the frequent incursions of Salvador's armed forces into Honduran territory in search of guerrillas, which was denounced by authorities in Honduras border department.[14] No longer able to postpone the problem, the Duarte government came to an agreement with that of Azcona Hoyo. Thanks to the good offices of the UN High Commission for Refugees, a bipartisan commission was set up in San José to prepare the repatriation of 20,000 Salvadorean refugees, which, both governments agreed, would be strictly voluntary.

These irritants, however, did not prevent diplomatic contacts from taking place at the highest level nor the two leaders from visiting one another, in accordance with Washington's best desires.

Relations between El Salvador and Guatemala have usually been most harmonious and continued so into 1986 despite the fact that, in recent years, the various Guatemalan governments had assumed a position of "neutrality" towards the Central American conflict, to the irritation of the Salvadoran military.

The bilateral agenda was limited; boundary problems were resolved through the Treaty of 1938. A Border and Waters Commission operated routinely ever since 1971, for the purpose of demarcating the boundary lines and of preventing the inevitable border problems from getting worse. There was no major flow of migrants which might cause friction.

During the operation of the Central American Common Market, Guatemala became (second only to the United States) the principal market for Salvadoran products. Due to the war between El Salvador and Honduras and the subsequent dropoff in regional trade, the Guatemalan market fell off slightly although it continued to have an important role.

By 1986 the level of trade had declined, in part because of the economic recession which caused production to drop in both countries but also because of the war in El Salvador, as much as anything else. The balance of trade between the two countries placed El Salvador in debt.[15]

In order to avoid an even greater decline of trade in the region, the *Derechos de Importación Centroamericanos* (DICA) was created as a Central American clearinghouse for foreign exchange to help prevent polarization of trade balances between the countries. It was hoped that its operation would result in greater trade activity between Guatemala and El Salvador.

From a political point of view, even though a Christian Democratic government was in power in both countries, no Guatemala-San Salvador axis was established, as might have been expected. Guatemala took a unique, relatively independent position towards the Central American crisis. Even more, President Cerezo siezed initiatives of regional leadership seeking to moderate the positions of his Salvadoran, Honduran, and Costa Rican colleagues towards Nicaragua. The most prominent of these was the summit meeting in Esquipulas, which brought together the five Central American presidents, and his proposal to create a Central American Parliament.

El Salvador's Foreign Policy towards the Region

El Salvador's position toward the efforts of the Contadora Group and its proposals has already been mentioned. Let us now take a brief look at its relations with the individual countries who make up that Group.

Regarding Venezuela, the government of President Herrera Campins maintained very cordial relations with President Duarte's *Junta de Gobierno.* However, after the victory of the Social Democratics in Venezuela, government-to-government relations cooled a little, although limited ties were maintained through party channels.

Relations toward Mexico evolved in reverse order; in effect, after reaching a high point of tension due to the Franco-Mexican declaration which, let us remember, recognized the FDR and FMLN as representative forces, that tension gradually dissipated. Nonetheless, Salvadoran authorities systematically excluded the Aztec capital from their Latin American tours not only due to the friction between their governments but also to forestall adverse public opinion generally.

However, El Salvador did continue to benefit from the cooperation of both countries, Venezuela and Mexico, through the Pact of San José, thanks to which El Salvador buys oil by paying only part of the regular price and using the difference as a soft loan, over a long period, for development projects.

Relations between El Salvador and Colombia have usually not been important, nevertheless the South American country's greatest projection into Central America and the Caribbean was to target El Salvador as an object of its foreign policy and possible ally. Thus we saw Napoleón Duarte visit Colombia twice in 24 months.

Regarding Costa Rica, while trade between the two countries declined in recent years, migration of undocumented Salvadorans took place.

Finally, regarding Panama, relations maintained their usual levels, in which ties between the two militaries held a privileged place.

After attending the inauguration of President Arias of Costa Rica, President Duarte accepted an invitation from Argentina and Uruguay to travel south to visit the countries who were members of the Contadora Support Group. The tour complemented one he had made to Panama, Colombia, and Venezuela in September of the previous year to advance the Salvadoran view of the Central American crisis, particularly the role of the Sandinista government, and to present El Salvador's armed opposition as the product of foreign intervention.

The Salvadoran delegation met with criticism from non-official groups wherever it went in the countries visited. There were street demonstrations in Montevideo, Rio de Janeiro and São Paulo, and Argentine parliamentarians absented themselves to indicate their lack of sympathy for the Christian Democratic regime in power in El Salvador. Nevertheless, the tour did produce two results at odds with the above-mentioned events: (1) the Salvadoran leader found himself obliged to give rhetorical support, through joint declarations, to the efforts of Contadora, and (2) he entered into a series of cooperative agreements of benefit to El Salvador (and, therefore, to the Duarte administration), among which should be mentioned the renewal, by the government in Buenos Aires, of a line of credit expanded by $25 million and the establishment of a Program of Migration and Settlement for Salvadoran families in Argentina. He also entered into an agreement with the Brazilian government whereby they pledged their mutual support in the International Coffee Organization.

El Salvador's Foreign Policy towards Western Europe

In regard to the major countries of Western Europe, Salvadoran diplomacy varied its objectives according to whether or not the country was governed by Christian Democrat.

The Salvadoran government's main objective regardingFrance and Spain at the time was to modify the attitudes of both countries towards the Salvadoran political process and to get them to view its own legitimacy more favorably. The fact that President Duarte was able to visit those countries at all in 1986 was considered a diplomatic coup by El Salvador's Ministry of Foreign Relations. As for economic cooperation, both Paris and Madrid funnelled their assistance through the multilateral machinery of the European Economic Community (EEC).

Relations with the West German Government were excellent. Due to their ideological affinity the attitude of Europe toward the PDC policy in El Salvador was basically favorable. El Salvador was the principal Central American beneficiary of aid from the Federal Republic of Germany (FRG). After Duarte's victory, he signed a government agreement for over DM50 million, and the government of Chancellor Kohl provided DM27 million more which had previously been held back by the Social Democratic government in reaction to that country's deplorable political conditions. The credit in question was to be used for agrarian reform. By the end of 1985, the FRG had placed DM95.6 million at El Salvador's disposal and had allotted DM42 million more for 1986, including assistance from the Konrad Adenauer and Hans Seidel foundations for political and administrative training.[16]

There was also a closer, more cordial relationship with the Italian government than had been usual in recent years. Rome intensified its bilateral cooperation with El Salvador, focusing on donations of agricultural and industrial equipment.[17]

With the other countries of Western Europe, relations functioned on a very low level, including those with Great Britain, whose Parliament decided to lower its profile in the region after having displayed unusual interest in Salvadoran affairs early in the decade.

III. FINAL CONSIDERATIONS

THE DUARTE ADMINISTRATION was at its midpoint in 1986. In the two and a half years remaining, it was doubtful that any significant change would develop in the parameters of his foreign policy:

1. So long as President Reagan remained in the White House, even though with a Democratic majority in Congress, the US policy of support to the counter-insurgency reform program and, thus, of Duarte as President, would probably continue.

2. Since the regime's major support came from abroad, the external dimension dominated and its need for international legitimacy will continue to be directly tied to the needs of Washington.

3. Within a context of domestic armed conflict, the regime saw itself pressured, on the one hand, by the Right to abandon the most interventionist aspects of its reform program and, on the other, obliged to satisfy the demands of those bases of support who hoped to improve their living conditions. Finally, given the nature of President Duarte's effort, at once personalistic and slightly contradictory, his regime cannot be expected to acquire a level of internal legitimacy sufficient to allow greater room for maneuver to develop in his foreign policy.

NOTES

1. See C. Eguizábal, "La situación actual de Centroamerica: entre la crisis y la normalidad," pp. 325-338 in J. Tokatlián and K. Schubert (eds.) Relaciones Internacionales en la Cuenca del Caribe y la Política de Colombia. Bogotá, Colombia: Library of the Chamber of Commerce, 1982.

2. Two cases received fairly complete coverage by the local media: that of the labor leader, Febe Elizabeth Velásquez, Secretary of Relations of the *Federación Nacional de Trabajadores Salvadoreños*, 7 July 1986, and, three weeks later, that of the Secretary-General of the *Administración Nacional de Acueductos* (ANDA), Rodolfo Andrés Prieto. Both, supposedly members of the *Resistencia Nacional* guerrilla organization, were captured in the street by members of the security forces and subsequently freed, at the express order of the President of

the Republic who interceded in response to the union pressure which provoked the arrests.

3. Strengthening agrarian reform has been one of the principal demands of the popular organizations since the law was first promulgated. The first stage was carried out between March 1980 and December 1982. According to data provided by the Central American University José Simeón Cañas, in the beginning 279 farms, the equivalent of 211,108 hectares, were affected. Nevertheless, by virtue of the so-called "right to reserve" (which permitted owners to keep up to 20% of their land), the area of the lands affected was reduced by 6%. The third phase legislated by the Constituent Assembly which was installed in 1982 concerned the rented land. The second phase included the expropriation of farms of 245-500 hectares. According to the decisions of the Constituent Assembly, expropriation could not take effect until three years after the law was passed in order to give the owners affected an opportunity to parcel or sell their land before being expropriated.

4. In this connection, it is worth mentioning statements made by Hugo Carrillo, Secretary-General of the PCN (*Partido de Conciliación Nacional*), official party of the old regime, when he announced his party's program of *Convergencia Nacional* and in which he was unusually tolerant of the guerrillas' proposal. It is also worthwhile to take into consideration the proposal by Dr. Antonio Rodríguez Porth, of the Chamber of Commerce, that a commission of deputies be organized to advance the dialogue, despite his adding "in case the latter modify their positions." He was referring to the fact that the leaders of ARENA (*Alianza Republicana Nacional*), the bastion of Right-wing opposition, PAISA (*Partido Auténtico Institucional Salvadoreño*), and even the PPS artido Popular Salvadoreño, continue to oppose any attempt to negotiate on the grounds that it would be unconstitutional, even under the aegis of the Christian Democrats or any other group (see Proceso 247, 23 July 1986).

5. Days before the catastrophe the Legislative Assembly approved (despite a negative vote by the opposition) the first taxes to finance the second stage of the economic stabilization plan. Among the new measures was a law to finance the defense of national sovereignty and one mandating compulsory military service (for Salvadorans 18-30 years of age of both sexes).

6. Figures from Inforpress Centroamericano 711 (16 October 1986): 2.

7. "Resumen del informe de labores de la secretaría de relaciones exteriores durante el período del 1 de junio de 1985 al 31 de mayo de 1986" (mimeo). San Salvador, El Salvador: Ministry of Foreign Relations: 2.

8. Op. cit., pp. 2-3.

9. J.N. Duarte. "La política exterior de El Salvador." Address of Ing. José Napoleón Duarte, President of the Republic, to the Legislative Assembly" (mimeo).

10. Proceso 229, 17 March 1986.

11. Proceso 243, 16 June 1986.

12. *op. cit.* Ministry of Foreign Relations: "Resumen del informe de labores…": 33.

13. J.N. Duarte. "La doctrina de Contadora" (mimeo). Address by Ing. José Napoleón Duarte, Constitutional President of the Republic, to the Argentine Council on International Relations, *passim.*

14. Proceso 223, 2 March 1986; and Inforpress Centroamericana 701, 31 July 1986.

15. Proceso 248-249, 6 August 1986.

16. Inforpress Centroamericana 689, 1 June 1986.

17. *op.cit.* Ministry of Foreign Relations: "Resumen del informe de labores…": 8.

HONDURAS: THE FOREIGN POLICY OF A COUNTRY UNDER DURESS

by DANIEL ASENJO

IN A FESTIVE ATMOSPHERE and attended by more than 50,000 people, including an encouraging number of represent-atives from foreign countries, Ingeniero José Azcona Hoyo was in-augurated as president of Honduras on 27 January 1986.[1] In this office, he replaced Dr. Roberto Suazo Córdova, who had governed the country since January 1982. Since both men were members of the Liberal Party, the inauguration signalled that the party would continue in power. The occasion took on particular meaning for the country because it was the first time since 1933 that a constitu-tionally-elected president had been able to transfer his mandate to a successor also chosen in general elections.

The first year of the Azcona administration witnessed no basic changes in foreign policy, such as had taken place during the previous administration.[2] Honduras maintained, with little varia-tion, its close identification with President Reagan's political-military strategy for Central America. The US-Honduran relationship continued to dominate Honduran foreign policy priorities and influenced important aspects of its domestic politics and economy as well. The country's greatest international strains were experienced along its border with Nicaragua, where friction was generated by the Honduran-based, armed anti-Sandinista groups (*contras*) who engaged with regular troops from both countries. Finally, the issues which commanded the

Daniel Asenjo is a Chilean sociologist and a researcher for PROSPEL-CERC.

most attention from the Foreign Ministry were those related to the regional crisis and relations with neighboring countries.

POLITICAL AND ECONOMIC DIFFICULTIES OF THE NEW GOVERNMENT

ALTHOUGH JOSE AZCONA MAY HAVE WON the November 1985 election, he also inherited the domestic political tensions which had been mounting throughout the year and which had appeared, on several occasions, on the verge of thwarting the redemocratization begun in 1981. His candidacy, rather than being a "people's choice," had been the outcome of *ad hoc* negotiations to choose the president that had taken place the preceding May.[3] Scarcely had the votes been counted when a call arose to annul the results of the election on grounds the whole proceeding was unconstitutional. Politically, Azcona was supported only by the *Alianza Liberal del Pueblo* (ALIPO), majority faction of the Liberal Party. There was no assurance that the remaining factions would be willing to put aside differences sufficiently to unite under his leadership. Even if this were to occur, government action appeared stymied by the virtual stalemate that existed between liberals and the opposition in Congress.[4] If this became the case, the new leader would have no alternative other than to initiate negotiations with groups outside the Liberal Party.

Only 5 days after assuming the presidency, Azcona reached a "gentlemen's agreement" (known officially as the *Acuerdo Patriótico Nacional*) with the largest group within the National Party, led by Leonardo Callejas.[5] This agreement created what was virtually a coalition government of the two parties which have traditionally governed Honduras, dividing the main responsibilities for public administration and the government between the Liberals and the *callejistas*.[6] One of the ministries sought by the Nationals (*callejistas*) was that of Foreign Affairs. Carlos López Contreras, a lawyer with broad academic experience and service in the Honduran Foreign Ministry, was chosen as foreign minister.[7] With this move, Azcona was able (1) to lay to rest any doubts about the stability of his regime, (2) to assure a comfortable majority in the Legislative Assembly, (3) to improve prospects of cooperation among the nation's three power groups, not to mention the participation and cooperation in governmental tasks of key Honduran economic groups and financiers.[8] He also emphasized the Right-wing nature of his administration in the process.

Adjustments in the seats of Honduran power also affected the armed forces. On 1 February 1986, after several announcements and false rumors to capture the country's attention in the days preceding, the office of Public Relations of the Armed Forces announced that Commander-in-Chief General Walter López had submitted a resignation of an "irrevocable" nature and that it had been accepted. Colonel Humberto Regalado Hernández was appointed in his place and was sworn in a few days later. This move seems to have been related to a series of power struggles that had been taking place within the armed forces, and to Honduras' new role in Central America. An intense struggle over promotions had erupted among Honduran colonels and lieutenant colonels, reaching to the highest levels of the army command. There were also differences within the army over its relationship with certain sectors of the civil government, as well as over the most effective way to institutionalize the role of the army as vital center of power in Honduran society. The army was also riven with disagreement regarding fallout from the country's alliance with the United States — particularly the *contra* presence in Honduras. Finally, some Honduran observers attributed the fall of Walter López to the fact that, towards the end, he exhibited increasing independence in making certain decisions, such as, for example, expediting aid for the *contras* and bypassing regular army channels in the process.[9] Beginning in March 1984, the Honduran military undertook a review and revision of certain areas of the agreements signed with the United States on grounds that Honduran national interests had been insufficiently safeguarded. For instance, they tried to use the *contra* issue to press the United States for more economic and military assistance.

Another of Azcona's motives for securing a firm political base with which to begin his presidency is the deep economic crisis into which Honduras has been plunged. In Honduras, problems of underdevelopment — it is the second poorest country of Latin America — go hand in hand with longstanding structural problems. The most visible signs of this crisis are unemployment, which affects more than 40% of the economically active population, a sustained fall in per capita income, and serious imbalances in Honduran foreign trade. To deal with these problems, the *Consejo Superior de Planificación Económica* (CONSUPLANE) has devised the "National Developmental Strategy 1986-1989," whose general goals are to repair the declining growth rate and inject more dynamism into the economy. Given the difficulties in generating decisive domestic savings in the private and state sectors, one of the assumptions of this plan is that there will be no problems in acquiring foreign credits and investments aimed at resolving the budget deficit.[10] On this basis, it is estimated that the foreign public debt will increase by only 51% over the next four years.

Renegotiation of part of Honduras' external debt, which had reached almost $ 2.5 billion dollars by the end of 1985, was one of the issues to which Azcona had promised to give priority during the electoral campaign. Of this, obligations which the state sector contracted with the international monetary bodies have been serviced in relatively normal fashion. Nevertheless, the state and private business still retain major debts with international commercial banks which have been accumulating unpaid payments since 1981. The former government broke off conversations with approximately 40 of the international banks, led by Lloyds International and the Bank of America, designed to reschedule a little over $200 million of these tardy balances, basically because the banks insisted that, as a first step, Honduras must regularize its relations with the International Monetary Fund (IMF), signing an agreement for monetary stabilization.[11] During 1986, new rounds of negotiations were held to reschedule the cancellation of overdue balances which had reached, by then, $285.5 million dollars.[12] Nevertheless, they did not succeed in bridging the gap between the Honduran proposals and those of its creditors. The areas of greatest difference were over (1) the time frames for payment of the debt, in which the Hondurans wanted more time than the banks were willing to grant; and (2) the amount of interest to be paid in the rescheduling, in which the Hondurans wished to pay less than the creditors demanded. However, one important obstacle was removed: the bankers ceased to insist that Honduras normalize its relations with the IMF as a necessary condition for continuing the negotiations.

In 1986, the Honduran government demonstrated no further inclination to obtain a *rapprochement* with the IMF, basically for two reasons. First, given the difficult conditions in which the Honduran people live, measures of the "tighten your belt" type, usually proposed by the IMF, would have exerted an immediate pernicious and destabilizing effect on the Azcona regime. As a preface, let us just say that the major Honduran labor organizations were extremely critical of governmental actions throughout 1986. Second, US aid and economic support to Honduras has, to a large extent, replaced the role played by the IMF as supplier of external financial aid. Moreover, the Interamerican Development Bank (IDB), the European governments and the European Economic Community (EEC), as well as some of the Latin American countries (mainly Venezuela and Mexico) have become important sources of financing for Honduras.

The optimistic economic forecasts made in Honduras at the outset of the Azcona administration quickly began to crumble. By August, it was estimated that inflation would reach 5% by the end of 1986, — greatly surpassing the official estimate of 3-3.5%. The prices of principal export products, such as coffee and bananas, showed a tendency to decline on the international markets, aggravating the deficit in the Honduran trade balance.[13] The tragedy of Honduras — so it is said — is that its economic stability depends on its exports, and the only thing it sells are desserts, like bananas and coffee.

RELATIONS WITH THE UNITED STATES

RELATIONS WITH the United States have always been a priority for Honduras. This was particularly apparent after 1983 when the Honduran government and military definitely aligned the country with the Reagan strategy for Central America. In return, Hondurans received a substantial increase in US economic and military assistance, though never as much as they wanted. During 1986, this situation remained basically the same. In fact, if any change could be perceived at all, it would be in an increased gravitation of Honduran foreign policy toward the United States.

Early in March 1986, Foreign Minister López Contreras addressed the Permanent Council of the Organization of American States (OAS) where he described the foreign policy of the new administration in the following terms:

> Honduras' friendship with the United States [is] one of its basic pillars ... This friendship, born of indisputable common interests, will be devoted to the benefits of democratic development and economic and social advancement of our peoples.[14]

At the same time, the foreign minister described Honduran-US relations in the 1980s as being based upon the "third dimension of the Honduran security system;" or, in other words, the search for complementary ways by which to safeguard peace, territorial integrity, and public security. "Under this concept," he added, "Honduras will maintain a special security relationship with the United States of America."

Formalizing this special security relationship — into a defense treaty similar to those of the US with its European and Asiatic allies — had been a goal long-sought by the previous administration. However, the most it had been able to come up with was (a) President Reagan's spoken word to come to the aid of Honduras in the event of external attack, and (b) inclusion of this commitment in the joint declaration issued following Suazo Cordova's visit to Washington at the end of May 1985, to wit:

> The United States government repeated, thus, its firm and unshakeable promise to defend the sovereignty and territorial integrity of Honduras, in accordance with the reciprocal obligations and rights relative to the legitimate defense, individual and collective, and of the use of the Armed Forces...[15]

The subject of economic assistance has been another of the constants in the Honduran-US relationship. Nevertheless, by the end of 1985 there were signs of tension in this area. Discussions between Honduras and the US Agency for International Development (AID) regarding the release of $67.5 million — final payment of Honduras' AID quota for 1985 which AID was holding back — had been suspended.[16] Officially, the snag was Honduras' refusal to restructure the economic stabilization program reached with AID in March of 1985. Other explanations linked suspension of talks (a) to the reluctance of the Suazo Córdova government to continue implementing economic measures which were becoming increasingly unpopular,[17] and (b) to its opposition to the US aid being channelled to the *contras* openly through Honduran territory.[18] In January 1986, government spokesmen described bilateral relations as being in a state of "tense calm," on grounds that the US did not seem disposed to deliver the $67.5 million, and the Hondurans were no longer disposed to expedite assistance to the anti-Sandinistas."[19]

On the US side, government spokesmen stated early in January 1986 that discussions had been suspended only until the new government could take office.[20] Aid was renewed the 30th of January when José Azcona and US ambassador John Ferch signed an agreement to initiate the second phase of the controversial economic stabilization program; Honduras was to receive the same $67.5 billion denied to Suazo Córdoba. Thus, Azcona began his administration with the tense atmosphere somewhat eased. What remained to be seen was whether, in order to bring this about, the government had changed its attitude in regard to the anti-Sandinistas.[21]

José Azcona made his first official visit to Washington at the end of May 1986. He left for the US capital the day after the meeting of the Central American presidents, held in Esquipulas (Guatemala) on the 24-25th of the month, had concluded. However, the outcome of the visit failed to come up to Honduran expectations since his main goal — to obtain an increase in economic assistance — was not achieved.[22] The US government merely reaffirmed its intention to complete the delivery of funds for the second stage of the economic stabilization program and to remit the last $30 million held since the end of 1985. Azcona did receive strong rhetorical support from Reagan, summarized in phrases such as the "promise to cooperate closely with Honduras in order to help it to reconstruct its economy as a bulwark for democracy," or "to stand at the side of Honduras in defending its national sovereignty and territorial integrity."[23]

What is the political cost of this economic aid to Honduras? Before looking for an answer, let's review the events which led up to Honduras' marked dependency on the United States. Between 1981 and 1986, US economic aid to Honduras rose from $47.3 million to $152 million. In 1985, nearly 22% of Honduran imports

US ASSISTANCE TO HONDURAS: 1981–1986

(In millions of US dollars)

Year	Economic Aid		Military Aid		Total
	Value	% of total	Value	% of total	
1981	47.3	83.9	9.1	16.1	56.4
1982	87.0	73.5	31.3	26.5	118.3
1983	102.7	73.4	37.3	26.6	140.0
1984	167.9	68.4	77.5	31.6	245.4
1985	135.5	68.5	62.4	31.5	197.9
1986(1)	152.0	63.3	88.3	36.7	240.3
	692.4	69.4	305.9	30.6	998.3

(1) Figures proposed for 1986.
Source: US Embassy in Honduras.

of raw materials, spare parts, and basic goods, besides various projects of agricultural development, of health, education, family planning, and nutrition, were financed through US economic assistance. Even more serious, if it had not been for US assistance, the GDP (Gross Domestic Product), which increased by 2.8% that year, would have fallen by 4%.[24] From these facts (see Table) one can draw certain conclusions. First, if US assistance is able to produce swings of 6% in Honduras' GDP, we ought to view it to a large extent as one more element in the economic structure of the country. Second, if this is so, any interruption in these flows would be capable of causing sufficient deterioration in the conditions of Hunduran life as to provoke social unrest and political instability in the short run. In the third place, maintaining and increasing present levels of this assistance becomes a sort of new "national interest" for the groups who want to stay in power. Finally, it is clear that, under these circumstances, the José Azcona government finds its freedom of action in the international sphere drastically reduced — politically, economically, and militarily.

US military assistance to Honduras affords another important parameter by which to view the bilateral relation. This measure has undergone constant increase since 1981, with its fluctuations producing sufficient percentile changes in overall military assistance to indicate the significance which Honduran-US relations acquired in the 1980s. More than the development of the country, it demonstrates that the US is more concerned with the role Honduras plays in its regional political-military strategy.

The White House commitment to the Honduran military to maintain the superiority of its Air Force at the regional level began to materialize in 1986. In September, the Honduran press announced the purchase of 10 US helicopters, valued at $30 million dollars, and financed by the US Military Assistance Program (MAP).[25] In October, this was augmented by the acquisition of military transport planes from Italy in the amount of $62 million. The US ambassador thought that the purchase would take place in Spain.[26] More important, however, was the announced updating of combat materiel.

According to a Honduran military spokesman, his country "has an obligation to modernize the Air Force because of the armed threat of Nicaragua, which possesses equipment of very advanced Soviet design." At first they spoke of acquiring Israeli KFIR planes to replace a dozen Super Mystere B-2s purchased from France in 1952. Nevertheless, at the beginning of November 1986, Azcona confirmed that the purchase would take place in the United States. The planes delivered would be F-5E hunter-bombers.[27] If we recall that Honduras already possesses the most powerful Air Force in Central America, introduction of this type of equipment would create an imbalance within the region, much more than the parity sought *vis-à-vis* Nicaragua. In the short run, this decision could give rise to an arms race in "modernization" that would involve its neighbors, Guatemala and El Salvador.

The other side of all this US economic and military assistance are the facilities granted to the United States in order to utilize Honduran territory for military purposes. This was graphically described by the president of the Central Bank of Honduras, Gonzalo Carías Pineda, who declared that "the United States gives economic cooperation because, in return, Honduras gives the country."[28] The plan for "joint military maneuvers," begun in 1983 and projected through 1988, continued to develop throughout 1986 without any change in either magnitude or design. For example, at the end of February, joint *Operación Lémpira* maneuvers were begun near the coast of Honduras to provide training in counter-insurgency. Between January and June, *Terencio Sierra 86* maneuvers were carried out, during which battalions of US engineers constructed 21 kilometers of highway, thereby finishing road projects begun some years before. In this way, the movement of troops and equipment was facilitated between the Caribbean Puerto Castilla and Yoro Province, which borders on Guatemala, and from there to the center and south of Honduras. In March, new "command and control" exercises took place, corresponding to the *Ahuas Tara* series started in 1983, designed to execute aerial and land attacks on a large scale. At the beginning of May, the *General Tosta 86* maneuvers, begun the year before, ended. Between March and July, *Cabañas 86* maneuvers[29] took place, which included "assaults" by special air transport units of the US Army and anti-guerrilla practice with veteran Green Beret groups from Vietnam. During the second half of July, "Guardians of the Caribbean II" naval exercises took place, in which Honduran and US units carried out operations of marine patrol, coastal interdiction, and training of marine infantry troops.[30] This brought to a close the most vigorous exercises planned for 1986, which brought more than 8,000 US soldiers to Honduras.

Throughout these years, the political-military purpose of these exercises has been obvious to, and shared by, both Honduras and the United States. The desire to pressure and intimidate Nicaragua is linked to the training of US troops in areas whose geography, climate, flora and fauna are very similar to those which they would encounter if the White House should decide to mount an invasion.[31] Moreover, these maneuvers have been accompanied by infrastructure projects designed to receive, house, and mobilize the Honduran and US troops who participate in them. Since this plan was initiated, US military engineers have opened routes of penetration and built more than a half dozen military camps consisting of an air strip capable of receiving medium transport C-130 and C-147 planes, besides "campaign" accommodations for the troops. The last of these bases was put up during the first half of 1986. It is estimated that the United States could quickly transport some 50,000 soldiers from these facilities to the Nicaraguan border. Of particular importance is the military base of Palmerola, located in the center of Honduras. Here one finds the most modern aviation and communications installations in the country, together with 1,200 US soldiers of the Bravo task force, who are periodically replaced.[32] Their main task consists of safeguarding the planes and pilots who continuously fly over Salvadoran territory, spying on the movements of the *Frente Democrático Revolucionario-Frente Farabundo Martí de Liberación Nacional* (FDR-FMLN).

The legal framework covering the US military presence in Honduras is the "Bilateral Treaty on Military Assistance between the Government of Honduras and the Government of the United States," which was signed 20 May 1954.[33] However, by the means of adding various *ad hoc* protocols to it, the United States has been able to acquire the ample facilities which it now enjoys. Up to now, three Annexes have been negotiated. The first dates from March 1982. Basically, it permits the United States to undertake "improvement programs" at any Honduran airport, to construct other new ones, and to " maintain airplanes in working order by, or for, the US government" able to make use of all of them.[34] The second was signed in 1985, and regulates the presence of US soldiers who participate in military maneuvers. Until then, these troops had enjoyed diplomatic status, placing them outside Honduran law. In March 1986, discussions were initiated to draw up a third protocol. It concerned regulating the use and maintenance of Honduran civil and military airport installations, as well as ones constructed during the course of the military maneuvers and already in existence. The Azcona government took the position that these expenses were the responsibility of the United States. But the outcome was somewhat different. Both countries finally agreed to share the costs of maintenance and repair. This new protocol was ratified by the Honduran Legislative Assembly in May 1986.[35] At the same time, the act provoked new demonstrations against the presence of US soldiers in Honduras.[36]

The nature of the Honduran-US relationship during the 1980s, the palpable US influence felt by Honduras, and the dependency of the latter on US economic and military assistance cannot be explained only by reference to the asymmetries of every kind existing between the two actors, to Honduras' limited economic development, to its geographical location in Central America, nor to US hegemony. An important aspect is due to the degree of encouragement and acceptance of this situation by various sectors — political, business, military, and government — within Honduras itself. One example. In 1986, an economic recovery plan was submitted for discussion to every body of power in Honduras. Before reaching their hands, the plan had already been approved by Washington. Officials from the US Embassy and from the AID office stationed in Tegucigalpa had participated in its preparation. Participation of Honduran *técnicos* was limited to compiling statistical information which served as the basis for the US work. Then, in the last stage of the discussions, President Azcona, Vice-President Jaime Rosenthal, US Ambassador John Ferch, and Honduran AID Director Anthony Cauterricci, took part.[37] Vice-President Rosenthal was one of the few Honduran officials well-informed about the plan. In commenting upon it, he was sufficiently realistic to note that "the US policy defends its own interests" and that within that perspective "countries like Honduras and Nicaragua are secondary." Within such a policy, he continued, "Honduras is only a *peon*." Nevertheless, he considered it "correct" that the strategy for Honduras' national economic recovery should be prepared by US diplomats. "This should not embarrass anyone," he concluded, because "without the United States, [Honduras] cannot progress."[38]

THE DIFFICULT ISSUE OF THE *CONTRAS*

DURING THE COURSE of the presidential campaign, José Azcona showed himself as opposed to the *contra* presence in Honduras. Nevertheless, just 2 months before his government took office, this position shifted toward that of the previous administration: the *contras* enter and leave Honduras because the country does not have resources necessary to keep close watch on the extensive wilderness on the border with Nicaragua, not because the military and government authorities are protecting them.

One of the principal risks of this situation for Honduras arises from the possibility that attacks against Nicaragua could get out of the control of the attackers and escalate into direct combat between the regular armed forces of both countries. This war of attrition translates into border incidents which take place almost daily. Between September 1985 and March 1986, there were more than 60 such incidents, in which soldiers of the Sandinista People's Army (*Ejercito Popular Sandinista* or EPS) crossed the Honduran border in pursuit of *contras* who had fled back towards their base camps.[39]

At the end of March 1986, an incident illustrative of the prevailing situation received considerable publicity, which exacerbated Honduran-US relations because of the use which the Reagan administration made of it. The events were made known on the 19th. The EPS had gone on the offensive and the *contras* were in full retreat. Predicting that the EPS push would not stop at the border, the Honduran Armed Forces decided to move 5,000 of its regular soldiers into the threatened area. Within the context of repeated border incidents as we have indicated, Honduras took rather normal preventive measures, alerting and reinforcing their military garrisons.[40] The White House, however, tried to elevate the incident to the level of a strategic crisis for Honduras and the United States, increasing feelings of belligerence: on the 23rd, certain "transcenders" surfaced in Washington who referred to an EPS "invasion" of Honduras;[41] the following day, the White House announced it was responding to an appeal by the Honduran government and was sending $20 million in emergency military assistance. Meanwhile, Secretary of Defense Caspar Weinberger sent General John Galvin, Chief of the US Southern Command, to Tegucigalpa "for an indefinite period," in order "to cooperate with the Honduran Armed Forces and repel the aggression of the Nicaraguan army."[42]

From the first, there was a series of discrepancies in the emphases which Washington and Tegucigalpa gave to this incident, owing to the policy of *fait accompli* instigated by the White House. The failure to consult bothered the Hondurans because it not only placed the new government in an embarrassing situation, but it impaired its national and international credibility. Until then, the official position had been that the *contras* were in Honduras, at best, illegally engaging in an occasional skirmish with the EPS only in passing. This was swept away by official White House announcements that the EPS was attacking, among others, important *contra* bases, such as that of San Francisco de Yamale.[43]

Something similar happened with the supposed appeal for emergency military assistance. An official communiqué of the Honduran government made clear that it was "completely false" that Honduras had asked for $20 million. What happened, it said, was that it had asked the United States to lend it some helicopters, then being used in military maneuvers, to move its troops quickly to the border.[44] Interestingly, 24 hours after Washington's "escalated announcements," the Honduran government was still refusing to confirm them.[45] While the Reagan Administration persisted in portraying the incident in the logic of "aggression," the Honduran government itself was playing down the confrontational image, making public assurances that it would maintain its pacific attitude of trying to avoid open clashes with Nicaragua. This attitude was reflected in an official communiqué made public by Foreign Minister López Contreras on the 26th. Affirming that "there is no belligerent climate in Honduras," but one of "prudence and a firm commitment to defend our sovereignty," he announced that the Honduran Armed Forces were "taking up positions and, if necessary, will proceed to evacuate any foreign force found on the national territory."[46]

The discrepancies did not stop there. President Azcona refused to make an official declaration, by radio or television, giving an account of the Sandinista "invasion." At the same time, officials of the Honduran government were given the job of publicizing Azcona's decision to travel "on vacation" to his home town of La Ceiba, taking advantage of the religious holiday of Holy Week.[47] With this step, management of the whole situation rested in military hands, both Honduran and US. Tension along the border lasted for several days, without any official reports of confrontations between Honduran soldiers and Sandinistas. Toward the 30th of March it was announced that the latter had returned home and the *contras* to their bases, which brought to an end the most icy stage of the incident.

In April 1986 rumors began to circulate that the Green Berets would be training *contras* on Honduran territory. Along with this,

Ambassador Ferch announced that the US was donating $11 mil-
lion to build a new military training center.[48] Officially, it would
only serve Honduran soldiers. But the idea that *contras* would
also be trained did not seem to elicit very strong denials in
Honduras. On this issue, again Washington and Tegucigalpa
seemed to be on different wave lengths. While the Chief of the
Honduran Armed Forces stated emphatically that "neither the
Green Berets nor any other US soldiers are going to come to
Honduras to train anti-Sandinistas," US officials indicated the exact
opposite.[50] All this discussion seemed to come to a head in
October 1986. What followed was a kind of intermediate arrangement, halfway between the Honduran position of observing the
greatest discretion in these activities and Washington's desire to
step them up. At the end of the month, US military leaders
announced that the United States "will establish" anti-Sandinista
bases on Honduran islands off the coast of Nicaragua.[51]

These cross-currents and tensions which went on throughout
1986 demonstrate the limits against which President Azcona strug-
gled in designing a foreign policy around Honduran interests.
Searching for a greater balance between costs and benefits, he
introduced some revisions in, and clarification of, the agenda
inherited from the previous administration. Thus, he repeated that
"there is no conflict between Honduras and Nicaragua," adding
that he could "guarantee that Honduran territory will not be used
as a platform for launching attacks against any neighboring
country, whether by guerrilla forces or the armies of third
countries."[52] Contrary to what may be believed, important sectors
in Honduras, particularly within the army high command, are not
really interested in an open war with Nicaragua. For purely
pragmatic reasons, war seems like good business as long as it
remains at the level of threat, but drops off when it turns into hard
reality. Even supposing the military downfall of the Sandinistas,
in the short run Honduras and its armed forces would find themselves among the losers. It is highly probable that once the
combination of circumstances that makes them essential to US
strategy disappears, the copious economic and military aid which
they have received in recent years will fall off to pre-1980s levels.[53]
Nevertheless, the willingness of Honduras' government and

military make up only some of the many factors which help or hinder this war, and not necessarily the most decisive.[54]

In 1986 the Honduran Government tried to reverse its former permissiveness toward the *contras* by letting responsibility for the *contra* presence in Honduras fall back on Nicaragua and its internal conflicts. As President Azcona remarked in his address to the Permanent Council of the OAS:

> Honduras, because of its geographic position, has historically been the victim of the internal conflicts of surrounding countries. Conscious of this reality, we encourage dialogues for national reconciliation to make room for structured democratic, representative, and pluralistic coexistence.

He then added that

> the length of the border [with Nicaragua], the wild, unpopulated condition of much of the border region, and the Honduran army's limited equipment, make complete control of the border extremely difficult.[55]

Azcona expanded on this idea even more vividly at various press conferences, saying that Honduras would not provide even one cent of its scarce resources to watch out for the Sandinistas.[56] From there, he went on to outline more clearly that his policy towards the *contras* would resemble a sort of "letting alone."

Subsequently, the Honduran government committed itself to cushion the impact which this "letting alone" could have on its domestic and foreign policy, indicating to US officials that they would persist in using cunning and discretion to handle the more sensitive aspects of aid to the *contras*. They were already quite concerned about complaints from farmers and residents in the south of the country of the difficulties they were encountering in carrying out their normal activities, and of the atrocities and assassinations committed by the anti-Sandinistas[57] — as if wanting to confirm their presence with open delivery of US aid into Honduran territory. The government did not want to see a repetition of the incidents such as in October 1985. Then declarations of government officials, military commanders, and leaders of the Legislative Assembly had displayed relative unanimity in assuring that aid to the *contras* would not pass through Honduran territory.[58]

But the Honduran government was not able to maintain its position unchanged for long. While to some extent this consensus of opinion made more difficult the task of US government and military officials who were in Tegucigalpa to break Honduran resistance all through 1986,[59] it was not sufficient to resist the pressure and overcome the limits placed on Honduran foreign policy by the nature of its relations with the United States. Thus, on 31 October 1986, the first major shipment of military equipment for the *contras* arrived in Honduras as part of the $100 million in aid approved by the US Congress.[60]

NEIGHBORING COUNTRIES AND REGIONAL CONFLICTS

THE ELECTION OF José Azcona to the presidency of Honduras did not signify any major changes in the parameters which had characterized its relations with El Salvador in recent years. Both governments defined the Sandinistas as aggressors and exporters of revolution with the United States, revealed by a series of common positions at the level of regional politics. Azcona's visit to his Salvadoran colleague, José Napoleón Duarte, at the end of July 1986,[61] showed that both leaders shared the opinion that "the real problem in Central America is Nicaragua's lack of desire for domestic democracy." According to Azcona, the *contras* were going to continue "fighting [the Sandinista Government] with arms in hand because they cannot do so with ballots or dialogue," a situation which "redounds negatively" on neighboring countries. A little more radical, Duarte expressed the need "to confront jointly with Honduras the terrorist ideological expansionism of the totalitarians" because this problem "cannot be challenged successfully by small democracies acting alone." In short, Azcona and Duarte sealed their alliance with the promise to "join forces" in the search for a peaceful solution to regional conflicts, emphasizing their right "to demand the democratization of Nicaragua."[62]

Accompanying these common interests, however, was an ongoing situation of bilateral tension and disagreement in other areas. For more than a century a border dispute had been hanging fire between Honduras and El Salvador, which had flared up into the brief 1969 war which had left 5,000 dead.[63] President Azcona returned to push for one of the last parts of the plan negotiated with El Salvador in the Peace Treaty, signed 10 December 1980 in Lima (Peru), which put an end to the state of war which still existed between the two countries and regularized diplomatic relations. This Treaty set a 5-year period in which to agree to a final arrangement *via* direct negotiations. The period ended 10 December 1985 without an agreement. Foreseeing this possibility, the Treaty had specified an additional 6-month period — until 10 June 1986 — in which both parties would prepare a joint presentation to be made to the International Court of Justice at The Hague (ICJ), whose judgment would be final. If by that time there were still problems, either Honduras or El Salvador would be free to appeal to the ICJ unilaterally.

The final period began to run out without the various rounds of negotiation having produced any firm agreement. By early 1986, Honduran diplomats had become pessimistic regarding El Salvador's promise to abide by an ICJ decision.[64] They remained tense right up to the last moment when Azcona and Duarte finally resolved their differences during direct talks which took place when they attended the meeting of Central American leaders in Esquipulas at the end of May.

However, the border conflict is only one of a whole range of problems that beset Honduras and El Salvador. For example, along the 472 square kilometers of territory under litigation, a series of camps houses a large part of the more than 20,000 Salvadoran refugees who have fled their country's devastating civil war. The Azcona government continues to link those refugees with the Salvadoran guerrillas, sharing President Duarte's opinion that they are part of the FDR-FMLN's rear guard.

Honduras is concerned for several reasons. First, the refugees place a heavy burden on a country which already ranks low on the scale of Latin American development.[65] Second, the tripartite commission — composed of representatives from Honduras, El Salvador and ACNUR (an organization formed to seek a solution to this problem) — made little progress in 1986 despite the fact that Salvador's foreign minister, Rodolfo Castillo Claramount, stated back in July that (1) his government was neither obstructing nor dampening efforts at repatriation and that (2) to the contrary, he was determined to "set up a calendar" which would "arrange for the transfer of those people in an orderly and systematic way."[66] On the other hand, the possibility always exists that, in order to strengthen its claim, El Salvador may argue before the ICJ that its citizens are already located in the disputed area.

One can be sure that the Honduran military sleeps with its eyes open: one directed toward El Salvador, its ideological ally but territorial adversary, the other toward happenings on the Nicaraguan border. When Azcona took over the presidency, Honduran-Nicaraguan relations were experiencing one of their more difficult periods. At any rate, the arrival of a new regime raised hopes for improvement. The inauguration of Vinicio Cerezo in Guatemala, on 14 January 1986, provided an opportunity for the newly-elected president to meet with his Nicaraguan counterpart, Daniel Ortega, for the first time. The fact that the latter did not attend Azcona's inauguration in Tegucigalpa two weeks later, on 27 January, dashed any hopes for a closer relationship that may have been raised. At any event, hope remained alive when Azcona met with Nicaraguan Vice-President Sergio Ramírez Mercado and agreed to a renewal of contacts — diplomatic, economic, and military.[67]

In this optimistic atmosphere, President Azcona sent a letter to the Nicaraguan leader at the beginning of February 1986 in which he stated:

> I take pleasure in demonstrating that ... my government is well disposed to expand and strengthen the ties of friendship which, by virtue of our common historical patrimony, unites us with Nicaragua and the rest of the fraternal countries of Central America, always searching for solutions which will benefit the whole Central American community.[68]

Along with strong anti-Sandinista rhetoric, there were other signs to indicate that the Honduran government was beginning to explore new paths in its relations with Nicaragua. Did this form part of a foreign policy plan designed — for example — to counteract the negative effects produced by the *contras* and the US alliance? It is highly probable. It is said that diplomatic contacts between Honduras and Nicaragua have been frequent, "though marked by great reserve," since January 1986; also mentioned is that both governments exchange intelligence information on the *contras*, and that Nicaragua uses indirect diplomatic channels to advise the Azcona government of punitive actions against anti-Sandinistas stationed in Honduras.[69] Another suggestive fact is that Honduras' new ambassador to Managua, appointed the beginning of June 1986, was Colonel Rigoberto Regalado, brother of Honduras' Commander-in-Chief of the Army. At the same time, it is maintained that there were preliminary contacts to set up a meeting between the Honduran and Nicaraguan military. However, the plan fell through when Managua went to the ICJ to press a claim against Honduras for the latter's alleged violation of international law in allowing armed anti-Sandinista groups on its territory.[70]

Underlying the atmosphere as well was the return home from Honduras of a significant number of Nicaraguan refugees (mostly Misquito Indians), whose numbers had risen to more than 4,000 by mid-1986 according to ACNUR sources.[71] Another achievement was the improvement of bilateral economic ties, which had suffered a major deterioration during the previous two years. Following various rounds of negotiations held in both Teguci-galpa and Managua, the two governments signed a mutual aid pact around the middle of May in order to strengthen and renew bilateral trade, to reschedule Nicaragua's $445 million debt with Honduras, and to set the terms by which Honduran fishermen would be allowed to harvest shellfish in Nicaraguan waters. Honduras also agreed to change the rules governing the transit of Nicaraguan businessmen through its territory, in order to avoid the situation of contraband and scarcity of goods in Nicaragua. Finally, they agreed to create a bilateral commission, to meet every three months, which would oversee fulfilment of the agreement.[72]

Nicaragua's charges against Honduras before the ICJ produced a strong reaction in Honduras, adding a new note of tension to their bilateral relations. While Foreign Minister López Contreras initially announced that the government would fight the charges, the following day it was no longer so certain that it would do so. President Azcona later made it known that, in order to safeguard Honduras from "any Sandinista sophistries," he had written to the International Court two months previously to withdraw Honduras from the Court's jurisdiction.[73] His decision to sidestep a judicial confrontation with Nicaragua, a secret up till then, provoked an outcry in Honduras. The Azcona government finally decided to present its side of the case before the International Court, even though that would bind Honduras to the Court's decision should Nicaragua's charges be upheld. No doubt Tegucigalpa trusted that the friendship of the United States would enable it to evade any adverse penalties.

During the year, Honduras' critical rhetoric toward the Sandinistas became even more aggressive at times, as border incidents worsened. For example, artillery battles between Honduran and Nicaraguan forces were reported in mid-November, and one of the worst crises of recent years began in December.[74] At the end of 1986, Honduran efforts to avoid events which could increase its involvement in the so-called "Central American conflagration" dimmed as every day the prospect of a Honduran-Nicaraguan war became more serious.[75] The dynamics imposed by the actions of US interests, added to the activities of the *contras*,[76] appeared to overwhelm the original intentions of the Honduran regime to achieve a more balanced relationship with Nicaragua.[77]

In mid-April, General Humberto Regalado, Commander-in-Chief of Honduran Armed Forces, visited Central American capitals accompanied by high-ranking Honduran army officials. The goal was to meet with the military heads of countries in the region to explore the possibility of reviving CONDECA (Central American Defense Council),[78] only now without Nicaragua, with the explicit objective "of checking the Communist ideology which is rapidly spreading in Central America."[79] Coinciding with the presidential meeting in Esquipulas, the military high commands of the region held discussions on this subject. But the Honduran urgings received only a lukewarm reception in the barracks of Guatemala, El Salvador, and Panama. Indeed, it was one more indication that Honduran politicians and military found themselves playing the role of *peon* to carry out US plans.[80]

Honduran trade with other countries of Central America was virtually paralyzed by mid-1986. As a result of its 1969 war with El Salvador, Honduras had dropped out of the Central American Common Market (CACM). From then on, its whole regional trade was based on bilateral agreements signed that same year with Costa Rica, Guatemala, Nicaragua and — in 1982 — El Salvador. The problems of 1986 derived from fluctuations in exchange rates in the other countries, which translated into losses for Honduras given its monetary stability. Added to this was the fact that, ever since 1982, Honduras has had an unfavorable trade balance with Central America. The situation became even more complicated when, in mid-year, El Salvador, Guatemala, and Costa Rica announced their resignation from the Central American Clearing House, a kind of regional exchange clearing house requiring payment for exports in dollars. This was a rude shock for Honduras, which faced a serious shortage of foreign exchange.[81] Cushioning the impact of these events and overcoming the shackles in regional trade were issues which consumed most of the efforts of Honduran political and economic authorities in 1986.

The Central American crisis and ongoing negotiations for regional peace were other high-priority issues in Honduran foreign policy during this period. José Azcona faced what was supposed to be the final stage in negotiations by the Contadora Group. Foreign Minister López Contreras outlined the position of the Honduran government at the meeting of the Contadora and Support Groups, held in Panama at the beginning of April, at which he announced its willingness to "redouble" its efforts to promote peace in Central America and insisted that

> discussions should focus specifically on concluding the Contadora Act as a comprehensive agreement which would take into account the basic interests of each and every one of the Central American states.[82]

Nevertheless, in the race against time to reach Contadora's deadline (6 June 1986) for final ratification of the Peace Accord, the Azcona government introduced elements which made it more difficult of achievement, and which ended by placing Honduras in unexpected isolation in the course of negotiations. For example, while the rest of the countries were disposed to prohibit the military exercises on their territory, Honduras — along with Costa Rica — remained supporters of them til the end. Even more telling, its thesis of discussing a significant reduction in the total number of soldiers and arms of the regional armies (including auxiliary bodies, militia, and paramilitary groups), to be achieved in progressive stages of 30, 90, and 120 days, brought it into conflict with particularly sensitive interests of its immediate neighbors.[83] El Salvador, Guatemala, and Nicaragua have organized armies significantly greater than that of Honduras, even leaving out auxiliary bodies, as a result of the existence of armed opposition groups of greater or lesser importance in those countries. These strategic considerations caused rejection of the Honduran proposal, provoking a crack in the tactical alliance which it had been able to maintain up til then with El Salvador, Costa Rica, and — finally — Guatemala within the ambiance of the Contadora Group.[84]

The Honduran government rejected the final version of the Peace Accord, presented by the Contadora Group on 13 June 1986, on the grounds that it did not establish "obligations reasonable and sufficient to guarantee the security of the nation," but reiterating "its desire to continue exploring new formulas which would offer effective guarantee of the legitimate interests of all the states," and endorsing the US position that any accord "ought to make verification of the reduction in armaments, soldiers, and foreign military advisors possible."[85] Honduran observers characterized this statement as a recognition that Contadora no longer offered the Azcona government a good peace alternative, an opinion which seemed to be confirmed when the Foreign Ministers of El Salvador and Costa Rica met in Tegucigalpa the following month. At the conclusion of that meeting, the Foreign Minister of Costa Rica — acting as spokesman for the trio — declared that they had exchanged views concerning the Central American situation which eventually would become a document to serve as a means for regional peace. "At no time have we considered eliminating Contadora," he emphasized, "but we want to form a democratic alliance to achieve peace in Central America."[86]

While the Contadora negotiations were paralyzed, conditions were once again ripe for restoration of a reduced "Tegucigalpa Group." Another factor bringing the Group closer was Nicaragua's accusations before the ICJ which impacted Honduras and Costa Rica alike. On the eve of departing for the 41st meeting of the UN General Assembly, Foreign Minister López Contreras declared that "the Nicaraguan charge in the International Court of Justice is incompatible with continuation of the Contadora process."[87] The conjunction of these elements, as much as the Reagan administration's decision to seek the military overthrow of the

Sandinistas, created a fairly pessimistic scenario for the progress of Central American peace negotiations.

NEW GOALS FOR FOREIGN POLICY

DURING THE ELECTION campaign, Azcona presented a program based on the following foreign policy goals:

(a) "To respect the principle of the people's freedom to choose the political regime they deemed most suitable;"

(b) "To maintain peaceful, cooperative relations with all nations;"

(c) "To fulfill international promises;"

(d) "To consolidate and promote ties of friendship, cooperation, and solidarity with other peoples to strengthen democracy and freedom;" and

(e) "To establish, and foster, international relations to promote Honduran interests."

Within this framework, he proposed two objectives of a functional nature:

(1) "to review the foreign service, professionalize it, and make it more dynamic, so that it will reflect a positive national image and be an agent of economic, cultural, and political exchange," and

(2) "to make an earnest effort to develop relations within Central America, above all with the countries on its borders, ... [and to] support all the organizations and mechanisms that favor the establishment and maintenance of peace."[88]

Another important goal in 1986 was for Honduras to increase its international ties.

In this regard, President Azcona's frequent trips out of the country played an important role. From his election until the following August, he attended meetings or other official events in Venezuela (December 1985); in the United States (January and May 1986); in Guatemala (January and May 1986); in Costa Rica (May 1986); in El Salvador (end of July 1986); and in Colombia (August 1986) — becoming one of Honduras' most travelled leaders in the process. Not only did the trips transform him into an activist in international relations, but they also helped him to project a direct, dynamic diplomatic image. His trip to Colombia to attend the inauguration of President Virgílio Barco (on 7 August) provides a good example. On 2 August, just prior to the ceremony, Azcona flew to the Colombian island of San Andrés to meet with outgoing President Belisario Betancur (1) to discuss the Central American situation and (2) to continue negotiations then pending regarding the sovereignty of various Caribbean islands. Discussions concluded with the signing of a treaty establishing, first, the Caribbean maritime borders of Honduras and Colombia, on the one hand, and, second, providing for the sharing of sovereignty over the Serranilla Keys.[89] Azcona then flew to the Colombian capital for the inauguration.

In another area, economic authorities made efforts to strengthen, diversify, and expand Honduran trade links. In August 1986, Economics Minister Reginaldo Panting announced that he had initiated discussions with Bulgaria and Czechoslovakia. According to Panting, the interest in establishing trade relations with socialist countries is in line with government policy. "We are going to try to promote our products with as many countries as possible," he pointed out, emphasizing that the Ministry he heads is limited to expanding trade activities, leaving the Foreign Ministry to define matters of political interest.[90]

This effort to expand the traditional limited diplomatic nexus of Honduras is accompanied by the relatively recent openings of new embassies. Among these has been its accreditation to The Hague, a requirement for the litigation with El Salvador, and that with Taiwan. In this context, we might mention the official announcement, made at the end of September, that President Azcona would visit Italy, West Germany, Holland, and Spain in 1987 — the first time that a Honduran leader would officially visit Europe. In preparation for this tour, during August Foreign Minister López Contreras made an extensive trip through Europe, which extended to Israel as well.

The need to make progress toward the above-mentioned objectives, together with internal and external tension and the pressure to which the government was subjected in 1986, was reflected in a serious reshuffling within Honduran diplomatic circles. At the end of December, the foreign minister confirmed that he had requested the resignation of all ambassadors and high-level personnel in the Ministry of Foreign Relations.[91]

FINAL CONSIDERATIONS

As IN FORMER YEARS, the conditions which its alliance with the United States imposed on Honduras remained apparent in 1986. The main themes of its foreign agenda, and important aspects of domestic policy and economy, showed a clear US interference. One demonstration of this was the limits encountered by the Azcona government when it attempted to lower its profile of participation in the Central American bellicose spiral imposed by the Reagan administration and to adhere to a foreign policy closer to the interests of Honduras.

On the other hand, diplomatic readjustments, expansion of foreign relations, and pursuit of a larger role in the international arena seemed to be part of an attempt to counteract the negative aspects of Honduras' alignment with the Reagan administration's political-military strategy for Central America. The perception that it has been converted into a political and economic vassal of the United States has in no way benefitted Honduras. We believe that this foreign policy is a hedge against the future, a form of security against the time when the Central American conflicts are resolved, or US policy toward the region takes on new goals, emphases or focus. In that case, Honduras will still need as much political and economic support as it does now. But it is also highly probable that US interest and aid will fall off to its former level as soon as Honduras loses its present geopolitical relevance. Faced with this eventuality, Honduran efforts to fill this vacuum should be directed to places away from the United States.

NOTES

1. These ceremonies were attended by Guatemalan President Vinicio Cerezo, President José Napoleón Duarte of El Salvador; Prime Minister Manuel Esquivel of Belize, US Vice-President George Bush, Vice-President Sergio Ramírez of Nicaragua, Vice-President Roderick Esquivel of Panama, Vice-President Blasco Peñaherrera of Ecuador, Vice-President

Victor Hugo Martínez of Argentina, and foreign ministers and members of 56 official embassy delegations.

2. For an account of the foreign policy of Suazo Córdova during his last 3 years in office, see Daniel Asenjo's "Honduras: Militarismo y Política Exterior," pp. 269-280 in Heraldo Muñoz (ed.) Las Políticas Exteriores Latinoamericanas Frente a la Crisis (Buenos Aires: Grupo Editor Latinoamericano, 1985), and "La Política Exterior de Honduras durante 1985," pp. 345-364 in Heraldo Muñoz (ed.) América Latina y El Caribe: Políticas Exteriores para Sobrevivir (Buenos Aires: Grupo Editor Latinoamericano, 1986).

3. In May 1985, the major political parties (Liberal and National) reached an agreement along the following basic lines: (a) each party would be officially represented by more than one candidate in the November elections; (b) the new president would be the candidate who obtained a majority of votes within the winning party; (c) in order to determine the winning party, individual votes for its candidates would be tallied. Thus, José Azcona was elected president with a 28% majority of the votes, whereas Leonardo Callejas, his principal rival from the National Party, had to give up his claim despite having received more than 42% of the ballots cast.

4. The November elections, in which the entire Legislative Assembly was replaced, also resulted in the following composition of the Honduran parliament: 67 legislators for the Liberal Party (46 from the Azcona faction, 18 from that of Mejía Arellano and 3 from that of Bu Girón; 63 for the National Party (all from Leonardo Callejas' faction); 2 for the Christian Democrats, and 2 for the *Partido de Innovación y Unidad* (Data from p. 2 of Boletín Informativo Honduras 56, December 1985, published in Tegucigalpa).

5. These parties reached a similar agreement in 1971 but were unable to avoid the military overthrow of President Ramón Ernesto Cruz, of the National Party, 15 months later.

6. President Azcona filled 10 of 12 ministerial positions, 2 of the 4 government vice-presidencies, the presidency and 2 of the 4 secretaryships of the Legislative Assembly. The remaining positions, plus the presidency of the Supreme Court, were filled by National Party *callejistas.*

7. Carlos López Contreras is an active member of the National Party and first cousin of the former Commander-in-Chief of the Honduran Armed Forces, General Walter López, to whose influence his appointment is, in great part, due. He is a lawyer and has worked as an official of the Honduran Foreign Ministry for several years. During the government of General Policarpo Paz García (1978-1982), he served as temporary Deputy Minister. He was one of the foreign minister's closest advisors during the former Eduardo Paz Barnica regime. He is a specialist in negotiations on the El Salvador border problem, a subject on which

he has written a book (see p. 6 of Boletín Informativo Honduras 58, February 1986, Tegucigalpa).

8. The top echelon of the ALIPO is made up of Jaime Rosenthal Oliva, Edmond Bográn and José Bueso Arias. At the time, they headed the 3 principal financial groups in San Pedro Sula, the most important commercial and industrial center in Honduras. The first of these businessmen was appointed vice-president of the republic, with specific responsibility for all economic negotiations with the United States (see p. 27 of Boletín de Prensa Latinoamericana No. 1-86, Hamburg).

9. For a detailed analysis of the fall of General Walter López, see Boletín Informativo Honduras 58, February 1986 (Tegucigalpa). Rivalry within the Honduran military claimed new victims at the end of September. Removed from their jobs and appointed to diplomatic missions were: Colonel Guillermo Thuman Cordón, former Commander-in-Chief of the army; Thomas Said Speer, former commander of the Blindada cavalry regiment; and Héctor Aplicano Molina, former director of the Command School and Chief-of-Staff of the army, accused of rebellion and trying to replace the head of the armed forces, General Humberto Regalado Hernández (see IPS Cable [Tegucigalpa] for 18 August 1986 and 21 October 1986; El Mercurio for 20 September 1986: A-7 and for 6 October 1986: A-3 and A-7; and pp. 1 and 12 of the Boletín Informativo Honduras 66, October 1986, Tegucigalpa).

10. Some of the goals proposed for the next 4 years are to increase private investment to annual rates of 18%, those of public enterprises to 4.5%, and exports to an average of 5.3%; that government consumption be held to 1985 levels, and that private consumption increase slowly — at no more than 4% annually — in order not to aggravate inflationary pressures; and that, altogether, the gross domestic product (GDP) grow at an annual rate of 4.5% (for more details, see pp. 26-28 in Boletín de Prensa Latinoamericana No. 1-86, Hamburg). According to figures released by CONSUPLANE at the end of 1985, Honduras had received offers for $1,200 million for the following 4 years: the IDB would provide $800 million at the rate of $200 million per year, and Japan promised $400 million to be payed in annual $100 million installments (see Excelsior, 26 December 1985: 2-A).

11. Honduras relations with the IMF were interrupted at the end of 1983. During the last half of that year, the government ceased to meet the conditions set by the IMF for stand-by credit. In mid-1984, discussions to arrange a new monetary stabilization accord began; however, the Suazo Córdova regime ended without such an agreement being signed.

12. This figure, modest by comparison with the external debt which is being renegotiated annually in Latin America, represents a considerable sum for Honduras — the equivalent of more than 50% of its total 1986 budget.

13. The first half of 1986 ended with a deficit of $152 million. This figure was $14 million higher than for the same period in 1985 (Central America, Latin American Monitor, September 1986: 336.)

14. This and the following quotes are taken from *Paz y Seguridad Democrática para Centroamérica*, a speech given by Foreign Minister Carlos López Contreras before the Permanent Council of the OAS on 28 May 1986, available as a brochure from the Honduran Embassy in Santiago. In this presentation, López emphasized that Honduran foreign policy has two main objectives: (1) to preserve internal peace and protect Honduras from the ravages of war; (2) to achieve an integrated security system for the country, composed of 4 parts. The first part is made up of means of defense already at the country's disposal; the second consists of those instruments which comprise the operation of the inter-American system (OAS, American Treaty for Peaceful Solutions, and the TIAR). The third part is based upon joining with "friendly" countries to draw up, or implement, security treaties which will complement the inter-American system in safeguarding peace, the security of the people and the integrity of Honduran territory. Finally, the fourth part is based on Central American agreements for security and disarmament which could be updated.

15. *Ibid.*: 10-11.

16. The total offered by AID for 1985 was $147.5 million, of which the balance, which was frozen, would be paid in October 1985 (Excelsior for 3 January 1986: 2-A, and for 4 January 1986: 2-A and 23.)

17. One must remember that general elections were held in November 1985, which placed the ability of the governing Liberal Party to continue in power at risk.

18. This denial remained in place even after a team of cameramen from one of the major US television networks filmed "non-lethal" aid destined for the *contras* being shipped from the United States on 10 October 1985 — and its arrival at Toncontin airport in Tegucigalpa. Honduras subsequently returned the shipment to the United States. Trying to arrange a new supply, both Admiral John Poindexter, member of the US National Security Council (NSC), and Colonel North, who served as liaison between the NSC and UNO (*Unión Nicaragüense Opositora*, a coalition of leading anti-Sandinista groups) arrived in Tegucigalpa (for details, see p.8 in *Boletín Informativo Honduras* 56, December 1985, Tegucigalpa).

19. Excelsior, 4 January 1986: 2-A and 23.

20. Informe Latinoamericano 2, 10 January 1986: 107.

21. Certain prior events indicate that this happened. During Azcona's visit to Washington just a week before taking office, he had reached a "secret" agreement with Vice-President Bush "to help the Reagan administration deliver aid to the Nicaraguan counter-revolutionaries" (quoted on p. 24 of Boletín de Prensa Latinoamericana 1-86, Hamburg)

22. The amount of aid which the US Congress finally wangled for Honduras at the end of 1985 came to about $231 million, of which $143 million was allocated for economic assistance and $88 million for military assistance. But Honduras wanted, at the very least, $483 million, a sum similar to that given to El Salvador (Miami Herald, 27 November 1985).

23. In what was described as preparation for this trip, the week before his visit a delegation of 7 Honduran legislators went to Washington at the invitation of US Congressmen, the first time in Honduran-US history that such a meeting took place (El Mercurio, 26 May 1986: A-7; and IPS Cable [Tegucigalpa] 27 May 1986).

24. Boletín de Prensa Latinoamericana 2-1986 (Hamburg): 16-17.

25. Boletín Informativo Honduras 65, September 1986 (Tegucigalpa): 1.

26. Boletín Informativo Honduras 66, October 1986 (Tegucigalpa): 5.

27. El Mercurio, 1 November 1986: A-7, and 2 November 1986: A-10; La Tercera, 1 November 1986: 19.

28. Boletín de Prensa Latinoamericana 1-86 (Hamburg): 25. Gonzalo Carias Pineda was the only high-ranking official of the former government to remain in his post during the Azcona administration.

29. This maneuver, characterized as "spectacular and without precedent in Honduras," included launching paratroops and heavy earthmoving equipment. Everything was transported from Fort Bragg (NC) to the Honduran zone of Urzuna, located 25 kilometers from the Nicaraguan border, in a 3-hour flight by 12 transport planes (Boletín de Prensa Latinoamericana 3-86 [Hamburg]: 28).

30. IPS Cable (Tegucigalpa) 6 June 1986, 5 April 1986, 23 April 1986, 3 June 1986, and 17 July 1986; Herald Tribune, 4 March 1986: 3.

31. At the beginning of the *Cabañas 86* exercises, US officials made it clear that the object of these exercises was to intimidate the Nicaraguan government and to prepare US troops for possible future military action against it (Herald Tribune, 4 March 1986: 3).

32. The US Congress did not authorized a permanent military presence in Honduras. This means that US soldiers are not able to remain there for more than six months. The only exceptions are the military attachés at the US Embassy and the commander of the base at Palmerola.

33. Text begins on p. 5 of Boletín Informativo Honduras 39, July 1984 (Tegucigalpa).

34. Complete text on pp. 7-8 of Boletín Informativo Honduras 39, July 1984 (Tegucigalpa).

35. IPS Cable (Tegucigalpa) 19 March 1986 and 1 April 1986; El Mercurio, 22 May 1986: C-1.

36. According to the results of a poll in Honduras, out of 200 leaders of different organizations interviewed, 64.5% disapproved of the presence of US in the country (Boletín Informativo Honduras, Special Issue 24, May 1986). An important factor in aggravating the climate of rejection were repeated denunciations of immoral behavior on the part

of the US soldiers (Boletín de Prensa Latinoamericana 3-86 [Hamburg]: 29; El Mercurio, 10 March 1986: A-B; Noticias Aliadas, 27 March 1986: 7).

37. Anthony Cauterrucci was known in Honduran economic circles as "superminister without portfolio" in the Azcona government. He, along with Ambassador Ferch, the trade attaché Shepard Lowman, and the head of the Bravo Task Force, Colonel William Comee, were removed from their posts at the beginning of 1986 (IPS Cable [Tegucigalpa], July 1986).

38. IPS Cable (Tegucigalpa) 24 September 1986; and Boletín Informativo Honduras 66, October 1986 (Tegucigalpa): 2.

39. La Tercera, 30 May 1986: 20.

40. In any case, Honduras southern border was not completely undefended at the end of March. Beginning in September 1985, several infantry brigades were located there, totalling some 5,000 men. In addition, at the time there were still some 3,000 US soldiers in Honduras, participating in various military maneuvers.

41. The office of Elliot Abrams was later identified as the source of the releases.

42. IPS Cable (Tegucigalpa), 25 March 1986.

43. The FDN maintains its "strategic command" in San Francisco de Yamale. Hospitals, supply centers, arms deposits, communication equipment, and other resources are located there (IPS Cable [Tegucigalpa], 25 May 1986).

44. Since President Reagan had already requested and received these funds, he forwarded them directly to the Honduran armed forces to supplement the military assistance for 1986 granted by the US Congress (IPS Cable [Tegucigalpa], 7 July 1986).

45. IPS Cable (Tegucigalpa), 25 March 1986.

46. El Mercurio, 26 March 1986: A-1 and A-12.

47. IPS Cable (Tegucigalpa), 29 March 1986; and La Tercera, 29 March 1986:15.

48. IPS Cable (Tegucigalpa), 16 May 1986. This news was confirmed at the end of July by Colonel Reinaldo García, head of US Special Forces stationed in Honduras, and also by Colonel Edmundo Torres, commander of Honduras 16th Infantry Battalion. The name selected was *Centro de Adiestramiento Militar del Ejército* (CAME). It was estimated that operations would begin in September, training 1,000 men in each session in the use of arms and counter-insurgency tactics (IPS Cable [Tegucigalpa], 16 June 1986).

49. For example, Carlos Montoya, the current president of the Legislative Assembly, who was constantly opposed to the training of Salvadoran soldiers when he was a deputy during the previous administration, now believed that "if [training of the *contras*] is contemplated in the assistance treaties with the United States, it could be carried out here" (IPS Cable [Tegucigalpa], 4 April 1986).

50. Statements reproduced in Proceso (El Salvador) 252, 27 August 1986: 14.

51. One of those chosen is El Tigre, located on the Gulf of Fonseca (Pacific Ocean) only 2 kilometers from the Nicaraguan coast, which, in 1983, housed a sophisticated radar station and was used to mine Nicaraguan ports. It will now become a supply base and detachment point for *contra* attacks. The others are the Swan islands in the Caribbean, 18 kilometers from Nicaragua, which will be used as a supply base. The latter provided one of the points of departure for the abortive Bay of Pigs invasion of Cuba, in 1961 (El Mercurio, 31 October 1986: A-7).

52. Concepts presented by President Azcona in his address to the Permanent Council of the OAS in Washington on 28 May 1986. The Honduran Foreign Ministry published the complete text of this speech in a pamphlet entitled "Paz Democrática para Centroamerica."

53. Between 1949 and 1979, US military aid to Honduras amounted to $29 million, or an average of less than $1 million per year. Economic assistance during the same period amounted to about $214 million, or an annual average slightly higher than $7 million (author estimates derived from several sources).

54. For more detailed analysis of why the Honduran Armed Forces did not want war with Nicaragua, see following issues of *Boletín Informativo Honduras* (Tegucigalpa): pp. 1 and 12 of issue No. 65, September 1986; pp. 1 and 16 of issue No. 67, November 1986.

55. Azcona *op.cit.*, "Paz Democrática para Centroamerica."

56. IPS Cable (Tegucigalpa), 28 May 1986; and El Mercurio, 29 May 1986: A-6.

57. In this sense, particularly revealing were statements by former Foreign Minister Edgardo Paz Barnica who stated, shortly after leaving office, that the anti-Sandinistas "committed horrible acts in the south and east of Honduras," and that "after 6 P.M … people had to shut themselves up in their houses because at that hour [the *contras*] began commit crimes against the Hondurans themselves." On the other hand, at the beginning of November 1986, coffee growers in the south of Honduras demanded $50 million in indemnity from the United States for damage done to their crops by the rebels (details in IPS Cable [Tegucigalpa], 19 March 1986, 16 May 1986, and 8 August 1986; Alasei 227-86, April 1986: 63; Hoy, 15-21 December 1986: 65.

58. These, for example, were the opinions of Vice-President Jaime Rosenthal, Foreign Minister López Contreras, and Armed Forces Commander-in-Chief General Humberto Regalado (IPS Cable [Tegucigalpa], 27 June 1986 and 26 August 1986).

59. For example, at the end of August the leaders of UNO — Adolfo Calero, Arturo Cruz, and Alfonso Robelo — travelled to Tegucigalpa to meet with William Walker, Assistant Undersecretary of State for Inter-American Affairs, and with Honduran authorities to discuss the flow of

assistance which at the time had been approved by the US Congress (IPS Cable [Tegucigalpa], 26 August 1986).

60. Boletín Informativo Honduras (Tegucigalpa) 67, November 1986: 16. In the interim, the United States tried to solve *contra* logistical problems by opening new air and land routes. For instance, at the end of June 1986, the CIA was accused of using a small clandestine runway for these operations in the area of Aguacate, Honduras (Newsweek, 30 June 1986: 13).

61. The trip was also historical because it was the first trip a Honduran leader had made to El Salvador in over 20 years.

62. IPS Cable (San Salvador), 31 July 1986.

63. The dispute is over the 472 square kilometers of border territory, the sovereignty of several islands, and the maritime limits of the Gulf of Fonseca (jurisdiction over which is shared with Nicaragua) on the Pacific side.

64. On the other hand, Honduras had been preparing for this presentation since 1985. The Suazo Córdova government had engaged a group of seven European jurists to advise the Foreign Ministry on this dispute and had accredited an official representative to The Hague to oversee the judicial process which was already considered inevitable at that level.

65. International help and cooperation do not allow one to reach a stable, definitive solution. Seeking to improve this situation, the Honduran government initiated plans to organize these groups into work cooperatives in order to ameliorate their situation by exploiting "available raw materials" (Hondpress Cable [Tegucigalpa], 28 July 1986).

66. Hondpress Cable (Tegucigalpa), 16 July 1986.

67. Boletín de Prensa Latinoamericana 1-86 (Hamburg): 25.

68. Full text published in Boletín Informativo Honduras 58, February 1986 (Tegucigalpa): 7.

69. In the case of the invasion during Easter, such a warning had arrived two weeks before (Newsweek, 5 May 1986: 9; El Mercurio, 7 May 1986: A-3; and Christian Science Monitor, 13 May 1986).

70. Foreign Minister López Contreras received confirmation that this claim had been presented at the end of July (IPS Cable [Tegucigalpa], 28 July 1986). The Nicaraguan presentation also includes Costa Rica.

71. IPS Cable (Tegucigalpa), 24 September 1986.

72. For events preceding the negotiating process, see IPS Cable (Managua), 9 April 1986; ANN Cable (Managua), 13 June 1986; IPS Cable (Tegucigalpa), 3 May 1986 and 5 August 1986; Hondpress Cable (Tegucigalpa), 6 August 1986; El Mercurio, 12 April 1986: A-8; Boletín de Prensa Latinoamericana 5-86, May 1986 (Hamburg): 38.

73. El Mercurio, 31 July 1986: A-7. In Honduras fear arose that such a decision might adversely affect Honduran interests in its border dispute with El Salvador before the International Court. The apprehension was assuaged when the Foreign Ministry sent an official communiqué clearly stating that it would have no effect on this case since Honduras and El

Salvador had signed an agreement to respect the decision of the International Court of Justice regarding the matter submitted to its jurisdiction (IPS Cable [Tegucigalpa], 4 August 1986).

74. In a fashion similar to Holy Week, on 1 December 1986 approximately 2,500 soldiers of the Sandinista Army entered Honduras in pursuit of *contras*. But they clashed with a platoon of Honduran soldiers, causing 3 deaths and capturing 2. Together with the diplomatic protest, Honduras decreed a rapid mobilization of its army; those transported by US helicopters quickly captured the Sandinista troops. These, in their efforts to break out of the encirclement, attacked 3 Honduran towns (Buena Vista, La Esperanza, and Español Grande). In reprisal, planes of the Honduran Air Force bombarded 2 Nicaraguan communities (Wiwili and La Congoja), leaving 7 dead and 15 wounded. This was the first time that the Honduran armed forces had carried their counter-attacks onto Nicaraguan territory (Hoy X, 491 [15-21 December 1986]: 64-66).

75. This idea was gaining ground in many sectors of Honduras during 1986. For example, at the end of December Carlos Montoya, president of the Legislative Assembly, said that he considered a war with Nicaragua to be "inevitable" and, in that perspective, added that "we must form a defense conscience and culture" (quotes from El Mercurio, 27 December 1986: A-7). However, President Azcona officially dismissed the idea by saying that Honduras had neither pending problems with, nor any interest in attacking, Nicaragua, adding that "it is not fitting for Nicaragua to war with Honduras because our powerful ally is closer than theirs" (El Mercurio, 30 December 1986: A-7).

76. Newspaper reports indicated that the Honduran Armed Forces began to evacuate communities on 28 October 1986, on the border with Nicaragua, particularly in El Paraíso Province, which was considered to be in preparation for a "war scenario" between the Sandinistas and the *contras* (IPS Cable [Tegucigalpa], 31 October 1986).

77. According to diplomatic sources in Tegucigalpa, the US decision to push the *contra* campaign to defeat the Sandinistas brought about the failure of a Nicaraguan proposal to carry out a high-level dialogue to alleviate bilateral tension. See IPS Cable [Tegucigalpa], 7 November 1986.

78. The *Consejo de Defensa Centroamericano* (CONDECA) was created in December 1962 as a body to coordinate a US-designed regional counter-insurgency strategy and to prevent possible conflict among its members: Honduras, El Salvador, Guatemala, and Nicaragua. The United States held member status by virtue of its Air Force Southern Command, whose headquarters were located in the Panama Canal Zone. The alliance withered when it was unable to forestall the Honduras-El Salvador war in 1969 or to prevent the Sandinista overthrow of Somoza. Since 1979, the only participants in CONDECA were Guatemala and El Salvador.

79. Boletín Informativo Honduras (Tegucigalpa) 61, May 1986: 1.

80. In 1983, General Gustavo Alvarez, former Commander-in-Chief of the Honduran Armed Forces, made some fruitless efforts to revive CONDECA or — if not that — the "Northern Triangle" of Honduras, El Salvador, and Guatemala.

81. For example, in 1985 Honduras exported $3.2 million to Guatemala, while imports amounted to $43 million (IPS Cable [Tegucigalpa], 1 November 1986 and 4 November 1986).

82. Hondpress Cable (Tegucigalpa), 8 April 1986.

83. Nicaragua was of the idea that any discussion of the control, regulation, and reduction of regional arms should make a distinction between defensive and offensive armaments.

84. IPS Cable (Tegucigalpa), 23 April 1986, 16 May 1986, 26 May 1986, 2 June 1986, and 6 June 1986; El Mercurio, 24 April 1986: A-6; and 29 May 1986: A-6.

85. El Mercurio, 14 June 1986: A-6.

86. There was no explanation of why Guatemala missed the meeting. The three foreign ministers agreed to exclude Nicaragua because they did not share Nicaragua's "vision of life and power" (IPS Cable [Tegucigalpa], 6 June 1986).

87. IPS Cable (Tegucigalpa), 24 September 1986.

88. Taken from *El Pensamiento del Presidente Electo Ing. José Azcona Hoyo*, a published pamphlet given out by the Honduran Embassy in Chile, s/d.

89. IPS Cable (Tegucigalpa), 1 August 1986 and 6 August 1986; El Mercurio, 3 August 1986: A-11. The signing of this agreement evoked sharp debate in the parliaments of both Honduras and Colombia when its ratification came up (Hondpress Cable [Tegucigalpa], 6 August 1986; IPS Cable [Tegucigalpa], 6 August 1986; and ALASEI 609-86, November 1986: 91).

90. IPS Cable (Tegucigalpa), 15 August 1986.

91. El Mercurio, 28 December 1986: A-10; 29 December 1986: A-8.

GUATEMALA: FOREIGN POLICY IN A FRAGILE DEMOCRATIC CONTEXT

by MLADEN YOPO

WITHOUT A DOUBT, the year 1986 marked a new starting point for Guatemalan foreign policy. After 32 years of brutal military regimes being in power, this Central American country took on democratic form when the young (42-year-old) Christian Democratic lawyer Marcos Vinicio Cerezo Arévalo[1] was inaugurated president — on 14 January 1986 — for a 5-year term. This transfer to civilian power, which had been anticipated by the previous Mejía Víctores administration,[2] had a decided impact on Guatemala's foreign policy in the year that followed.

Nevertheless, despite this change in regime, the major variables which had influenced the country's foreign policy in the past continued to cast their shadow during the new president's first year in office, suggesting that a major part of the military regime's goals would persist into 1986, altered only to the extent needed to support the democratic pocess.

1. CONTEXT OF DEMOCRATIC TRANSITION AND FOREIGN POLICY GOALS

WITHIN THE CONTEXT of Guatemala's foreign policy decision-making framework, the most salient fact is that, though the armed forces have apparently ceded authority to a civilian government, they have lost neither their power base nor their ability to

---

Mladen Yopo is a researcher for the *Programa de Seguimiento de las Políticas Exteriores Latinoamericanas* (PROSPEL-CERC).

maneuver. In this sense, one must not forget — as political leader Carlos Gallardo Flores put it — that

> in the last months of Mejía Víctores, which were characterized by a great power vacuum, the public quickly realized that the army was made up of 3 factions: (1) those, basically motivated by economic self-interest, who opposed handing the government over to civilians; (2) the Mejía group, which wanted the army to retain its position, based on a process of agreement; and, finally, (3) the faction, made up of young officers, who wanted a transfer of power "without any compromise."

Of these factions, the Mejía group won out, and President Cerezo was forced to make a series of concessions to the armed forces and/or to limit the scope of some of his policies. For example, during a period of just a few days, almost 40 decree-laws were issued and published, 16 of which took effect on the eve of the new government taking office.[3] This series of pacts and concessions explains why so many officials in the Cerezo government, both military and civilian, are holdovers from, or have ties to, the previous regime.[4]

On this point, the former Head of State, General Oscar Humberto Mejía Víctores, had this to say about the continued influence of the military: "the politicians must understand that the elections constitute an opportunity the Army was gracious enough to grant. Never before has there been an opportunity like it and they should take advantage of it."[5] After leaving office, Mejía Víctores made this point again when he said "we are not an army overthrown, we are a victorious army ..." and "those who want to pass judgment on the military would be wrong if they did so."[6]

Vinicio Cerezo himself recognized this fact when he stated, shortly before assuming his post, that he respected the judgment of the armed forces and took a realistic and objective attitude: "if I were to judge those officials, I would be committing suicide ... Nobody assumes total power the day after. I am a good politician but I am not God to perform miracles ... " Even before his election, he had stated

> even if I am elected, the door to democracy will scarcely be opened. Only my successor will be able to push for those social changes so desperately needed in Guatemala, including agrarian reform.[7]

Together with the negotiated exit plus influence of the military over much of the decision-making, the new administration inherited an enormous crisis facing the country. The day after his inauguration, President Cerezo acknowledged this when he said: "We have found the country to be in the worst condition ever to be inherited by any head of state of this nation. We are in a terrible crisis."[8] He did not exaggerate. Among other things, the new Christian Democrat administration had to contend with the following adverse socioeconomic indicators: a 47% unemployment rate; poverty affecting two-thirds of the nation (65% of the population can be classed as extremely poor); 50% illiteracy; infant mortality of 85%; inflation that had soared to 145%; a fiscal deficit soon to border on 2.6 million quetzales; negative growth indicators; loss-es (due to reduced imports) of US$1.2 million; and a foreign debt that surpassed $3 billion.[9]

To this bleak picture and its consequent social demands (particularly in a democracy), must be added corruption and smuggling plus an influential concentration of economic and financial power — the latter in the hands of no more than 350 families with well-known links to the military.

The third major conditioner arose from the issue of human rights and political violence. According to incomplete data, political violence since 1954 — when the Jacobo Arbenz administration was overthrown — has left 130,000 persons dead and/or disappeared, thousands of refugees (45,000 in Mexico alone, 75% of whom are women and children), and more than 110,000 orphans.[10] This situation, within the context of returning democracy, has presented the Cerezo government with 3 problems over and above that of the refugees: (1) the *Grupo de Apoyo Mutuo* (GAM or Mutual Support Group) and the case of the detainees-disappeareds; (2) the death squads and organs of repression; and (3) the guerrillas. These three major issues — the armed forces, socio-economic crisis, and human rights and political violence — have indeed placed restraints on domestic policy and strongly conditioned the international policy of the new government.

Nevertheless, not everything was grim for Vinicio Cerezo's exercise of power. Besides inheriting a country eager for democracy, Cerezo could also count on (1) a majority in Parliament,[11] (2) some members of the military who, despite the negotiated exit, had suffered during the long-drawn-out process of maintaining power for 32 years and the crisis thus generated, and (3) the support of the international community, which had given him a warm reception at the outset of his term and during the transition. Evidence of the latter can be found in the official statements of high-ranking personnel and reports in the media of the two superpowers, the United States and the Soviet Union. For example, *PRAVDA*, official newspaper of the Kremlin, declared that Cerezo's triumph in the elections heralded "a new process of transformation begun in Guatemala with a truly constitutional chief of state;"[12] and *Izvestia* described it as "extremely positive." US government advisor Mark Falcoff went as far as to say in an interview that "we are so willing to help Cerezo that it is almost not important what he does."[13] And Richard G. Lugar, Chairman of the Senate Foreign Relations Committee, seconding Falcoff's views, said that:

> the Guatemalan people demonstrated their desire for democracy and the United States clearly supports this objective. These elections are certainly not the final step on what will be a long and difficult road. Nevertheless, what I saw in Guatemala represented a practical and long-awaited opening that deserves the strong support of the United States.[14]

This fulsome rhetoric was echoed by other international spokesmen as well and given tangible expression through the number and variety of countries represented at the Cerezo inauguration. Notable guests included US Vice-President George Bush, all the Central American presidents (with the exception of Luis Alberto Monge of Costa Rica, who excused himself due to the turbulent domestic electoral campaign taking place in his country), the presidents of Panama (Eric del Valle) and Colombia (Belisario Betancur), and the foreign ministers of Argentina, Brazil, Mexico, Peru, Uruguay, and Venezuela.[15] Most important for Cerezo foreign policy goals was the presence of Foreign Minister Claude Cheysson, of France, whose mission was to deliver "the unconditional support of the European Economic Community to the new Guatemalan democracy."[16]

Within this context of crisis and international good will, the Christian Democratic government set forth its primary goal: "to have ... the best democracy;"[17] in other words, to achieve legitimacy and internal strength — to consolidate civilian power — and, at the same time, to increase its options *vis-à-vis* the hegemonic power of the United States. Since the international community, due to its favorable attitude, was viewed as fundamental in achieving this goal, Guatemala directed its foreign policy toward: (a) breaking out of its isolation and improving the country's international image; (b) increasing and diversifying its financial aid and improving the terms of its debt payments to enable it to respond to the socio-economic crisis; (c) achieving a peaceful settlement of the Central American conflict and/or at least strengthening mechanisms to defuse the tension;[18] (d) joining Latin American integration efforts;[19] and (e) maintaining friendly, but neutral, relations with the United States.

In pursuit of these objectives, Vinicio Cerezo defined his foreign policy as one which "will maintain the best possible relations with everyone; will accept all — unconditional — help that is offered; and will continue to support the country's neutrality on the question of the Isthmus."[20] He also described this policy — of active neutrality — as one of "international leadership in search of peace ... in order to convert the international community into a natural friend of Guatemala."[21]

2. THE FOREIGN POLICY OF VINICIO CEREZO

2.1 Activism, Central America and the United States

IN THIS AREA OF diplomatic activism, President Cerezo attacked foreign policy goals "at full speed ahead." In the latter part of December 1985 and before assuming office, he followed the pattern instituted by presidents of other newly-democratic Latin American countries by setting off on a quick tour of all the Central American countries, the United States, and the countries of the Contadora Group. By including Nicaragua in his schedule, he not only reaffirmed his policy of rejecting confrontation in favor of dialogue and negotiations, but also indicated the direction of his foreign policy and the countries it deemed important. He met with all the presidents of the countries visited, seizing the opportunity to reaffirm his intention to respect neutrality (a policy characteristic, to some extent, of the previous military governments) while promising to promote it in dynamic fashion at the same time. During his stay in Managua, he not only met with President Ortega but also attended a reception, hosted by the Guatemalan ambassador, at which the invited guests included those who were active critics of the Sandinista regime.[22]

In the United States, he met with Vice-President George Bush, Assistant Secretary of State John Whitehead, Assistant Secretary of State for Inter-American Affairs Elliott Abrams, National Security Council Chairman John Poindexter, and with leaders of the House and Senate. Even though Cerezo declared himself a "friend" of the United States, he steadfastly refused to criticize the Nicaraguan government or to discuss the regional crisis in an East-West context. Not only did President Cerezo disagree with Secretary of State Schultz that the Soviet-Cuban influence was a "cancer," and with President Reagan that Nicaragua was the principal source of instability in the region, but with respect to the confrontational outlook, which he compared to Lebanonization, he declared that "his regime would seek the development of a forum appropriate for the peaceful resolution of regional disputes and with respect for regional pluralism."[23] These declarations, which found a positive response among various ideological circles in Latin America and among such members of the US Senate as Michael Barnes and Edward Kennedy, also established the limits of the friendship of his Christian Democratic government toward US foreign policy. In response, Lawrence Birns, chairman of the Committee on Hemispheric Affairs, commented: "To judge by his first speeches, Washington is going to have trouble getting Cerezo to swallow its Central American policy."[24]

In order to crystallize Guatemalan leadership at the Central American level and to take advantage of the attendance of four of the Central American presidents at his inauguration, President Cerezo seized the initiative to call a "regional mini-summit" meeting to revive negotiations within the Contadora framework. Indeed, the outcome was the so-called Guatemala Declaration, in which all the points that had been spelled out by the foreign ministers of the Contadora Group and its Support Group — in the Caraballeda Declaration — a few days earlier were, almost naturally, set forth again, such as that the solution of the conflict is Latin American; this necessarily means [that] self-determination, non-interference, territorial integrity, pluralistic democracy, no military bases or armaments, no hostile actions, no foreign troops or advisers, respect for human rights, resumption of dialogue between the United States and Nicaragua ... provide the conditions for reducing regional tension.[25]

The policy of active neutrality toward the Central American conflict endorsed by Cerezo since the beginning of his campaign — as opposed to his runner-up, Jorge Carpio, who endorsed alignment — responded to a variety of facts and situations. In the first place, he had a distinctly different analysis of the isthmian crisis than did President Reagan. This analysis was basically influenced by (1) the increased internationalization of the conflict 10 years after its inception, (2) the unusual length of the crisis, and (3) the extent to which its symbolic significance for the great powers had constantly increased.[26]

In the second place, this analysis was an extension of the policy followed by the previous administrations of General Ríos Montt and, especially, Mejía Victores, i.e., one based on the overriding concern with internal security: not to internationalize a conflict considered "already won" against internal subversion; resentment of the Guatemalan armed forces towards the United States dating back to 1977, when then-President Jimmy Carter suspended military aid to Guatemala for its systematic violation of human rights; a feeling that the regional conflict was not their own (Guatemalan nationalism);[27] and a desire for good, friendly relations with the region to ensure the free flow of trade, including trade with Nicaragua.

Finally, there was also the fact that any Guatemalan *rapprochement* with the US policy of confrontation in Central America would necessarily imply an upgrading of the armed forces — in soldiers, in training, in modernization of weapons, and so on. Such a situation would directly contradict Cerezo's objective of transferring and strengthening civilian power.

In line with his policy of leadership in the area of negotiation, President Cerezo used his inaugural address to invite the Central American presidents to a summit meeting in Esquipulas — a small town in the department of Chiquimula, Guatemala — on 24-

25 May 1986. The agenda, to which all the Central American leaders agreed, dealt with reducing tension and promoting integration in the region: creating a Central American Parliament, revising Contadora Group initiatives, financing the foreign debt, and strengthening intra-regional commerce.[28]

According to Francisco Villagrán, Guatemala's Deputy Minister of Foreign Affairs, Cerezo's proposal for a Central American parliament would create an instrument intended to complement, not conflict with, the Contadora peace process.[29] As a matter of fact, the Christian Democratic government valued the work of the Contadora Group very highly; Cerezo had even said that this process "is peace." Nevertheless, consonant with its view of the crisis, the Cerezo administration also emphasized that, in order to achieve a solution, "other permanent political instruments are required." According to Cerezo, the Central American parliament would help in this direction in two ways: (1) as "a forum for discussion and (2) for resolving differences by political means."[30] At the same time, Guatemalan Finance Minister Rodolfo Paiz implicitly broadened its scope when he indicated that

> the integration of Central America — which comprises a network of interests — is one of the key elements for overcoming the socioeconomic crisis now affecting nations in the area. It is an indispensable element for our future development.[31]

In this way, the idea of a Central American parliament took on a more strategic aspect than offering just one more vehicle for dialogue with which to try to defuse tension. It was also planned as an option for joint effort to overcome the structural barriers to the crisis.

Attending the Esquipulas summit, in addition to President Cerezo, were the presidents of El Salvador (José Napoleón Duarte), Honduras (José Azcona), Nicaragua (Daniel Ortega), Costa Rica (Oscar Arias), and the four deputy foreign ministers of the Contadora Group. Over and above the signing of the Esquipulas Declaration, the meeting sent out conflicting signals. While, on the one hand, some agreement was reached to create the parliament and to formalize meetings of the presidents in the area, on the other hand, and even though the Esquipulas Declaration assumed the desire to sign the Contadora agreements (its second point), it was known at the meeting that the Act would not be signed — a fact confirmed by the Guatemalan leader on 2 June 1986.[32] Further statements by Guatemalan officials, and by Cerezo himself, indicated that the Esquipulas meeting was but a first step in a process launched by the Christian Democratic government to relieve the tension and that its results were still unclear.[33] So, while foreign affairs officials announced that Vinicio Cerezo "is very satisfied," he himself said "the Esquipulas summit concluded with differences but without opposition."[34]

The importance of the meeting, from the Latin American perspective at any rate, was clear upon its receiving prompt support from the foreign ministers of the Contadora Group and the Support Group (meeting in Panama City on 6-7 June 1986) who issued the Panama Message. In it, among other things, they expressed "their satisfaction at the historical meeting" and urged the countries of the isthmus to put into effect as quickly as possible the revised Contadora Act, "the only path to a just and effective peace in Central America."[35]

Although Esquipulas produced few concrete results, the proposed Central American Parliament made slow progress throughout 1986. One such indication was the meeting that took place on 13 August — which was delayed for some days due to the difficult regional situation — of the Parliamentary Planning Committee. The meeting was attended by the vice-presidents and foreign ministers of, and three representatives from, each country. Guatemala provided a constitutional treaty for the regional parliamentary system as the Committee's working paper. It provided for the establishment of 3 bodies: a Parliament, a Forum of Vice-Presidents, and a Summit of Central American Presidents. It also specified that the parliament "should be finally operational by June or September 1987, with democratically elected representatives."

At the conclusion of the meeting, there was sufficient consensus among the participants to agree on general guidelines or the proposed constitutional treaty and to sign a joint declaration, released on 14 August. In it they agreed "to create a constitutional committee of two working members from each country ... in order to implement suggestions for the project ... and to present its report no later than 15 September."[36]

Nevertheless, declarations from representatives of those Central American governments aligned with the United States presaged a rough road ahead for the project. Rodolfo Castillo Claramount, vice-president of El Salvador, announced, on 13 August, that the fundamental problem for peace "is the negative attitude of Nicaragua toward the concept of democratic values as understood by the rest of the countries." The same sentiments were expressed by the vice-presidents of Costa Rica and Honduras. Already, on the eve of the 11 August meeting, the representative from Guatemala, Enrique de León, stated that "there is pressure from the United States that the Parliament not be formed, since it is a forum for discussion in which the world powers would not be able to interfere."[37]

At these high levels, in any case, one must emphasize that if the policy of active neutrality put forth by the Christian Democratic government did not produce immediate results toward agreement, it is also clear that, in its first months in power, it did add to the administration's maneuverability in foreign affairs. First, besides the support gained from the Contadora and Support Groups, the policy was highly regarded by two major actors in the Central American crisis who are also important to Guatemala's internal stability: the *Frente Farabundo Martí para la Liberación Nacional* (FMLN) of El Salvador and the Sandinista government of Nicaragua. So, to cite one example, the FMLN guerrilla commander Venancio Salvatierra announced in July that

> in the last weeks Washington pressured Guatemala into joining El Salvador, Honduras, and Costa Rica — its allies in the region — for the purpose of liquidating the peace efforts of the Contadora Group ... However, the position adopted by the present government is a praiseworthy one.[38]

For his part, Vice-President Sergio Ramírez, of Nicaragua, at the meeting of the Planning Committee for the Central American parliament responded to the hostility of his neighbors and recognized the moderate Guatemalan position when he stated that

> Guatemala's active neutrality is valuable because it offers a balance in the Central American situation. We hope that it maintains this policy.

This recognition, besides favoring Guatemalan initiatives regarding the isthmus, assured the Cerezo government that it would be more difficult for Guatemalan guerrillas to obtain help from these actors in the future, despite their ideological affinity.

In the second place, this neutrality policy allowed Cerezo to use his goals as a counterweight to the pressure the United States has been bringing to bear on Guatemala and the rest of the Central American nations. In this sense, at least in part, it lent prominence to the mutual understanding between the Guatemalan proposals and the actions of the Contadora Group, in spite of Assistant Secretary of State for Inter-American Affairs Elliot Abrams saying that it was "a farce." The day before taking office, Guatemalan Foreign Minister Mario Quiñonez declared:

> Guatemala is as impartial in the conflict as Panama. Why not then consider making us a part of the Contadora Group like Panama, and take advantage of our geographic location, political situation, and our strategic importance to prove ourselves as privileged mediators?[39]

This position, advocated by Quiñonez, was endorsed by Philip Habib, the Reagan administration's special envoy to Central America, during his visit to Guatemala (on 2 June) where he went to inform himself about the meeting of the presidents at Esquipulas. In the course of their conversations with him, the Guatemalan government announced that "it would continue to participate in the Contadora efforts." [40]

Guatemala, without rejecting the West nor the advantages attendant upon being part of that world (particularly with the United States), generally rebuffed efforts of the Reagan administration to involve it in the US strategy for dealing with the Central American conflict. In keeping with this view, Cerezo refused US military aid from the outset on the grounds that his country did not need it, [41] reproached Reagan for allocating $100 million to the Nicaraguan *contras* but less than half of that to support Guatemalan democracy, [42] and even hailed — as a triumph for democracy — the initial vote, by the US House of Representatives, to reject the $100 million aid to the *contras* that had been proposed. He also tactfully turned down a proposal of the US Southern Command for Guatemalan forces to participate in joint military maneuvers near the Central American coast [43] and called for the United States to "respect" Latin America as a way to guarantee lasting peace. [44] The Minister of Foreign Affairs, Mario

Quinoñez, declared that his country would not be part of any Central American bloc to isolate Nicaragua[45] and refused to join in any peace initiative outside the Contadora process — as proposed by Costa Rica, Honduras, and El Salvador.[46] Finally, the Christian Democratic government emphasized its mandate by declaring that it would not accept "either now or in the future" any proposal to train Nicaraguan *contras*.[47] Indeed, in mid-year and in the months during which the road to a negotiated solution was rockiest, Cerezo even declined to meet with Reagan envoy Philip Habib.

Despite these signs, which the United States must have viewed negatively, Cerezo's position of "maintaining a balanced relationship" with the US while still declaring Guatemala a country within the Western orbit,[48] permitted Cerezo to avoid points of difference and to emphasize those areas of agreement advantageous to his country.

On its side, Washington — which had viewed the democratic government favorably during the period of free elections — abandoned its hope to involve Guatemala in its strategy to place Nicaragua under siege. In an article published in the April issue of *ALASEI*, the position of the US State Department was described in the following terms;

> it is more important to the United States that democracy be consolidated than that the Cerezo government fully share our views on Central America. In any event, we are sure that in a situation that is, by definition, limited, Guatemala is on our side.

This logic was confirmed when — despite the declaration of US Senator Mark Hatfield, in December 1985, that Cerezo's election "will not automatically renew military aid" until Guatemala improves its human rights situation[49] — the Guatemalan ambassador to the US announced (23 January, 1986) that military aid had indeed been renewed and that the Reagan administration had approved a first installment of $10 million.[50] (Other sources indicated the amount would rise to $15 million).[51]

Faced with Cerezo's refusal to receive military aid, at least for a year (the Guatemalan President sought aid to upgrade the professional ability of the police), US officials announced they would hold the sum allotted to Guatemala in reserve.[52]

In this area, the Christian Democrats had succeeded in having their point of view prevail. *First*, according to Jaime Hernández, Minister of Defense, this was because the US sent only $5 million in aid to the armed forces, and Guatemala hoped that it would allot $15 million in *non-lethal* aid for 1987.[53] In the *second* place, the US held out the lure of helping to reorganize the Guatemalan police force. Among others, Second Secretary Thomas Shannon, of the US Embassy in Guatemala, had sent a team to Minister of the Interior Juan José Rondil that would help him develop a modern criminal investigation unit worth $30,000 dollars. The US Department of Justice is sending this team outside the US for the first time.[54]

In any case one must remember that, despite the embargo imposed by former President Jimmy Carter (in 1977), US military aid continued to arrive indirectly from Israel,[55] so that by 1985 — as a result of the "opening" planned by the Guatemalan military — the US Congress had approved $300,000 in aid to train Guatemalan soldiers. At the same time, economic aid in 1985 grew substantially over that of 1984: from $33.3 million to $61.3 million, respectively.[56]

Financial aid was essential for Guatemala's internal stability (Cerezo claimed he needed $300 million to stabilize the economy), and the US was considered to play a vital role in this area as well as in that of military control. The favorable US attitude, particularly since the restoration of democracy, signified (despite some delay) eventual approval of funds. Thus, for example, the Agency for International Development (AID) approved (6 June) a loan of $47.3 million to Guatemala, of which $23.4 million is to paid over a 25-year period (with ten years grace) and the balance as a gift.[57] To its credit, approximately $25 million of the aid was earmarked for development projects, and $19 million was to import food (wheat and oil) — which the US administered to Guatemala as part of its PL-480 program.[58] At the same time, the Interamerican Development Bank (IDB) approved (November 1986) a loan of $25.8 million to finance the fourth stage of a project to build neighborhood and rural roads;[59] the Christian Democratic government also solicited another $20 million from the IDB to be invested in an evaluation of the upper and mid reaches of the Chixoy River.[60]

During the early months of the Cerezo administration, this US aid was not forthcoming, which some observers attributed to Cerezo's adherence to his neutrality policy. Although there is no way to be sure, it is a fact that these funds only began to be released after the Economic and Social Reorganization Program, as envisioned by US Ambassador to Guatemala Alberto Martínez Piedra, was announced.[61] On the same day, (22 June), the World Bank announced the grant of a loan of $81 million to Guatemala to finance expansion of the country's electrical capacity.[62]

In its relations with the United States, Guatemala steered a careful course between adherence to its neutrality policy on the one hand and its need for increased US assistance to overcome its economic crisis on the other. Consequently, Guatemala has not only seen its financial aid to carry out its announced economic plan conditioned, but also its own policy of neutrality and activism — as carried out by Cerezo — under US pressure as well. Examples of the latter, according to a Guatemalan official, are (1) that the US tried to impair the Esquipulas (Guatemala) meeting by promoting an alternative meeting in San Pedro Sula (Honduras);[63] and (2) that President Cerezo himself — between the end of July and the beginning of August — asked the US State Department to "clarify" persistent rumors that US Embassy personnel were working, through members of the military and businessmen, to influence the Christian Democratic government to support the *contras*.[64] Among these contacts, General John Galvin, Chief of the US Southern Command, suggested to Guatemalan Minister of Defense Jaime Hernández, and to the US military mission there, that he should be invited to visit Hernández at the government palace early in November 1986.[65] Moreover, there have been persistent — but unconfirmed — rumors that these pressures included a campaign against Cerezo while the latter was touring Europe.

Thus, US-Guatemalan relations in 1986 were marked by contradictions, ranging from friendliness on both sides through tolerance, to situations that were frankly tense. As far as the tension goes, on some occasions Cerezo found it wiser, in order to avoid obstacles in his path, to modify his conduct of foreign affairs or at least to pursue a more relative line. Thus, there was the unfortunate approach which Guatemala made to the countries comprising the Tegucigalpa Group, at their meeting in Panama (6 April, 1986) with respect to international maneuvers and suggestions for disarmament, a situation which it finally amended. During the meeting and at a time when Nicaragua was included, regional disarmament — something which Nicaragua obviously could not accept — was discussed, among other topics — as Nicaraguan Minister Miguel D'Escoto made clear.[66] On the other hand, the appetite of the Guatemalan armed forces for a resumption of US military aid and contacts was whetted. Thus toward the end of November, General Hector Alejandro Gramaio, Guatemala's Chief of Staff, mentioned that the armed forces would like to receive $50-60 million in the year to come "in order to convert itself into a force capable of driving communism from the region," alluding to Guatemala's precarious position *vis-à-vis* its neighbors. At the same time, he referred to conversations planned with the guerrillas as "insincere."[67] These statements by the Chief of Staff undercut two policy positions of the civilian government: (1) of inclusion and internal pacification, and (2) of regional neutrality and co-existence.

In every way, President Cerezo has been more than clear on the kind of relations he wants with the United States. Thus, within the framework of the 16th General Assembly of the Organization of American States (OAS) — held in Guatemala on 10 November 1986 — the Guatemalan chief executive declared: "we respect the US position, but we have told them that we wish to be partners, not instruments of their policy."[68]

For his part, the young chief executive has been persistent in his search for a negotiated settlement to the Central American conflict. Thus, while talks among countries of the isthmus were being held up (on the pretext that Nicaragua's charges before the International Court of Justice (ICJ) that Honduras and Costa Rica offered refuge to, and served as bases for, the *contras* who harassed the Sandinista regime, each time freezing the Honduran-Nicaraguan border ever more owing to the enclave policy fostered by the US),[69] Guatemalan Minister of Foreign Relations Mario Quiñonez began a tour — the last week of October — to the two Central American countries in an effort to revive the issues of peace and a new presidential summit within the framework of the OAS meeting which was to be held in Guatemala.[70] On his brief visit, the Guatemalan representative proposed to raise such issues as (1) the Nicaraguan charge (made the previous July) against Honduras and Costa Rica before the ICJ, and (2) the arms, military maneuvers, and conditions/requirements that each country wanted to see complied with before resuming the Contadora dialogue. However, the Guatemalan official said he would not raise the issue of either country — Nicaragua or El Salvador — renewing dialogue between their governments and the guerrillas operating within their borders, as certain persons had attempted in the past.

According to a high Guatemalan official, at the 16th meeting of the OAS President Cerezo announced that he would put his personal prestige on the line in a serious effort to re-establish dialogue among the Central America and Contadora countries at a time when threat of war in the region was imminent.[71]

2.2 Regional Relations

WITHIN THE REGION, Guatemala continued to maintain friendly ties with all of its neighbors despite a few problems during the period in question. These ties were essentially cemented in the first place by a tradition of good relations arising out of Guatemala's position as the largest, most powerful country on the isthmus, which has given it a dominant role to play. In the second place, and complementing this comparative advantage, is the dynamism with which Cerezo has approached his policy of neutrality via his various regional proposals for peace and integration, i.e., by an auspicious policy for regional coexistence which could be termed a "policy of international pluralism without complex ideologies."[72]

Both factors, added to certain "Messianic" aspects of Guatemalan nationalism and, certainly, the present CD government,[73] have contributed to the perception of Guatemalan leadership in the area, which facilitates its good neighborly and/or cooperative relations.

Regarding Guatemala's relations with El Salvador, and taking into account that both countries are led by Christian Democratic governments, one might think there would be sufficient agreement on regional issues as to be conducive to ameliorate their relations towards the rest of Central America. Nevertheless, Cerezo emphasized the differences between the two countries from the very outset:

> We are each facing two different situations which is why Napoleón (Duarte) and I emphasize different things. We [in Guatemala] place more emphasis on political opening because we want to lessen polarization. They [in El Salvador] are in the midst of a war and, thus, their international posture varies accordingly.[74]

These differences are sufficiently clear to explain why Guatemala's options — i.e., active neutrality and inevitable support of Contadora — are opposed by Duarte's El Salvador, which takes a highly ideological position allied to the US policy of confrontation. Among other things, El Salvador's position can be explained by its civil war and its need to legitimize the Christian Democrat government, as well as by the aid it receives from the United States to carry on the war (it has been estimated that the US finances almost 60% of its national budget and about 15% of its GNP). El Salvador has defined its own situation, as well as that of the isthmus, as one of defending itself against Soviet aggression which it describes as "at times direct and at times indirect" through Cuba and Nicaragua.[75] At the same time, the Duarte government gave as its reason for withdrawing from the Contadora mediation effort (June 1986) that the Panama declaration, particularly as recently modified, failed to meet the region's need for peace.

In any event, these differences have not ruptured their traditional harmonious relationship, even though they have limited the bilateral agenda. Border problems were resolved by the 1938 treaty and safeguarded by the Commission on Boundaries and Waters, which has been operating since 1971, so that bilateral relations between the two, over and above Guatemala's regional proposals, center upon trade. One must not forget that in years past, Guatemala sent 94% of its industrial sales and 30% of its exports to the Central American Common Market.[76] Even though trade between the countries fell off for many reasons (such as the El Salvador-Honduras war, the decline of the Common Market, the ongoing regional crisis), the basic relationship remained a good one. This explains, for example, the establishment of DICA (*Derechos de Importación Centroamericanos*), and the resultant extension (to 20 September 1986) by the Bank of Guatemala and El Salvador's Central Reserve Bank of the mechanism by which each country could pay for goods imported from the other, prior to 20 May 1986, in national currency.[77] This extension, aside from being framed in a formula designed to prevent further deterioration of exchange rates, was also linked to a Guatemalan proposal regarding El Salvador's debt to Guatemala: in 1984 alone, Guatemalan-Salvadoran trade created a debt for Guatemala of 83 million Central American pesos.[78] At the same time, presidents of both countries inaugurated an electrical energy link-up which will enable El Salvador to cover its energy shortfall.[79]

In keeping with past ties, Guatemala's relations with Nicaragua, though not entirely free from problems, were open and relatively friendly for the greater part of the year. Cerezo, quoting the dictum that "isolation means confrontation,"[80] not only succeeded in lowering his country's profile as a US ally but also opened up a space for dialogue which acted as a "buffer" in the escalating regional conflict. The Managua government has greatly appreciated this on more than one occasion, despite Guatemalan comments on Nicaragua's need for greater internal democratization.

This stand, combined with the Christian Democrats' policy of active neutrality, enabled them to keep up their strong economic ties. It is pertinent to point out that, within the region, Guatemala and Costa Rica vie for first place as purchasers of Nicaragua's exports, valued at 15.7 million, and 16.4 million (Central American pesos) respectively.[81] On the other hand, Nicaragua has also proven to be a good market for Guatemala, who exported goods worth 32.4 million (Central American) pesos in 1984 alone[82] — which helps to explain Nicaragua's debt with Guatemala ($150 million plus interest).[83]

However, the relationship was not totally without friction, mostly stemming from certain ambiguities in Guatemala's application of active neutrality. First, Guatemala reached a certain amount of *rapprochement* with the Tegulcigalpa Group on the issues of international maneuvers and disarmament measures. Second, the member countries of CONDECA (Central American Defense Council) held a meeting, parallel to that of Esquipulas, at which its new president and Guatemala's Minister of Defense, General Jaime Hernández, declared, in an allusion to Nicaragua, that

> if we had strengthened the union of the six countries, we would not now be experiencing the aggression of a country which has tried to destabilize peace in the region.[84]

Third, Guatemala generated an incident when its representatives to the Latin American Parliament first agreed to condemn the Nicaraguan *contras* and then refused to ratify that stand at the meeting of the World Inter-Parliamentary Union two weeks later.

The chilling effect upon the bilateral relationship became evident when Nicaragua's Deputy Minister of Foreign Affairs, Victor Tinoco, openly accused Guatemala of sympathizing with the Tegucigalpa Group — thus implying that it was violating its own neutrality policy. However, this confrontation was overcome after high-level meetings between both governments, at which Guatemala clearly re-affirmed its commitment to neutrality (1) by supporting the most recent Contadora revisions, and (2) by General Hernandez declaring that Guatemala would continue as a member of CONDECA "since no one had asked it to resign," implying that that military group posed no threat to Nicaragua.[85] Guatemala's Foreign Minister, Mario Quiñónez, also declared (16 June) that his country would not participate in any bloc of nations that desired to isolate Nicaragua.[86] Finally, General Hernández announced the possibility that he might visit Nicaragua at the express invitation of President Daniel Ortega, an invitation which he described as "sincere."

The chill in the relationship had been almost entirely overcome when *Comandante* Daniel Ortega, Nicaragua's Head of State, proclaimed that "Guatemala respects our revolutionary process."

Neither were Guatemala's relations with Honduras free from problems. Beyond the obvious differences over the Central American crisis — such as Honduras' decision to withdraw from all international fora in which the isthmus situation was to be discussed until Nicaragua withdrew its suit against Honduras in the International Court of Justice (which Foreign Minister Quiñonez called "an obstacle to peace in the region...that his government deplored")[87] — difficulties centered on bilateral trade. Two factors compelled Honduras to close its trade border with Guatemala: (1) the existence of a trade balance overwhelmingly favorable to Guatemala — in 1985 Guatemalan exports to Honduras totalled more than $43 million and imports only $3.2 million — and (2) Guatemala's mid-year withdrawal from the *Cámara de Compensaciones Centroamericana* (a Central American currency clearinghouse), a move which forced the rest of the nations to cancel purchases made in dollars. According to Guatemala's Minister of the Economy, Lizardo Sosa, this restrictive measure not only "caused serious problems for Guatemala's exports,"[88] but also, as reported in the local press, created a strong incentive to smuggle goods across the border, including, among other products, sugar, basic grains, and cattle.

To resolve this problem, Minister Lizardo Sosa went to Tegucigalpa at the end of October, as head of an official mission, to meet with Reinaldo Panting, his Honduran counterpart. At the early November meetings, which included leading businessmen from both countries, the Honduran authorities demanded better terms of trade and maintenance of the traditional monetary system. Despite the fact that the meetings were considered only preliminary, they did not end well once the Guatemalan minister announced that his country could not join the Central American clearinghouse operation at that time. However, he did disclose the intention of his government to revive several joint Central American organizations, such as the Central American Institute for Industrial Research and Technology, in order to overcome serious problems affecting production on the isthmus. He also advocated implementing the Central American import laws (DICA) on the grounds that this system would be able to initiate negotiations to normalize trade.[89]

In another area, a landmark for both countries was the relative ease with which they resolved the problem of refugee and/or undocumented Guatemalans in Honduras.

As President Cerezo said to the United Nations regarding his government's priorities: "first the national interest, second the regional interest, and then the international interest,"[90] essential to the success of the first priority was the unconditional security of the region as a whole. Thus, it was difficult for the Guatemalan democracy to think of security with a conflict at its doors, a deteriorating international trade, and an undervalued peso with which to renegotiate a swollen debt and to improve its level of trade with the developed world, etc. In similar vein, Guatemala's General Secretary for Economic Planning, Hermes Marroquin, declared at the plenary session of ECLA (Economic Commission for Latin America), held in Mexico at the end of April: "Central America is determined to achieve and to maintain peace in the region, not only as an historical inalienable right, but also as a condition for development."[91]

Finally, relations with Costa Rica, most important of all, centered on negotiating the conflict on the isthmus. If Costa Rica demonstrated continuity in its foreign policy, from the end of the Luis Alberto Monje government to the present one of Oscar Arias, this centered mostly on the military aspects: denouncing the *contras*, calling for a dismantling of their bases and the need to establish a firm frontier with Nicaragua. On the political plane, however, this neutrality had gradually acquired a more hostile tone, particularly under the present PLN (*Partido de Liberación National*) government, toward both Nicaragua and the Contadora process. Arias generally focussed on the issue of security — a position similar to Honduras and El Salvador — and advocated a regional democratization subject to verification. These positions, added to the facts that (1) he did not sign the Act of Contadora and (2) Nicaragua made charges against Costa Rica (28 July 1986) before the International Court of Justice, implied that Costa Rica was withdrawing itself from the regional negotiations.

These positions indicate that there were certain discrepancies between the policy of Costa Rica and that of Guatemala. This was illustrated at the OAS meeting in Guatemala by the declarations of President Cerezo as compared with those of Rodrigo Madrigal, Costa Rica's foreign minister. While the former was optimistic *vis-à-vis* the resurgence of the Contadora Group's efforts and expressed the opinion that the meeting "would revitalize the Contadora Group by strengthening both the Latin American and Central American decision and conviction to be actors for their own destiny," the Costa Rican minister maintained that the path to peace would be difficult because "peace in the region is a very complex issue because, aside from the arms escalation problem, there are others of a very profound political nature."[92]

2.3 Isolation and Latin America

ONE OF THE MOST important items on Guatemala's foreign policy agenda was to re-evaluate and diversify their relations abroad. Due to their brutal and persistent violation of human rights, the military regimes had gradually isolated the country diplomatically, and one of the first tasks of the new government was to embark upon a selective diplomatic offensive to diversify Guatemala's international relations.

To do this, Guatemala looked first to the Latin American community, especially those involved in the Contadora process and/or those who were perceived to be regional powers. The government identified Mexico as particularly important, given the multiple ties between the two countries. Among those which favorably disposed Guatemala toward Mexico were the following: (1) Mexico's perception of Guatemala as falling within its sphere of influence, owing to its proximity and unequal weight; (2) the great number of Guatemalan refugees on Mexican territory; (3) the coincidence of views between the two countries *vis-à-vis* the Central American conflict and how to resolve it; (4) the fact that both countries maintained ties with Nicaragua; and, finally, (5) the financial/economic links between them.

This evaluation was evident from the outset of the Vinicio Cerezo administration, when he included the Aztec capital on his pre-inaugural tour. Bernardo Sepúlveda Amor, Mexico's Foreign Minister, confirmed it when he stated, upon his return from Cerezo's inauguration, that: "Mexico strengthened its political, economic, and cultural ties with Guatemala at the inception of President Marco Vinicio Cerezo Arévalo's new democratic process."[93]

There were several important topics on the bilateral agenda. In order to address these, President Cerezo travelled to Mexico City early in July, accompanied by 16 government officials, including six ministers of state and his wife, Raquel Blandón.[94] After three days of negotiations, the two governments drew up an agreement covering 6 separate issues. The first dealt with a line of credit for $10 million — to be handled jointly by Mexico's Bank of Foreign Commerce and the Bank of Guatemala — to promote trade between the two. At the time (1986), the balance of trade favored

Mexico: in 1985 Guatemala imported goods from Mexico valued at $101,193,000 whereas, during the same period, it exported to Mexico goods valued at only $15,983,000 dollars, creating a deficit of $85,210,000.[95] Lizardo Sosa, Guatemala's Minister of Economy, stressed the need to increase the number of free trade products in the Mexican-Guatemalan border area.[96] Another issue addressed was renegotiation of Guatemala's debt with Mexico, which had reached $72 million.[97]

The other agreements concerned: (a) fiscal/financial cooperation; (b) cooperation in the area of socio-economic planning; (c) technical cooperation in the areas of public health and welfare; besides (d) signing various cooperation agreements.[98]

A very important issue of discussion was that of the 46,000 Guatemalan refugees living in the Mexican southwest. The two presidents (de la Madrid and Cerezo) signed a joint agreement to facilitate the gradual return of the refugees, in compliance with the United Nations High Commission for Refugees, taking into account the free will of those involved and guaranties of their security. Mexico considers it vitally important that Guatemala's spiral of violence come to an end in order to resolve the refugee problem and restore border security. Nevertheless, Abraham Talavera, Mexico's Ambassador to Guatemala, gave assurances that Mexico "will not expel those Guatemalan refugees who do not wish to be repatriated."[99] One must not forget reports that almost 700 persons were assassinated in Guatemala during the first half of 1986 (a number which does not include those kidnapped), though the Christian Democrat government gives an official figure of 560, of which 40% are characterized as political.[100]

As the Guatemalan leader emphasized upon his arrival in Mexico: "Relations between Mexico and Guatemala are excellent,"[101] and this evaluation is reflected in the transfer of products vital to Guatemala. For example, Mexico agreed to grant Guatemala a $10 million line of credit for various programs of social and economic development some days prior to Cerezo's visit. On the other hand, Guatemala continued to benefit from the San José Accord, whereby Mexico and Venezuela supply oil under preferential conditions, including a rebate of 20% to be used for development projects on very favorable terms.[102] For this reason,

Julio Sánchez, a spokesman for the Guatemalan president, denied, at the end of August, that his government had plans to purchase oil from any other source.[103]

These good relations have been re-enforced by the fact they share the same view of the regional crisis. On more than one occasion, both governments have expressed their commitment to the efforts of the Contadora Group and to the principle of non-intervention, demanding support from those countries directly involved in the conflict as well as from those with interests in the area. At the meeting in Mexico City, Cerezo and de la Madrid expressed confidence that creation of a Central American Parliament (suggested by Guatemala) would help to consolidate democracy and bring peace to the region. These joint views also took on a broader range. For example, Cerezo and de la Madrid supported a resumption of talks between the United States and Soviet Union as a way to promote world peace, and they condemned armaments. Both leaders also expressed concern over the failure to resolve the foreign debt problem, the need to adjust interest payments to allow for economies to grow, and they demanded that creditors assume some responsibility for the financial crisis.

Another demonstration of the very real good will and cooperation between the two countries was reflected by holding the first Mexico-Guatemala Inter-Parliamentary Meeting in Mexico City (29-30 September) to discuss bilateral concerns on 17 different subjects, involving such issues as science and technology, health, fishing, and trade, among others.

Another Latin American country targeted for Guatemalan attention was Venezuela. This country, besides being a member of the Contadora Group, is considered a regional power who can perform a function similar to Mexico in being able to serve as a balance in Guatemala's relations with the United States.

Clear evidence of the positive nature of Guatemala-Venezuelan relations, in addition to the similarity of their views on the isthmian conflict, can be seen in the many bilateral visits which have (1) promoted Guatemala's domestic stability and (2) buttressed its foreign policy. Not only did the Venezuelan Foreign Minister attend the inauguration of Cerezo, but one of the latter's first acts to assuage his country's economic problems was to initiate a dialogue with Venezuela regarding both the supply of oil and possible financial aid. In mid-February, Eduardo Castillo Controux, Guatemala's Minister of Energy, was sent to Caracas to discuss possible changes in the way oil was supplied under the San José Accord. Under the terms of the Accord, Guatemala currently receives 17,000 barrels of crude oil daily, with Venezuela and Mexico each supplying half. With the huge hydroelectric complex at Chixoy, Guatemala is now able to save $19 million on its imported energy account (now up to $40 million). Nevertheless, to do this, it now needs to import 22 million barrels of crude oil daily, whereas its purchases under the Treaty of San José cover only 77% of this amount. Aside from this, the Chixoy complex requires certain changes in the composition of the Guatemalan oil imports. Before Chixoy, a package of residual petroleum products was needed to feed the electric generators; now, lighter crude oils are needed.

Cerezo, who had included Venezuela in his pre-inauguration trip, made a second trip to Caracas in March 1986 to hold talks with Jaime Lusinchi, his Venezuelan counterpart, the agenda being devoted primarily to the Central American problem: ways to advance the peace and discourage war, the need for democratic governments to seek for political solutions, etc. For Vinicio Cerezo and Jaime Lusinchi, the countries of Contadora and its support group constituted 90% of Latin America's democratic governments.[104] Later it was revealed that Cerezo's visit also had an economic and financial purpose:

> Guatemala refinanced a debt contracted with the FIV [Venezuelan Investment Fund] because of its [Guatemala's] delay in interest payments and reactivated a $210 million loan that the prior military government had not used.[105]

Moreover, an agreement was also concluded which would permit Guatemala to sell 120 non-traditional products to Venezuela. Eduardo Estrada, Deputy Minister of Economy and part of the official mission headed by Lizardo Sosa, announced that the agreement allowed partial elimination of tariffs on such products as molasses, kaolin, and essential oils, among others.[106]

Shortly afterwards (25 April), Guatemala's Minister of the Interior Juan José Rondil made a brief stopover in Caracas, while en route to Europe, to speed the disbursement of a special credit earmarked for modernization of the police force. In a local interview, Rondil explained that attempts were being made to change the orientation of the police, which had been — for 30 years — directed "towards repression rather than crime prevention," adding that this program was already underway with the dissolution of the DIT (Department of Technical Investigations) and "is being reinforced by a reform of the judiciary system."[107] Rondil held interviews with Venezuela's President Lusinchi, Minister of the Interior Octavio Lepage, and Minister of Foreign Affairs Alberto Consalvi. Before leaving for Spain and the Federal Republic of Germany on a similar mission, Rondil announced that Venezuela had granted his country a $10 million credit, at a low rate of interest, to buy police equipment, most of which would be made in Venezuela.[108]

Before Rondil's visit, Venezuela had offered Guatemala technical assistance to restructure and modernize the police force. Early in 1986, Venezuela's security agencies had sent a special mission to Guatemala to help evaluate and diagnose Guatemala's police needs.[109]

The coming to power of a democratic government and its policy of active neutrality also reaped dividends for Guatemala with another regional power and member of the Contadora Support Group: Argentina. This country, which naturally supported Cerezo's neutrality policy (also supported by Peruvian President Alan García during his visits), granted Guatemala a line of soft credit of $15 million — payable over an 8-year term at 5.5% interest — which, according to Argentine Ambassador to Guatemala Alberto de Simone, could be expanded to US$10 million more. The ambassador also declared that Argentina extended its "support and solidarity to Guatemala regarding neutrality…," observing that Guatemala did "not need military aid, but social and economic assistance."[110] Bilateral arrangements also included various projects of a technical nature. Accordingly, representatives from some of Argentina's laboratories presented Guatemala's president and minister of health with a program to construct plants for clean drinking water in rural areas; at that time only 19% of the rural population had access to clean drinking water.[111] Similarly, the scientific and technical cooperation included Argentinian aid to develop nuclear energy.[112] In return, and reflecting its long-stand-ing dispute with Great Britain over Belize and the strong Latin American bias of its foreign affairs, Guatemala did not hesitate to support the Argentine position on the Malvinas/Falklands Islands at the November meeting of the OAS in Guatemala.[113]

Thus, in one way or another, Guatemalan diplomacy has employed all the means within its reach opened up by other Latin American and Caribbean countries. Prominent in this regard is the trip Cerezo made to San Juan (Puerto Rico) in March to take part in an international conference of businessmen and government representatives from a dozen Caribbean countries and the United States. For the same reason, Minister Mario Quiñónez travelled to Colombia in early August to attend the inauguration of President Virgílio Barco. Taking advantage of the presence of foreign ministers from the countries of Central America and the Contadora Group, he lobbied for renewed dialogue in the region. Colombia was also one of the countries included in President Cerezo's pre-inaugural tour.

Latin American unity and democracy have not been neglected items on Cerezo's external affairs agenda. During the SELA (*Sistema Económico Latinoamericano*) meeting in Caracas at the end of March, for instance, President Cerezo advocated Latin American unity as a way to deal with the problems facing the region:

> Before the economic and technological power of the developed countries, Latin America faces the enormous challenge of convincing itself to unite in order for our countries to advance, seeking to work together and overcome differences.[114]

This policy explains why the Guatemalan Congress ratified (7 October 1986) the agreement to establish the Latin American Organization for Fishery Development (*Organización Latinoamericana de Desarrollo Pezquera* or OLDEPESCA) together with Bolivia, Costa Rica, Ecuador, El Salvador, Guyana, Haiti, Honduras, México, Nicaragua, Panamá, and Perú.

Guatemala's president has also been frank regarding those authoritarian regimes still existing in South America, such as the following comments on Chile:

> I can say that, in view of the historic process now taking place in Latin America, it would be very praiseworthy for the Chilean army and the current president to follow the example

> of those other Latin American armies who have understood
> that peace in Latin America can only be based on democracy
> and take rapid strides to ensure democratic participation by
> all sectors.[115]

Also, to consolidate its domestic situation and improve its international image, Guatemala ratified the OAS Human Rights Convention on 27 October 1986.

The CD government has also brought its policy on foreign debt — $3,000 million according to Eduardo Castillo Controux, Minister of Energy — more in line with that of the rest of Latin America. Don't forget that the day after he took office, Cerezo criticized the policy of the international banks, particularly that of the International Monetary Fund, because, as he said: "I never knew, because I never inquired, how much of that money was diverted into the pockets of the previous government officials." He emphasized that he "would not pay a penny while people go hungry."[116] Just a few days before, Minister Mario Quiñónez had declared, in a similar vein, that "the foreign debt, a common problem among Latin American countries, must be paid, but without massive interest rates and on reasonable terms."[117]

Even though the Guatemalan government pleaded for justice in this matter in every international forum, Cerezo himself announced (3 September 1986) that he had renegotiated 90% of the foreign debt — equal to $400 million — on terms that were "reasonable" under the circumstances. Had he not been successful in rescheduling the due dates for 1986, Guatemala would have had to designate almost 50% of its hard currency earnings exclusively for debt service. During the negotiations, like the majority of Latin American countries, Cerezo had to weight domestic needs against the possibility of new foreign borrowing. In the beginning, the government renegotiated only the most urgent, short-term debt, and then only the debt held by the private banks — without resorting to the Paris Club and without changing the terms on long-term debt held at low interest.[118]

Up to the early days of September, despite diversification and renegotiation, the Cerezo government had not been able to raise the financial assistance it had hoped for; the latter amounted to only $181 million.[119]

2.4 The World Context and Human Rights

GIVEN THIS SITUATION and Western Europe's favorable response towards Guatemala's return to democracy (remember Claude Cheysson's comments at the Cerezo inauguration), the Cerezo government viewed that part of the world as fundamental to achieving its objectives. Thus government spokesmen gave assurances that Europe had not only "indicated great interest in supporting the policy of active neutrality," but had given it concrete expression — aid — which "permits us to consolidate and increases our credibility around the world, not only *vis-à-vis* the United States but also with the rest of the Central American community."[120]

Beyond this goal of diversifying support for its foreign policy abroad, the Cerezo government had 3 other goals: (1) it wanted aid to restructure its police force; (2) it needed financial cooperation and trade; and (3) it needed to reverse the negative image incurred by the previous regime, due to human rights violations — most important in securing cooperation from Western Europe, for whom it was a prerequisite to any increase in trade and/or financial assistance.

In this regard, besides dissolving the DIT and annulling the Mejía Víctores amnesty decree (which the GAM had denounced because it did not provide for initiating trials to investigate the cases of *desaparecidas*),[121] the Christian Democrats began a program to restructure and modernize the police force. To do so, Cerezo — through Minister of the Interior Juan José Rondil — solicited the aid of Germany, Spain, the United States, and Venezuela. When Rondil arrived in Germany at the end of April, he said that "in order to consolidate democracy and to ensure respect for human rights … it is necessary to strengthen those institutions that endorse democracy and safeguard public security."[122] Rondil met with ministers of the German government — Friedrich Zimmerman (Interior) and Jurger Warnke (Economic Cooperation) — as well as with representatives from Foreign Affairs and the Konrad Adenauer Foundation to negotiate, successfully, an increase (of 58 million marks) in the aid already granted to Guatemala by the Bonn government. West Germany's entire grant of aid totalled 80 million marks: 30 million as a gift and 50 million as loans on extremely good terms (at 7.5% interest over 50 years, with a 10-year grace period). In addition, the Bonn government donated 55 Mercedez-Benz radio-patrol cars, 60 motorcycles, communications equipment and other goods to help the police function better.[123] Rondil included Spain on his tour, and the Spanish government also promised some help in this area.

At the end of September, President Cerezo, accompanied by a sizable entourage, embarked on his own tour of the United States and of Europe in order to cement relations with the Old World. In the United States he had two major functions to attend: he was awarded a presidential medal and received an honorary degree from Loyola University (in New Orleans), and he addressed the United Nations. On this stopover, Cerezo had an interview with Secretary of State Schultz to discuss possible ways of resolving the Central American crisis.

The 20-day tour of Europe, which was controversial on the domestic level and omitted countries where the president might encounter pro-human rights demonstrations, included Spain, the Federal Republic of Germany, Belgium, the Netherlands, France, Italy, and the Vatican. During this tour, he met with presidents, prime ministers, foreign ministers, businessmen, and even Pope John Paul II. As Cerezo triumphantly announced upon his return, the trip was most successful:

(1) in obtaining more than $200 million in loans and donations;[124] (Italy alone donated almost $45 million over a 3-year period and granted a line of credit of $100 million dollars);[125]

(2) in opening new markets (Cerezo met with representatives of France's 25 largest companies, who agreed to purchase, over the next 4 years, over $50 million of Guatemalan foodstuffs; besides which, France granted a line of credit of $10 million);[126]

(3) in renegotiating part of the national debt (Spain not only agreed to renegotiate some of the debt but also extended $18 million in new credit); and

(4) in garnering support for Guatemala's foreign policy.

Clear proof of the trip's success was Claude Cheysson's announcement that the EEC (European Economic Community) would quintuple its economic aid to Guatemala the following year

(1987). In mid-October, President of Congress Alberto Cabrera went to Europe to follow up, and finalize, among other assignments, these pledges to Cerezo.

While in Europe, the large Guatemalan mission took advantage of the opportunities afforded by their economic and political diplomacy to better Guatemala's negative image. For example, Cerezo declared that "we have not come to Europe to say that all violence has miraculously ceased, because that is not true, but that it is now the violence of common crime," and, in Italy, that the International Association against Torture had not found a single instance of abuse of human rights in his country.[127]

An important milestone in Guatemala's relations with the Old World was its resumption, after 23 years (since 24 July 1963), of diplomatic relations with Great Britain. This process was set in motion at Oscar Arias' inauguration as President of Costa Rica when the new Guatemalan president met with the British delegation attending the event to discuss the possibility of re-establishing relations.[128] The central issue blocking relations between the two governments was Guatemala's territorial claim (since 1859) to the former British colony of Belize. Despite this claim, Great Britain had unilaterally granted independence on 21 September 1981 to its former colony, which led to a total break in the relations — both consular and commercial — still existing at the time.

When Cerezo took office, he took a more realistic position on this issue than his predecessors. He declared (16 January 1986) that

> Guatemala is now taking a completely different position on Belize ... We don't want Belize to be Guatemalan. We only want, and we are going to propose, that Guatemala have access to the sea, either through consultation or negotiations with Belize, for a strip of territory.[129]

Furthermore, the new Guatemalan constitution, which went into effect on 14 January 1986, recommended that the president reach a negotiated solution on Belize and did not propose making this territory a part of Guatemala.[130]

Guatemala knows full well that it can get some compensation for the "loss" of this territory, whether it be a strip of land or economic indemnity. Even more important, however, is the opportunity to resolve a problem which has both domestic as well as international implications. Among the former is the fact that any unresolved border dispute increases, in one way or another, the role of the Armed Forces, a situation which the Christian Democratic government wants to avoid. As to the international implications, there would be two political results: (1) the definitive removal of this territory from any disputes with Mexico and (2) resolving a conflict with an important member of the EEC. Furthermore, Britain has its own view of the Central American conflict which does not always coincide with that of the United States and sees re-establishing relations with Guatemala as a way to consolidate its presence in the area. Thus, consular relations were restored on 18 August[131] and full diplomatic relations at the end of December 1986.[132]

At the time, Guatemala had no relations whatsoever with the socialist world but not, as Foreign Minister Quiñónez expressed it, "for ideological reasons, but because our economic and trade interests are not compatible."[133] With regard to Asia, a few ties are maintained with Japan, which granted $250,000 to Guatemala to pay for material for an archaeological museum.[134]

Relations with the Third World were minimal until September, when Foreign Minister Quiñónez announced the government was considering opening embassies in Saudi Arabia, Malaysia, Australia, Indonesia, and Portugal, and missions of less importance in Singapore, Thailand, Morocco, and Zaire.[135] In line with this *rapprochement* with the Third World and alignment with pro-human rights positions, the Guatemalan Congress urged the president to sever relations with the racist regime in South Africa. Nevertheless, by the end of 1986 no such step had yet been taken.

3. CONCLUSIONS AND TRENDS

IN GENERAL, 1986 was a dynamic, upbeat year for Guatemala's foreign policy. This is true despite the fact that the various conflicting factors which conditioned its policy in the past continue to exist, that some of its main goals did not materialize, and that, ultimately, there were certain failures of execution.

Regarding its international image, an important component affecting not only its ability to achieve domestic goals but also its ability to assert some independence *vis-à-vis* the United States, considerable progress was made compared to the past. Here, taking advantage of the international good-will towards his regime, Cerezo buttressed this perception by actively emphasizing positive values. In the first place, the Christian Democratic government made an effort to strengthen the democratic process in various ways.

In the second place, the policy of active neutrality stood out in the Central American arena, a policy whose proposals — like the meeting at Esquipulas and for a Central American Parliament — not only conferred continuity and leadership on Guatemala, but also stimulated three other achievements: (1) greater margin for maneuver towards the United States without confronting it directly; (2) preventing escalation of the crisis by breaking out of its isolation and utilizing the concepts of dialogue and peaceful resolution; and, finally, (3) a fundamental *rapprochement* with those in the Latin American and European community who shared its views.

In the third place, we must call attention to the pragmatic, balanced activism with which Cerezo directed his policy of diversification — in Central America, in Latin America, and in Europe — to attain his internal and external goals. Outstanding in this respect were his strengthening of ties with the regional powers, with Europe, and with his handling of the debt. Over and above the benefits these conferred in and of themselves is the fact that, together, they helped break down the isolation in which Guatemala dwelled for so long.[136]

Nonetheless, despite the positive aspects, there has been no solution to a number of pending problems and deficiencies. Here one must mention, first of all, the human rights problem which, though it has seen some positive development, has yet to be finally resolved. This means that Guatemala remains subject to controversy and censure regarding the questions of the refugees, deaths by violence, and of the *detenidos-desaparecidos* (detainees and persons who have "disappeared"). For instance, in October 1986, the Interamerican Commission on Human Rights deplored "the horrific practice of disappearances which has not totally ceased."[137] According to the Mexican government, by midyear the violence had resulted in about 700 deaths and, as a result, caused at least 6,000 refugees to flee the country. In the context of human rights and political violence, a dialogue with the guerrillas had failed to materialize — which both Spain and the local Catholic Church officials had offered to mediate — nor had they been incorporated into political life, causing them to continue their activities and the armed forces, in persecuting them, to overstep the bounds of their authority.

On the other hand, the socio-economic area remained critical despite measures undertaken and aid obtained, such as the economic reorganization plan (which the General Surveillance Society continued to criticize for taxing exports), renegotiation of the debt, re-insertion of Guatemalan products into the international market, the acquisition of gifts and loans (like the 40 million quetzales granted by the World Food Program).[138] Thus, domestically, while the per capita GDP descended to a new low of 2.8%,[139] there was no redistribution of wealth; and, on the international level, the United States continued to be the main financial benefactor to the extend of a little over $100 million.

It is also important to mention that, despite the many positive steps taken during this time, the Guatemalan Ministry of Foreign Relations could not always count on the human and financial resources to cope successfully — always — with the pressures to which it was subjected. This explains, for example, why Guatemala's international efforts were undertaken almost entirely by officials of the regime, while the embassies were relegated to secondary place. There was also its temporary abandonment of neutrality and the fiasco of its relations with POLISARIO (Popular Front for the Liberation of Saguiat al Hamra and Rio de Oro),[141] besides its failure to establish any strong relationship with other Third World countries.

The continuation of many of these problems (and the context in which they take place) into 1987 will certainly reinforce the main lines and trends of Guatemala's foreign policy as it developed in 1986. These include the policy of active neutrality with its sense of leadership within the isthmus; a more balanced relationship with the United States; greater unity and integration with Latin America (particularly with the region's superpowers); strengthening its new ties with Europe and making them more viable; cultivating relations with key countries in the Third World (as indicated by opening new diplomatic offices); and, perhaps, making contact with one or another socialist country, mainly in pursuit of trade. All this in pursuit of its principal goal, which is to secure its democracy.

NOTES

1. In his second electoral campaign, Vinicio Cerezo succeeded in consolidating his victory (of 8 December 1985) by winning 63.3% of the votes against Jorge Carpio of the Right-wing *Unión Centro Nacional* (UCN), who won 31.6% (Noticias Aliadas, 19 December 1985: 1 and 8).

2. In the Mejía Víctores administration, the announced constitutional normalization became another important factor in diminishing Guatemala's isolation and improving its international image. It was, however, also seen as a way to strengthen certain legacies of the military government as well as to consolidate the winning position of the armed forces. The timetable was as follows: 1 May 1985: promulgation of the Political Constitution, the electoral law, and *habeas corpus*; 27 October 1985: presidential election and election of representatives and municipalities; 24 November 1985: second round of elections; 15 December 1985: installation of representatives and municipal officials; 14 January 1986: inauguration of the president-elect. Subsequently, the dates of 27 October and of 24 November were changed to 3 November and 8 December respectively. (See Florinda Castro, "La Política Exterior de Guatemala," paper presented at the VIII RIAL Meeting, Notes, p. 2; and Daniel Asenjo, "La Política Exterior de Guatemala: Continuidad en Medio de la Crisis," in América Latina y el Caribe: Políticas Exteriores para Sobrevivir [Anuario de Políticas Exteriores Latinoamericanas], 1985, ed. Heraldo Muñoz [Buenos Aires: Grupo Editor Latinoamericano, 1986], p. 239).

3. Among the decree-laws issued out General Mejia Victores outgoing government are the following: that of 8-86 which establishes a general amnesty "for every person or union responsible for committing political crimes and *comunes conexos* during the period from 23 March 1982 to 14 January 1986," on the grounds that it "is the obligation of the State to establish the condicions needed the strengthen peace and harmony;" that of 17-86 which created the Council of State Security, made up of the President of the Republic, the ministers of Defense, Foreign Relations, Government, Communications, Finance, Energy and Mines, and of Economy, as well as the head of the *Estado Mayor de la Defensa*, the Secretary of National Defense and Security (a post that had not existed before and which came under the Minister of Defense), and other officials appointed by the President; that of 19-86 which gave legal recognition to the Patrols for Civic Self-Defense (in this decree called Committees for Civil Defense), known counter-insurgency organizations, which "must be auxiliaries of, and coordinated by, the Ministry of

National Defense;" and that of 25-86 which creates 3 new ministries, that of Urban and Rural Development (although its functions are not defined, it is supposed that it will handle the civil part of the military programs of the counterinsurgency that will no longer come under military control, like the Inter-institutional Coordinators and the Poles of Development), that of Culture and Sports and Specific Affairs (see El Salvador, Bulletin of Analysis and Information No. 20, January-February 1986: 17).

4. President Cerezo's cabinet comprised the following: Foreign Relations, Mario Quiñonez; Development (a new ministry), Rene De Leon Schlotter; Public Finance, Rodolfo Paiz; Public Health, Dr. Carlos Soto; Work and Soc.Prev., Catalina Soberanis; Culture (a new ministry), Elmar Rojas; Agriculture, Rodolfo Estrada; Education, Eduardo Meyer; Energy and Mines, Rolando Castillo; Communications, Eduardo Goyzueta; Economy, Lizardo Soto; Interior, Juan José Rondil; Defense, General Jaime Hernández.

As one might guess, four members are related to the previous regime: General Jaime Hernández (Defense), who was Commander of the Honor Guard and is considered a man *desdibujado*; the ministers Juan José Rondil (Interior) and Mario Quinonez (Foreign Affairs), who are alleged to be the main authors of the government statute that established the military regime in 1982 and suspended the Constitution; and the Minister of Economy Lizardo Sosa, who was Deputy Minister of Finance under Mejía Victores. To these may be added the appointments of General Héctor A. Gramajo (commander of the Justo Rufino Barrios military base) as Commander-in-Chief of the Army; Colonel Roberto Natta Galvez, former commander of the Playa Grande (El Quiché) military zone, as Presidential Commander-in-Chief; and the holder of the post of Head of the *Guardia de Hacienda* (until 29 June 1986) of Miguel Eguizábal who was appointed by Mejía Victores and the cases of Ambassadors Lobos (Panamá) and Andrade (OAS), to mention only a few (Informe Latinoaméricano, 24 January 1986: 41; El Excelsior de México, 10 January 1986: A-2; Inforpress, August 1986: 50; Le Monde Diplomatique, June 1986: 12-13).

5. Florinda Castro, "La Politica Exterior de Guatemala," paper prepared for the 8th meeting of RIAL (*Relaciones Internacionales de América Latina*): 8.

6. El Excelsior de Mexico, 6 November 1986: A-2.

7. La Nación (Argentina), 12 December 1985; The Washington Post, 9 December 1985; Pensamiento Propio (Nicaragua), August 1985: 45.

8. La Tercera (Chile), 16 January 1986: 16.

9. El Excelsior, 13 January 1986: A-16; Noticias Aliadas, 19 December 1985:1.

10. El Excelsior, 18 January 1986: A-2; IPS Cable, 27 November 1986; Nuevo Diario (Nicaragua), 11 July 1986.

11. El Excelsior de Mexico, 18 January 1986.

12. Vinicio Cerezo can count on 51 of the 100 representatives who make up the Guatemalan Congress and on 50% of the mayors from the 330 existing municipalities (La Nación (Buenos Aires), 10 December 1985: 2).

13. Le Monde Diplomatique, June 1986.

14. The Washington Post, 1 December 1985.

15. The Miami Herald, 15 January 1986.

16. El Excelsior de México, 10 January 1986.

17. The Miami Herald, 18 December 1985; El Excelsior de México, 15 December 1985: A-2.

18. El Excelsior de México, 22 January 1985: 2-3.

19. El Excelsior de México, 22 January 1985: 2-3.

20. La Nación de Buenos Aires, 10 December 1985.

21. ALASEI, October 1986; COSAS 265, 27 October 1986: 8.

22. New York Times, 27 December 1985.

23. Miami Herald, 18 December 1985; El Excelsior de México, 18 December 1985, A-2.

24. *Ibid*.

25. ALASEI, January 1986; El Excelsior, 12 January 1986, pp. 1 and 13.

26. Luis Maira. "Proyecciones de la Crisis Centroamericana." Convergencia 10 (December 1986): 73ff.

27. On a regional level, this country ranks first in population, third in territory, and possesses one of the strongest economies. Until the present crisis multiplied the armies of El Salvador, Honduras, and Nicaragua, it also had one of the largest armed forces. One indication of its ability was that, for at least the last 7 years, it demonstrated that it could contain domestic subversion without US assistance. Above all, it seemed natural for Guatemala to assume a leadership role in any kind of "regional defense alliance" and thus take over the role of the Hondurans, which seemed to be the wish of the United States before General Gustavo Alvarez was relieved of his post as Commander-in-Chief of the Honduran armed forces (31 March 1984). Besides, from the perspective of its "strategic interests," Guatemala probably did not find it very reassuring to witness a buildup of military power in its neighbor to the south, Honduras. Even if Guatemala did not anticipate any "strategic" response to threats posed by its immediate neighbors, certainly Honduras' military buildup would create questions for its military planning agenda (see Daniel Asenjo, "Guatemala: Contradicciones en una Política Exterior Alineada," in Políticas Exteriores Latinoamericans Frente a la Crisis [Anuario de las Políticas Exteriores Latinoamericanas] 1984, ed. Heraldo Muñoz [Buenos Aires: Grupo Editor Latinoamericano, 1985]: 262).

28. Florinda Castro, "La Política Exterior de Guatemala" (paper presented to 8th meeting of RIAL): 27.

29. IPS Cable (Panamá), 28 May 1986.

30. As Cerezo explained during his visit to Caracas (May 1986), in his opinion a Central American Parliament would create an excellent alter-

native to promote dialogue in the area. To give his proposal a more precise definition, he studied the way the European Parliament (EP) worked very closely, to which end he had recently hosted an EP mission in Guatemala. He also analyzed the functioning of other deliberative bodies in the sub-region. He came to the conclusion that the Central American Parliament must have legislative powers from the outset, in view of the constraints the European Parliament had confronted due to its consultative character. He also felt that members of the Parliament would have to be appointed during the constitional phase, not to last more than a year (IPS Cable [Caracas], 19 March 1986; and COSAS 265, 27 November 1986: 10).

31. IPS Cable (Guatemala), 9 April 1986.

32. El Mercurio, 3 July 1986, A-8.

33. IPS Cable (Panamá), 28 May 1986.

34. Florinda Castro. "La Política Exterior de Guatemala" (paper presented at 8th meeting of RIAL): 27.

35. Mensaje de Panamá, 7 June 1986.

36. El Salvador Proceso 251 (20 August 1986): 14.

37. *Ibid.*

38. IPS Cable (La Habana), 17 July 1986.

39. ALESEI, 14 January 1986.

40. IPS Cable (Guatemala), 3 June 1986.

41. El Mercurio, 18 December 1985, p. A-9.

42. El Mercurio, 4 May 1986, p. A-6.

43. ALASEI, April 1986.

44. El Mercurio, 23 May 1986, A-9.

45. IPS Cable (Guatemala), 16 June 1986.

46. Informe Latinoamericano, 3 July 1986.

47. Day before the arrival of the first aid package of $100 million, which the US Congress had voted for the anti-Sandinista rebels, Philip Habib, special White House envoy, made a surprise visit (his fifth) to the countries in the region. The tour, shrouded in secrecy, took place 8-10 September and, as on previous occasions, omitted Nicaragua from the itinerary.

According to Central American officials, the Habib mission was related to "the Reagan administration intention to gain the consent of some of the region's authorities to train counter-revolutionary troops on their territory."

This strategy, besides its political objective, also had a military component: any US invasion of Nicaragua would lead to an inevitable territorial expansion of the war, drawing into the line of fire landing strips, bases, and US military installations in Honduras (such as the one at Palmerola). Consequently the Pentagon needed to be able to count on an infrastructure of support or alternatives and considered that Guatemala offered the best conditions for this within the area. This theory was first mentioned in the magazine Newsweek and reprinted in

La Hora (3 November, the Guatemalan newspaper: see further ALASEI, September 1986; El Salvador Proceso 255, September 1985: 12; and La Hora de Guatemala in INFORPRESS, 14 November 1986).

48. La Nación de Buenos Aires, 12 December 1985.

49. Noticias Aliadas, 19 December 1985.

50. El Excelsior de México, 24 January 1986: 2.

51. It appeared that the $15 million figure, besides the $10.3 million in military aid proposed by the United States for FY1986, would include $5 million as part of President Reagan's program (sent to Congress in November 1985) to fight terrorism in Central America (see Daniel Asenjo's article "La Política Exterior de Guatemala: Continuidad en Medio de la Crisis," that appeared in PROSPEL's 1985 Anuario: América Latina y El Caribe: Políticas Exteriores para Sobrevivir: 336).

52. Informe Latinoamericano, 28 February 1986: 105.

53. El Heraldo de México, 22 September 1986: 8.

54. El Excelsior de México, 26 September 1986: 16.

55. According to *The Link*, a US publication specializing in Middle Eastern affairs, Israel's activity in Central America has been a cooperative effort with the United States after both countries signed an agreement of strategic cooperation.

According to *The Link*, General Alexander Haig admitted the existence of this agreement — in relation to Guatemala — on only one occasion (in 1981) when military cooperation "outside the zone of the eastern Mediterranean" was brought up and covered questions of arms sales to third countries. Israel became the main source of military equipment after the end of the 1970s when the United States ceased supplying arms. The first large sale of arms and equipment took place in 1975, consisting of 10 Arava transport planes, artillery pieces and light arms. Another shipment of 15,000 Galil rifles, UZI machine guns, armored tanks, grenade-launchers and patrol boats, was sent to the Guatemalan army in 1980.

Israel has been helping Guatemala's military regimes through supplying arms, computerized information centers, and radar equipment, besides taking direct part in counterinsurgency campaigns against native communities (Informe Latinoamerican, 10 January 1986: 18).

56. National Research on Military Complex (NARMIC). American Friends Service Committee, January 1985.

57. Central America Report, 6 June 1986.

58. USIS Communique, 7 June 1986.

59. IPS Cable (Guatemala), 27 November 1986.

60. Prensa Libre (Guatemala), 16 June 1986.

61. La Palabra (Guatemala), 3 June 1986.

62. Diario de Centramérica (Guatemala), 27 June 1986.

63. ALASEI, April 1986.

64. ALASEI, September 1986.

65. Prensa Libre (Guatemala), 11 November 1986.

66. El Mercurio, 7 April 1986: A-1.

67. Washington Post, 17 November 1986.

68. El Mercurio, 12 November 1986: A-10.

69. See Mladen Yopo, "Honduras-Nicaragua: Una Frontera Caliente," in the magazine APSI, 188 (15 December 1986): 55-56.

70. IPS Cable (San José, Costa Rica), 25 October 1986.

71. El Mercurio, 12 November 1986.

72. Prensa Libre (Guatemala), 1 October 1986.

73. This was reflected in Vinicio Cerezo's address to the United Nations, on 29 September 1986, which he ended with the following thought:

> As president of the Guatemalans, and conscious of the historic moment in which we live, I place myself at the service of the nations of the world so that with the port of a magic country, full of history and hope, we can give light to humanity and realize that utopia which, since the second world war, this esteemed organization was founded to achieve: the consolidation of peace (Prensa Libre de Guatemala, 1 October 1986).

74. La Nación (Buenos Aires), 12 December 1985.

75. *Cuenta* of the El Salvador Ministry of Foreign Relations, June 1 1985 to 31 May 1986.

76. Diálogo Social 184 (November-December 1985): 38.

77. Prensa Libre (Guatemala), 30 August 1986.

78. See María E. Gallardo and José R. López: Centroamérica, La Crisis en Cifras (IICA-FLACSO, San José, Costa Rica, 1986): 106.

79. IPS Cable (San Salvador), 12 September 1986.

80. Miami Herald, 15 January 1986.

81. See María E. Gallardo and José R. López, Centroamérica, La Crisis en Cifras (as mentioned above in note 78): 107..

82. *Ibid*.

83. INFORPRESS 642 (30 May 1985): 2.

84. IPS Cable (Guatemala), 9 April 1986.

85. IPS Cable (Guatemala), 24 June 1986.

86. IPS Cable (Guatemala), 16 June 1986.

87. El Excelsior (México), 24 September 1986: 1.

88. IPS Cable (Tegucigalpa, Honduras), 1 November 1986.

89. IPS Cables (Tegucigalpa), 1 and 4 November 1986.

90. Prensa Libre (Guatemala), 1 October 1986.

91. IPS Cable (México), 25 April 1986.

92. IPS Cable (Guatemala), 11 November 1986.

93. El Excelsior (México), 2 July 1986.

94. Prensa Libre (Guatemala), 3 July 1986.

95. La Palabra (Guatemala), 3 July 1986.

96. Several years ago, Mexico and the Central American countries signed agreements which enable products from the isthmus to be sold,

tax-free, on a strip of Mexican territory several miles long, parallel with the Guatemalan border (see Diario de Centroamérica [Guatemala], 26 June 1986; and Diario de Guatemala, 3 July 1986).

97. El Día de México, 2 July 1986.

98. El Gráfico (Guatemala), 3 July 1986.

99. IPS Cable (Guatemala), 27 November 1986.

100. Latin American Monitor (August 1986): 322.

101. Prensa Libre (Guatemala), 3 July 1986.

102. IPS Cable (Caracas, Venezuela), 25 April 1986.

103. IPS Cable (Guatemala), 29 August 1986.

104. ALASEI, March 1986.

105. IPS Cable (Caracas, Venezuela), 25 April 1986.

106. IPS Cable (Guatemala), 17 March 1986.

107. IPS Cable (Caracas, Venezuela), 25 April 1986.

108. Miami Herald, 26 April 1986.

109. IPS Cable (Guatemala), 25 April 1986.

110. La Palabra de Guatemala, 9 September 1986.

111. Integración Latinoamericana 112 (May 1986): p. 39.

112. La Palabra de Guatemala, 9 September 1986.

113. La Tercera, 11 November 1986: 4.

114. Análisis, 1-7 April 1986: 40.

115. *Ibid.*

116. El Excelsior (México), 17 January 1986.

117. El Excelsior (México), 13 January 1986.

118. IPS Cable (Guatemala), 4 September 1986.

119. *Ibid.*

120. El Heraldo (México), 21 September 1986: 17.

121. Comercio Exterior, February 1986: 163.

122. La Hora (Guatemala), 10 May 1986.

123. El Heraldo (México), 22 September 1986: 8.

124. El Gráfico (Guatemala), 21 October 1986.

125. La Hora (Guatemala), 17 October 1986.

126. Prensa Libre (Guatemala), 13 October 1986.

127. Prensa Libre (Guatemala)7, 18 October 1986.

128. ALASEI, May 1986.

129. El Excelsior (México), 17 January 1986.

130. El Mercurio, 26 December 1986.

131. El Mercurio, 20 August 1986: A-7.

132. El Mercurio, 30 December 1986.

133. El Mercurio, 9 February 1986: A-8.

134. El Mercurio, 25 December 1985: B-3.

135. Informe Latinoamericano, 18 September 1986.

136. El Gráfico (Guatemala), 7 October 1986.

137. El Día de México, 11 October 1986.

138. Prensa Libre (Guatemala), 25 April 1986.

139. Notas Sobre La Economía y El Desarrollo. Santiago de Chile: Comisión Económica para América Latina (CEPAL), December 1986: 15.

140. One event that went unnoticed by the general public was that the Guatemalan government recognized the POLISARIO Front, and then retracted it, all in one day.

COSTA RICA: DEEPENING POLITICAL BELLIGERENCE AND MILITARY NEUTRALITY

by FRANCISCO ROJAS ARAVENA

COSTA RICA'S FOREIGN POLICY in 1986 was concerned — as it has been since the Central American crisis began — with four main points of tension: Nicaragua, the United States, Central America, and Contadora. Costa Rica was searching, through its neutrality policy and aggressive promotion of democracy, for the best way to respond to the demands emanating from these four sources.

The regional crisis bore upon Costa Rican foreign policy so heavily that it increasingly became a determinant of domestic policy, as the election of Oscar Arias Sánchez to the presidency made clear. It also ranked high on the agenda of the new government after it took office.

This analysis will show how courses of action designed to deal with tension in one area gave rise to new tensions in the others. At the same time, due to domestic politics, the government encountered major difficulties in forging a foreign policy without getting involved in the regional war.

Francisco Rojas Aravena is a political scientist and Research Coordinator in the School of International Relations of the National University of Costa Rica. During 1986, he was a Fulbright Research Scholar at the Latin American and Caribbean Center of Florida International University (Miami, FL).

THE ELECTION CAMPAIGN AND ITS RESULTS

As THE CANDIDATE for the Social Democratic PLN (*Partido Liberación Nacional*) in the 1986 elections (held 2 February), Oscar Arias won with 52.35% of the vote. His opponent, Angel Calderón, candidate for the PUSC (*Partido Unidad Social Cristiana*) obtained 45.8%. At the same time, the PLN also won a majority in parliament — by only one vote.

The PLN victory broke the tradition whereby the two major parties alternated in power, long considered a hallmark of Costa Rica's modern political system. The election results seem to mark the PLN as the major party, guaranteeing that it will increasingly dominate the two-party system.

The fact that the two major parties together captured 98% of the votes served to confirm not only the bipartisan nature of the system but also the marginal position of the parties on the Left. The latter organized themselves into two electoral coalitions, which considerably lowered the total number of votes cast. The preference for two parties was expressed in both the presidential elections and in the election of deputies. Given this recent electoral performance, it may well be that effective participation of the smallest parties, not just those on the Left, will become even more limited in the future. The trend towards a two-party system may result in another kind of limitation as well, i.e. towards more passive campaigns, in which the emphasis will be more on propaganda than on differences in program and/or issues.[1]

Not only did the election results confirm the legitimacy of the system but its legality as well. Abstention from voting sank to its lowest level ever: only 18% of registered voters abstained. This marks a major difference between Costa Rica's political system and that in the rest of Central America where, though elections take place, they fail to convey the legitimacy necessary to stabilize the party system and develop democracy.[2]

The main difference between elections in Costa Rica and elsewhere in Central America is that elections in Costa Rica offer a real possibility for change in the political elites of the two principal parties. The electorate can express its desire for social change, confirming or promoting policies which the government will then put into effect. It must be remembered that Costa Rica's current political system began after a civil war (in 1948) in which one of the central issues was defense of the suffrage. One outcome of the war was the establishment of legal institutions, like the *Tribunal Supremo de Elecciones*, whose purpose was to improve and guarantee the system of electoral participation.

Some of the reasons which led to the victory of the PLN and its candidate, Oscar Arias, are the following:[3]

1. The great popularity of incumbent President Monge (also a PLN member). At the end of his term (1982-1986), Monge was the most popular politician in the country, who, according to opinion polls, received an 85% approval rating by the public. In the public's estimation, his greatest achievements were enhancing the stability and security of the country.

2. The second major issue was that of Central American war and/or peace. Oscar Arias ran on a peace platform, emphasizing the themes of neutrality and the need to find political solutions to the regional crisis.

3. In addition to the two above-mentioned points was the fact that the voters linked the *Partido Unidad Social Cristiana* (PUSC) to the Carazo administration (1978-1982), which had governed during a period marked by economic crisis and inflation and which coincided with the development of the regional crisis. The public associated it with fear of instability.

4. Other important elements that affected the outcome of the election were: (a) a more unified campaign strategy by the PLN (though it came late); (b) a change in PLN campaign strategy from one emphasizing the candidate and his personality to one that placed its emphasis on the party — its philosophy and program — itself; added to (c) the overconfidence of the PUSC, which banked on the tradition of change and alternation of parties.

5. Also the PLN, despite a failure to play up its government program, did present a series of specific slogans on sensitive subjects: promises to work for peace, to construct housing, and to create new jobs.

THE NEUTRALITY POLICY

NEUTRALITY WAS THE CORNERSTONE of the Monge foreign policy, and Oscar Arias indicated he would continue and strengthen that commitment. The main differences between the PLN and the PUSC in the campaign revolved around the Central American crisis and how to deal with it (i.e., the options of neutrality and Contadora), creating public perceptions of positions based on either *guerrerismo* or "peace and neutrality."[4]

In his final presidential address, Luis Alberto Monge re-affirmed his commitment to neutrality, which he said had enabled him to keep Costa Rica from being drawn into the regional conflict. In his view, this policy had undeniably played a vital role in that achievement, and therefore no one should try to change it.[5]

Monge was equally emphatic that neutrality did not mean being impartial in the ideological sense but, rather, in the military sense. Near the end of his administration (November 1985), the government tried to pass a *Ley de Neutralidad*, which, though approved by a committee in the Parliament, failed to obtain the votes needed in the full house.[6]

The neutrality of the Monge and Arias administrations has essentially been more a government policy than a state policy. This explains the difficulty it had in gaining parliamentary approval and its weak support in the private business sector in contradistinction to its strong support by the general public. Many businessmen find it difficult to support the Neutrality Law since they find their business activities already constrained as a result of the US support of Nicaraguan *contras*, as some US newspapers have described.[7] Consequently, these groups support their own interests politically, through their representatives, although the government defines the national interest differently. Here Oscar Arias has pointed out:

> there is no full agreement in this area [neutrality]; I have not
> heard the echo that I expected. It may be that my position is
> wrong, but I believe that we ought to make a superhuman
> effort to keep our country removed from violence and this
> can only be done through neutrality.[8]

FOREIGN POLICY PROMISES OF
THE NEW GOVERNMENT

IN THE VIEW OF Costa Rica's Social Democrats and its new government, the national interest can only be served by pursuing a policy of aggressive democracy and military neutrality. This would allow the country to distance itself from war on the one hand, and to promote democratic development in the area on the other. However, this policy creates disparate tensions with the four major poles: Nicaragua, the United States, Central America, and Contadora.

Ever since the beginning of the 1970s, Costa Rica, under PLN guidance, developed an international image of importance. Today these same principles apply, but in a completely different regional/international situation. Decisions taken can affect the independence and very survival of the national political system.

The new government made two basic foreign policy commitments: (1) to search for peace and (2) to develop democracy, especially in Central America. Toward these ends, President Arias has consistently relied on international law as the basis of international stability.

The new president opposed aid for the *contras* but, at the same time, declared himself anti-Sandinista.[9] He expressed these positions politically by stepping up his advocacy of pluralistic democracy, especially toward Nicaragua, and of military neutrality in the Central American conflict. Carrying out this policy has not been easy; it produced friction and few friends. Neither Washington nor Managua understood it, creating tension with these poles as well as repercussions with the other two, Contadora and Central America. At the same time, since this policy has not provided any kind of peace in Central America, it has gained few major allies in Latin America. Oscar Arias has pointed out the need for others to "understand" a state that does not base its foreign policy on military strength: "We have no squadrons; we should have the sympathy of other nations."[10]

Costa Rican policy is based on making the fullest use of the limited autonomy available to a small country, particularly one located in a crisis area close to superpower which has defined that area as one of central importance to its national interest.[11] The different perceptions of danger, the solutions to the crisis, and the ways of dealing with them create rising levels of dissension with other important actors. In this respect Oscar Arias has pointed out:

> We are a sovereign country and want the best for Costa Rica, and if that means that we must disagree with friendly nations, we will have to do it and they will have to understand, since the only objective [of the President] is to do what is best for the Costa Ricans and this should be respected.[12]

At the press conference following his victory in the elections, Oscar Arias enumerated eight basic points for his government's foreign policy:

1. Neutrality in military conflicts between countries.
2. Respect for the principle of self-determination and non-intervention in the internal affairs of other countries.
3. Only multilateral dialogue with Nicaragua.[13] The Nicaraguan government of Nicaragua should reestablish liberty in its country.
4. To serve as an agent for peace in Central America by adopting an active role in seeking peace in the region.
5. Support the Contadora Group in their peace efforts without relying exclusively on that effort as the only way to attain peace in the region.
6. Maintain friendly relations with the United States and search for aid for the country's development programs.
7. Always keep flexible lines of communication open with the European Economic Community (EEC).
8. Renegotiate the foreign debt, amounting to US$4,000 million. Relations with the International Monetary Fund (IMF) will not include submission to their severe austerity programs when such are detrimental to the country's societal interests.[14]

The government enunciated these principles on many occasions from the time it took office on 8 May 1986, particularly in the president's inaugural address, in his address to the United Nations (UN), and on the many presidential visits.

The external factors which the government needed to carry out its foreign policy were identified as crucial: "It is not possible to talk about peace and liberty or to make decisions about our own development without first taking into account events which take place beyond our country's borders."[15] In over to overcome these conditioning factors, the Costa Rican leader stressed the need to form good-faith alliances based on shared values and principles.

Arias expressed his conception of such an alliance — the so-called *Alianza Democrática* — in a letter of reply to the Contadora Group. He repeated this suggestion to the United Nations (24 September 1986) where he stressed that an alliance based on the principles of liberty and democracy could serve as a foundation by which to strengthen the development of democracy in the area.

In addition to his country's democratic traditions, this proposal was legitimized by Costa Rica's ratification of its neutrality and its defense of international law.[16] Arias pointed out to the United Nations that his government would respect this policy "with all necessary courage" and clarified the point by adding that he would not permit the nation's territory to be used to attack· neighboring countries.[17]

In equally emphatic fashion, he criticized the domestic policy of the Sandinista regime.

> Costa Ricans worry that a totalitarian regime with a Marxist ideology is being consolidated on our borders. The course of the Sandinista revolution, neither desired nor foreseen, has transformed Central America into another scene of East-West conflict. There is no relief for anyone in the path chosen by the *comandantes* who have betrayed a revolution designed to return democracy to those who have known only oppression for many generations.[18]

The president also singled out Contadora's mediation efforts as another area of his continued support by stating, in his inaugural address, that the date of the 6th of June was sacred to Costa Rica. He told the United Nations that "Contadora is not dead," declaring that Costa Rica would continue its support of Contadora so long as there was the slightest hope.

THE FOREIGN MINISTRY

ARIAS APPOINTED Rodrigo Madrigal Nieto, an attorney with extensive political experience in the country, as Minister of Foreign Relations. He is the Cabinet member with the greatest political experience. Since Madrigal Nieto considers himself a friend of the United States, his appointment to the government team was interpreted as designed to provide an appropriate avenue for communication with the White House. Madrigal Nieto was one of the promoters of the Caribbean Basin Initiative (CBI) and, as early as 1982, had indicated the need to develop a "Marshall Plan" for Central America.[19]

Although Madrigal Nieto was one of its founders, he is not a member of the PLN, a fact which led to severe intra-party criticism of Arias.[20] The president did appoint Carlos Rivera Bianchini as Vice-Minister of foreign affairs, a man who is not only a former PLN deputy but who also represents the younger generation within the party.

Concerned about the professional caliber of the Ministry, the foreign minister and his team have undertaken a major reorganization in order to improve its capability. This takes on even greater importance, from the Costa Rican viewpoint, since other foreign ministries in the area have already made strides in that direction. In order to meet his foreign policy objectives, the new foreign minister announced his desire to gain bipartisan support for his policy and, to that end, would seek consensus among the two leading parties.

As far as the regional crisis goes, this policy is based on the fundamental concept that peace in Central America must not be understood merely as the absence of war, for there can be no peace without a pluralist democracy. Neither will the government concentrate all its efforts on relations with Nicaragua. However this latter goal proved difficult to achieve and will probably remain so due to the charges which Nicaragua brought against Costa Rica in the International Court of Justice at the Hague. Despite this situation, the Foreign Ministry has developed policies that are generally oriented toward democratization and *rapprochement* with the Arab countries, as will be discussed later.

RELATIONS WITH NICARAGUA

RELATIONS BETWEEN Costa Rica and Nicaragua, commanding the most attention, redounded on the other poles of Costa Rica's foreign policy, impacting them in the process.

1. Normalization of Diplomatic Relations

The Monge administration normalized relations with Nicaragua just before leaving power. After the "Las Crucitas" incident, contacts between the two countries dropped to their lowest level, with Costa Rica recalling its ambassador from Nicaragua.[21] To normalize relations, the Costa Rican government demanded that Nicaragua explain the incident, which it did a few days after the presidential elections (13 February 1986).

Thus came to an end the most serious incident between the two countries since the advent of the new regime in Managua. Argentine President Raúl Alfonsín took on the role of mediator to resolve the situation. Arias gave his support to the joint arrangement developed by Alfonsín, although he indicated that, due to the ideology of the Nicaraguan government, future relations would not be free of problems.[22]

Generally speaking, the period between "Las Crucitas" and subsequent normalization was one of calm along the border. This could have been because the Sandinista government exercised greater caution along its southern frontier as well as because "Operation Sovereignty" — newly implemented at the time the incident took place to remove the Edén Pastora forces from Nicaraguan territory — proved successful.[23]

2. The Border Commission

This point demonstrates how one bilateral relationship can impact other poles of its relations and, at the same time, have an impact on domestic policy.

Costa Rica and Nicaragua made various attempts to establish a commission to supervise and control their common border: in April 1982, in 1983 (at the request of the OAS), and again in 1984 (supported by Contadora). Once the two states normalized relations (upon acceptance of the Monge initiative), they tried to find some means, with the participation of third countries, by which they could finance the experts needed to carry out the tasks. On 20 February 1986, Foreign Minister Carlos José Gutiérrez, of the Monge administration, announced an agreement to establish a force to inspect and guard the border. The Contadora Group accepted this proposal at their meeting in Punta del Este, Uruguay.

The US government frowned upon the Costa Rican initiative because, at the time, it was involved in a major effort to secure congressional support for what the Reagan administration liked to call "freedom fighters." Rumors circulated that the US government was putting pressure on Monge, who declared: "If the installation of a border commission does not please the United States, I am very sorry; this time, as on many other occasions, one is dealing with a sovereign decision of Costa Rica."[24]

Nevertheless, the initiative did not fare well. An agreement was signed[25] which had different meanings for Costa Rica and for Nicaragua. For Costa Rica, it constituted the basis of an agreement which ought to be presented to Contadora; for Nicaragua, it was a signed agreement (between the two of them). The impasse which followed the Contadora negotiations eliminated all possibility of this type of agreement. Finally, the Nicaraguan accusations before the International Court of Justice (ICJ) eliminated all hope for the near future.

3. Costa Rica, Oscar Arias, and the *Contra* Problem

The Costa Rican president has been emphatic in opposing military and economic aid to the *contras*. He considers them incapable of overthrowing the Sandinista regime and, on the contrary, to be counterproductive. He made this clear during an interview on US television in which he indicated that, if the decision were up to him,

> ...I would give this money to Guatemala, El Salvador, Honduras, and Costa Rica for economic aid, not for military aid to the *contras*. I do not believe that military aid is going to produce the desired effect. On the contrary, the consequence of aid to the insurgents has been more dictatorship, more totalitarian government in the north. They abolished individual liberty because they had an excuse — aid to the *contras* by the US Congress — so there is not going to be a more open society in Nicaragua, nor is there going to be a negotiated solution with the Sandinistas by giving more money to the guerrillas.[26]

Following his statement, the US Department of State claimed it was "perplexed."[27] Elliot Abrams stated that the president of Costa Rica was forgetting history and insinuated that Oscar Arias had taken several different positions on the subject. Arthur L. Tambs, the US ambassador in Costa Rica, was recalled for consultation, and disbursement of an AID loan was held up due to "bureaucratic problems."

Arias has been equally categorical, both before as well as after assuming the presidency, that he will not allow the *contras* to abuse the national hospitality, i.e., he will not permit them to undertake military actions within the country. These statements (which Monge criticized) on eliminating *contra* action within the country took on added importance in March when US Secretary of State George Shultz told the US Congress that "the problems of aid transit through Honduras and Costa Rica had been overcome" and assured "that there will be few difficulties in the future."[28] The Costa Rican Foreign Ministry issued an immediate denial.[29]

If its policy toward the *contras* has been clear and acted upon, Costa Rica also exerted political pressure on Nicaragua to sign the *Acta de Contadora* and institute some kind of internal political "opening," thus permitting processes of national reconciliation to develop with a view to establishment of a democratic pluralistic regime. These goals serve to support the aggressive policy that Costa Rica is developing.

4. From the San José Meeting to Esquipulas

The presidents of Argentina, Colombia, Ecuador, El Salvador, Guatemala, Honduras, Panamá, and Perú met in San José for the inauguration, i.e., the leader of every Central American country except Nicaragua,[30] at which time a dinner was planned to discuss issuing a joint declaration.

The Costa Rican proposal (well-known after being "leaked" to one of the country's major newspapers) sought to establish a timetable for Nicaragua's democratization. It was proposed that this would be a "rough working draft" of ideas on the subject and the statement made reference to this. Among the ideas proposed for the timetable were: a system would be set up to take effect in a series of steps, starting with (1) changes in the Nicaraguan constitution to effect a separation of powers and then, (2) within two years, the holding of legislative and municipal elections which would permit the other major states of the region to recognize the Daniel Ortega presidency as legitimate. The draft even implied that a parliamentary regime could be established, thereby weakening the power of the FSLN *Frente Sandinista de Liberación Nacional*).

In fact, the "mini-summit" didn't produce any document. The Contadora Group issued a communiqué asking those countries with interests in the area to guarantee that they would not take any steps that would disrupt the consolidation and execution of the *Acta*.[31]

It would have been hard for the "mini-summit" to have committed more errors in the planning and design of the proposal. In the *first* place, Nicaragua was not even invited to the meeting despite being the subject of discussion and the one who would have to carry out the hoped-for responsibilities. In the *second* place, the proposed changes were of such a nature that they went far beyond what would be acceptable in the way of political intervention. Even a minimum of consideration would have suggested that the countries of the Contadora and Support Groups would find it extremely difficult even to discuss the ideas contained in the proposal. This became even more true when the Costa Rican authorities declared that the Act was interventionist by its very nature. In the *third* place, the presidents who attended the meeting came for only 48 hours and were on a very tight schedule which precluded any time for prior informal discussions, an absolute necessity given the scope of the document. In the *fourth* place, the preliminary draft was late in being sent to the various foreign ministries, which meant that the foreign ministers arrived in Costa Rica without having seen it. *Finally*, the meeting took place in a regional political environment full of contradictions: not only was the signing of the Contadora Act viewed as something possible, but also the approval of $100 million in US aid to the Nicaraguan *contras* was imminent.

During the month of May, the Contadora Group made significant efforts to reach a consensus; nevertheless, their meetings did not produce an accord. Meanwhile, President Vinicio Cerezo (Guatemala) suggested establishing a Central American Parliament and called a meeting — in Esquipulas on 26-27 May[32] — to discuss its feasibility. At the same time, this meeting would provide an opportunity, not only for discussion, but for signing the *Acta*. However, instead the meeting served to emphasize differences among the participants, not just the expected ones of a military nature — like verification and control — but of a political nature as well.

Costa Rica opposed the draft of the Contadora declaration, circulated earlier, which stated that "we the Central American presidents freely elected by the will of the people" on the grounds that it would imply recognizing the legitimacy of the Nicaraguan elections. It was proposed that the declaration say only "we the presidents of Central America…" instead. Foreign Minister Madrigal Nieto pointed out that Esquipulas would serve "in order to illuminate clearly the problems involved in the search for democracy" and reaffirmed that "there has been no change in the aim to establish a timetable to keep alive the processes of national reconciliation and, with it, the strengthening of democratic processes."[33]

The meeting failed to live up to expectations; it did not succeed in advancing regional peace. The declaration was revised to incorporate the change proposed by Costa Rica and reflected the point of dispute as follows: "in the dialogue we have analyzed the points of agreement as well as of disagreement which persist with respect to the conception of the life and structure of pluralist democracy."[34] During the meeting, major differences arose between Oscar Arias and Daniel Ortega over the meaning of democracy.[35]

Before Esquipulas, Costa Rica's position was that it could not accept, with the *Declaración*, the legitimacy of either the Daniel Ortega presidency or Nicaragua's process of constitutional discussion; a true process of national reconciliation — the only basis for developing a democracy — just did not exist there. This view coincided with US interests, in the sense that a declaration of that nature plus the Contadora action placed no new obstacles in the path of getting the Congress to approve aid to the *contras*. US special envoy Philip Habib emphasized the Costa Rican position, pointing out that Costa Rica "assumed a position of leadership on the isthmus by confronting the Nicaraguan leader at the meeting and defending the democratic system."[36]

The Arias administration, like the Monge government before it, finds that its pro-democracy policy meets with a warm reception from, and support by, the United States whenever that policy is asserted. However, differences between the two countries arise whenever the subject changes to the implementation of that policy. To Costa Rica, neutrality is the only way that it can prevent war from reaching its territory and resist those pressures which would involve the country in military actions.[37]

5. Costa Rica before the International Court of Justice (ICJ)

Nicaragua's charges against Costa Rica before the ICJ strengthened the sense of national unity, the feeling of democracy under assault, which led it to increase its belligerent rhetoric of denouncing *sandinismo* for being undemocratic and holding Nicaragua responsible for Contadora's failure to achieve a peaceful solution. For Nicaragua, this was just part of its military strategy.

These accusations constituted the greatest problem between the two countries, reverberating throughout the region. For Costa Rica, the Nicaraguan accusations — besides being unfounded and ill-conceived — ruptured the regional dialogue and any possibility of reaching an accord through Contadora. Costa Rica refused to participate in Contadora unless Nicaragua rescinded its allegations.

The Sandinista government lodged its charges against Nicaragua before the ICJ on 28 July 1986; on the same date, it filed similar charges against the government of Honduras. In its letter of complaint, Nicaragua stated:

> The situation is becoming increasingly dangerous, provoked by the systematic refusal of the government of Costa Rica to end its complicity in those activities the United States has instigated against Nicaragua, violating international norms, particularly in the use and threat of force against Nicaragua.[38]

The Costa Rican government responded immediately with a categorical denial of the charges, pointing out that the judicial process would offer an excellent opportunity to "demonstrate the aggression to which Nicaragua has subjected Costa Rica in recent years."[39] Costa Rica accepted the jurisdiction of the Court immediately, ratifying Monge's statement to the Court during his visit. President Arias declared it was absurd to think that a democracy like Costa Rica's could possibly represent a threat, adding: "Those who export war and violence accuse us before the Court at The Hague."[40] Costa Rican society and its political class rallied in defense of the country to reaffirm their national unity. Former presidents spoke out in support, which included the launching of a campaign to raise funds to defray the costs of the case.

A commission composed of Gonzalo Facio and Fernando Volio (both former foreign ministers) and Ulises Odia, a former president of the Supreme Court, was appointed to study the Costa Rican defense strategy. Edgar Ugalde was appointed as the country's legal counsel to the Court; he handles international affairs for the PLN and has had a long political and academic career. Faustino Jiménez de Aréchaga, a well-known Uruguayan lawyer and former president of the ICJ, was named as one of the defense attorneys.

Following the filing of the charges, the general reaction was that it would not be a difficult defense, perhaps its major weakness as their self-confidence in their democratic system as the basis of their defense. What is at issue is not Costa Rica's merits as a democratic republic or its internal mechanisms for negotiation. Within Costa Rica, it was thought that it would be impossible to demonstrate the country's *complicity* with the United States to attack Nicaragua. This is true, but the accusation is not based on this point, even though it was used in the Nicaraguan charges. Support for the Nicaraguan accusation can be found in the various links which certain Costa Rican individuals or groups have with the *contras*, even though official policy is to avoid involvement and to make serious efforts to limit such actions.

A given event may be viewed from different angles, such as the following will illustrate: when the Costa Rican government dismantled a *contra* hospital for which they exonerated various public officials; or when the government deported several *contras* apprehended while carrying on military operations. For some, this may be the best demonstration of Costa Rica's neutrality policy and the government's serious efforts to put it into practice. For others, it could constitute proof positive that *contras* do operate in Costa Rica with the support of government officials. Both points of view will be brought up at The Hague.

How can this Sandinista action be understood? It is clear that it has introduced a new dynamic into the bilateral relationship, making any kind of border agreement impossible and seriously impairing any possibility of a multilateral accord. Whatever the evaluation, Nicaragua must have taken this viewpoint into consideration in the early stages of planning this move. Even more, Nicaragua must have guessed that it would have a negative effect on its relations with other countries but went ahead anyway. The explanation seems to be that Nicaragua defined its immediate major problem as a military — not a diplomatic — one, or that the latter was only a secondary consideration compared to what occurred in the military area. From this, every course of action has war as its starting point.

In this sense, the Nicaraguan action compels Costa Rica to prove its neutrality by renewing its efforts to prevent armed elements from engaging in activity hostile to Nicaragua from Costa Rican territory. At the same time it will place Costa Rica under an international magnifying glass, a process which could extend over some time — it has been estimated that the case could drag on for almost 5 years — during which the basic war situation may change drastically before the case is concluded. The Court has allowed a year and a half — 9 months for each side — just for the charges to be brought and for Costa Rica to reply.

From a larger perspective, the charges can be linked to Nicaraguan actions on Honduran territory during Holy Week. Not only did Nicaragua demonstrate its capacity for action but also how easy it would be to regionalize the conflict. If war comes, it will be regional. Daniel Ortega has indicated that he fears an incident with Costa Rica more than one with Honduras since the consequences of a confrontation with Costa Rica would be unpredictable.[41] President Oscar Arias is in complete agreement: "The day that Daniel Ortega tries to attack our nation is the day he will fall."[42]

Viewed in this way, Nicaragua's charges have a certain rationality and could fulfill certain of its objectives, even if it does produce political problems in Contadora, in the Socialist International (SI), and in its relations with the European Economic Community (EEC) and with Latin America.

Costa Rica's *Partido de Liberación Nacional* has taken an international line in combating *sandinismo*. The Secretary-General of the PLN declared that the charges exceeded the bounds of tolerance and made plain the aggressive nature of the Sandinista policy toward Costa Rica.[43] Subsequently, PLN Secretary-General Rolando Araya announced that the PLN would not take part in the Socialist International (SI) if *sandinismo* was present. This was demonstrated at a meeting the Friedrich Ebert Stiftung organized in Costa Rica, from which the PLN representative withdrew when the FLN representative appeared.[44] The same thing happened at an SI meeting in Panama in September; as a result the SI Vice-President for Latin America offered, at the meeting, to serve as mediator to persuade Nicaragua to withdraw its accusation.

COSTA RICA AND CONTADORA MEDIATION

As MENTIONED, the problems with Nicaragua were reflected in Costa Rica's relations with the other countries in both Central America and the Contadora Group. Costa Rica had made withdrawal of Nicaragua's charges a condition for its continued participation in the Contadora process (similar to that in the Urbino Lara case).[45]

Under the Monge administration, Costa Rica had defined its objectives in Contadora as political; on matters of security it generally agreed with the positions of Honduras and El Salvador.[46] Under Arias, the government gave greater emphasis to democratization measures — including their verification. Furthermore, it insisted that a timetable should be set up for the establishment of national reconciliation and democracy.

Although the Executive branch made a great effort to have the Contadora Act signed and put into effect by a fixed date, this did not happen. Contadora issued its *Mensaje de Panama* and a revised version of the Act, announcing that the Central Americans would continue to negotiate. The Foreign Ministry approved of this move in principle, viewing it as bringing the period of Contadora *tutelage* to an end. However, its primary criticism was that Contadora had failed to exert sufficient pressure on Nicaragua.

From Costa Rica's point of view, the Group should have functioned as "a fraternal center of pressure to democratize Nicaragua."[47]

This political assertiveness plus its apparent close ties to the Honduran and Salvadoran positions narrowed the country's room for maneuver and brought into question its own neutrality, on which its foreign policy was based. As reality made itself felt, Costa Rica gradually began to assert itself in the dialogue, particularly in those areas which pertained to peace in the region. Oscar Arias made this clear when he told the United Nations (UN) that "Contadora is not dead." Even though the Contadora mediation efforts did not achieve their final objectives, any alternative means for achieving peace or a negotiated settlement would have to be an accord of the Contadora type. If Contadora did not exist, it would have to be invented in order to open up the room to negotiate.[48]

Costa Rica's reply to the Contadora Group regarding its revised Act[49] emphasized five points:

(1) Costa Rica would comply with all the basic commitments therein;
(2) security matters would be of only indirect concern to Costa Rica;
(3) restoring democracy in Central America was vital;
(4) a timetable for democratization should be established;
(5) a Democratic Alliance, in which Europe would play an important role, should be created.

Foreign Minister Madrigal Nieto's response revealed some continuity with the position of the previous administration. Around the same time, former President Monge, attending a meeting in Strasbourg, had suggested the need for "Europe and Latin America to form an alliance for peace and democracy."[50] Costa Rica has consistently sought *rapprochement* with the Europeans and, with this proposal, tried to provoke some sort of concrete action, of which the first result had been the meeting in San José (Conference of European and Central American Foreign Ministers, September 1984).

From Costa Rica's perspective, involving the Europeans could help to break the circle of tension in which Costa Rica found itself.

This response also indicated Costa Rica's desire to put a certain distance between itself and the Tegucigalpa Bloc, enabling it to recover some of that room for maneuver which had been lost by its too-close association with Honduras and El Salvador. Costa Rica is the only country in Central American whose democratic legitimacy is unquestioned, giving it the strength to call for creation of a democratic alliance. Pursuing more European participation would enable it, from the point of view of the West, to break out of the narrow East-West definition of the conflict which some actors insist upon imposing.

If the regional crisis, escalating war, and lack of democracy is viewed primarily as an East-West conflict in an area of vital interest to one of the superpowers, this will lead to only one outcome: a military one, without alternatives. If this tragic situation should occur, it would necessarily affect, and very profoundly, the interests of all the others, particularly those of the West. Moreover, such an outcome would produce a solution that was neither political, nor social, nor economic and, almost certainly, not even a military one. Instability would spread and be prolonged over time, placing the Central American countries in a situation fraught with danger and allowing only a very narrow range for national autonomy.

Such a situation would have fatal consequences for a country like Costa Rica, given its military vulnerability. This explains the president's insistence on placing so much hope on mediation. Nevertheless, Madrigal Nieto did not seem to share this hope when he declared before leaving Mexico: "Contadora has failed to solve the Central American problem and has tolerated Nicaraguan ambiguity."[51]

RELATIONS WITH THE UNITED STATES

COSTA RICAN POLICY has many points in common with that of the United States. Basically, these are expressed in the calls for democracy and in the insistence on a clear verification process, but when they reach the point of how to achieve these goals, important differences appear.

During the first months of the Arias administration, relations between Costa Rica and the United States were not easy. Differences over aid to the *contras* and Arias' condemnation of the US punitive action toward Libya were major points of friction. In addition, there was a specific problem concerning an agreement to fish for tropical tuna in Costa Rican waters.

It would have been difficult for Costa Rica to have taken any other position, not only because of its neutrality policy but also because the country has long advocated the need to strengthen international law. Violations of international law bring into question the very foundations of Costa Rican security. During his Latin American tour, Arias had said that "as a small country, we have to believe, have faith, and be optimistic about international law and international organizations."[52]

Costa Rica's most basic concern is to prevent war from reaching its territory. This means that civil conflicts must not turn into regional conflict. It also means preventing an armed force — like the *contras* — from operating on its national territory. Not only does this risk the security of its borders but also its own internal security. Not being able to control an armed group, whose arms and experience are possibly superior to those of the Costa Rican police, brings into question the state's own monopoly of the use of force. At the same time, it is also of major importance that Costa Rica continue to receive the flow of US aid, which has risen to a half million dollars per day (see Table).

Costa Rica's main dilemma has been to establish a policy able to secure strong national support and achieve its desired objectives while maintaining cooperative relations with the four main poles of tension which affect its foreign policy. On the domestic plane, the administration has been severely criticized for its policies. While the most critical sectors have not suggested any alternative policy, they do consider that US-Costa Rican relations are tense, particularly since President Arias had not yet secured an interview with President Reagan (finally scheduled for 4 December 1986).

It is unlikely that these differences will be overcome in the immediate future, as evidenced by Arias meeting with [US Secretary of State] Shultz at the United Nations. On the contrary, granting aid to the *contras* will maintain the tension between Costa Rica and Nicaragua and, in so doing, confirm Costa Rica's perception that its only alternative to war is neutrality. Nonetheless, the pressures and counterpressures to change its neutrality policy create sufficient tension within the Costa Rican political

TABLE

ECONOMIC ASSISTANCE FROM THE UNITED STATES
(In millions of dollars)

Fiscal Year	1982	1983	1984	1985	1986	1987*
Development						
Aid	11.5	27.5	15.5	20.5	11.0	16.0
Loans	9.7	20.2	12.4	10.7	6.3	9.0
Gifts	1.8	7.0	3.1	9.8	4.7	7.0
Other						
Economic Aid	1.1	1.7	1.9	3.4	3.8	3.2
Loans	---	---	---	---	---	---
Gifts	1.1	1.7	1.9	3.4	3.8	3.2
Food Aid	19.1	28.2	22.5	21.4	23.0	18.0
Loans	18.0	28.0	22.5	21.4	23.0	18.0
Gifts	1.1	0.2	---	---	---	---
ESF	20.0	157.0	130.0	160.0	120.6	150.0
Loans	15.0	118.0	35.0	---	---	---
Gifts	5.0	39.0	95.0	160.0	120.6	150.0
Military	2.1	4.6	9.1	13.2	2.6	3.4
Loans	---	---	---	---	---	---
Gifts	2.1	4.6	9.1	13.2	2.6	3.4
Total	53.8	218.7	179.0	218.0	160.2	190.5
Loans	42.7	166.2	69.9	32.1	29.3	27.0
Gifts	11.1	52.5	109.1	185.9	130.9	163.5

These amounts put Costa Rica in 12th place (1985) and 14th place
(1986) among US aid recipients. .

Source: Steven R. Harper. "US Assistance to Costa Rica: Foreign
and Facts." Washington, DC: Library of Congress, Congressional
Research Service (8 April 1986).

*Estimates

---

system that government action becomes increasingly difficult. In
this situation, the entry of foreign investment and income from
tourism (one of the country's three principal sources of income)
could be seriously affected, making economic growth and stability
even more difficult .

To this may be added the massive influx of refugees, which the
government estimates as about 240,000 (or almost 10% of the
country's population). The presence of the refugees in certain
areas of the country has awakened strong opposition. Internation-

al cooperation to establish joint programs (national and refugee) is very limited, and Costa Rica is in no condition to resolve the combination of problems which this new situation requires. This is another element which could lead to greater tension within the Costa Rican body politic.

From the US point of view, it would appear that it has fixed its gaze on its immediate goals related to Nicaragua without giving any consideration to the adverse affects of that policy on countries like Costa Rica, which are not among its priorities. To date, US policy has not resolved the problem of how to confront the policy of neutrality without tragic consequences. For some observers this is not so serious, as they feel Costa Rica is already engaged in a low-intensity war, only one being played out in the political arena.[53] My own analytical perspective indicates that, despite the points of agreement regarding political objectives, differences over how to achieve them could take on increasing importance.

PROBLEMS OF PUBLIC SECURITY

As THE CENTRAL AMERICAN crisis has increased, so have Costa Rica's security problems, deriving not just from the narrow area of politics but from the use of its national territory as a transit point for international traffic in narcotics.

The Arias government has indicated that, while it will not change the country's tradition of remaining unarmed, it will continue, at the same time, with its program of professional police training. Preparedness and militarism are very different things, declared Hernán Garrón, Minister of Public Security and a major defender of the neutrality policy.[54]

A peaceful Costa Rican-Nicaraguan border is in the common interest of both countries, not only for the usual reasons of stability which states desire on their international borders, but for other reasons as well: for the Costa Ricans, it means reducing the danger of finding themselves involved in the regional conflict; for the Nicaraguans, it means reducing the risk of a second front, in which a large part of their troops would be "tied" to the southern border, preventing deployment to the north and the Atlantic area. However, it is impossible to reach any bilateral agreement since Costa

Rica has followed a broad, multilateral policy from the very beginning of the Contadora negotiation process.[55]

Costa Rica's security problems are not confined to its northern border alone. A great number of problems originate from the presence of the international drug traffic in the country. This fact became evident, and has been gathering strength, ever since the capture and deportation of Rafael Caro Quintero, a Mexican drug-trafficker. Surveillance and control of the national territory and air space requires increasingly modern and technologically sophisticated equipment — which Costa Rica does not have. It means organizing special units, incorporating sophisticated listening devices, and acquiring airplanes for reconnaisance.

The drug traffic plus the regional crisis has prompted various sectors to express doubts about whether to militarize or not, as well as about the ultimate end use of the military technology.[56] Whether this will be used in relation to the regional conflict or to repress the illegal drug traffic, especially now that US military aid has become significant compared to what Costa Rica received in the past, loses importance when we compare these amounts with those received by other countries in the area (see Table, p. 139).

All the declarations of government officials and major political leaders point to a reaffirmation of modern Costa Rica's historical calling: to be a demilitarized country.

PROMOTING DEMOCRACY

THE FOREIGN POLICY to promote democracy did not refer to Central America alone. The Foreign Ministry also took specific action in relation to at least two countries: South Africa and Chile.

Costa Rica broke both diplomatic and consular relations with South Africa on 5 July 1986. This measure was based on its traditional policy of promotion of, and respect for, a country's human rights record, and on the fact that the South African regime has continued its policy of racial segregation, ignoring the international community's call to eliminate *apartheid*. The two countries had cut off trade relations in 1967.[57]

When Costa Rica severed its relations with South Africa, Oscar Arias made a speech in which he referred to democracy on the continent, pointing out that "Paraguay does not have democracy, and Chile is farther than ever from attaining it." The Foreign Ministry has repeatedly sent notes of protest to Chile protesting the detention of leaders in the democratic opposition. At the beginning of September, the head of the foreign minister's cabinet visited Chile to evaluate the situation. Various factions in both the PUSC and the PLN had asked the government to close its embassy in Santiago. The government position has been that it would be difficult to carry out any work in the field of human rights without an embassy.

During these first months, the new administration also initiated a program of *rapprochement* with "moderate" Arab countries. It re-established relations with Morocco (25 September 1986) and seeks to continue this process. It has also initiated contacts with Egypt and Saudi Arabia.

The administration has also sought *rapprochement* with Mexico, a country with whom its traditional relations of friendship and political cooperation had fallen to a minimum. To this end, the foreign minister visited that country in November 1986.

REORGANIZING THE FOREIGN MINISTRY

COSTA RICA HAS diplomatic relations with almost a hundred countries and maintains offices to represent the government in 46 of them (23 of which are located in the Americas). The basic premise of the new government team is that, since Costa Rica has no armed armed forces, it can't afford the luxury of doing without a professional diplomatic corps. Traditionally, representing Costa Rica in a foreign country has been viewed as a "political plum" and, as a result, diplomats have not generally attained the level of professionalism and efficiency which the regional crisis requires.

On that kind of reasoning and once the new government took office, the Foreign Ministry began to reorganize, creating new positions to coordinate functions, reorganizing departments, and establishing technical procedures. This process took place at the same time ambassadors were being appointed and went on for more than three months. This whole practice was severely criticized, given the fact that Costa Rica had no overseas representation while Nicaragua was presenting its case to the International Court.

One problem complicating the appointment of ambassadors was that the government had so little money with which to pay salaries and maintain offices. This meant that the foreign service ran the risk of *oligarquizarse* since the only persons able to serve were those who could supply their own funds in emergencies. As a result of this situation, Guido Fernández, appointee to the White House, never assumed his duties til November. The same thing happened with Nicaragua.

PERSPECTIVES

FOREIGN AFFAIRS will continued to center around the four poles of tension: Nicaragua, the United States, Central America, and Contadora. Of these, the United States and Nicaragua are the two poles which will exert the greatest impact on relations in the future. In turn, this triangle of relations will create other tensions in a kind of ripple effect that will affect Costa Rica's other international relations. Costa Rica will continue to try to draw the European Community into this nexus as a way to reduce tension.

Costa Rica will maintain its policy of military neutrality and will increase its political assertiveness.

NOTES

1. Costa Rica: Balance de la Situacíon (No. 14, January-May 1986). San José, Costa Rica: Center for the Study of Social Action.

2. Miguel Gómez and Mitchell A. Seligson. "Ordinary Elections in Extraordinary Times: The Political Economy of Voting in Costa Rica." Paper presented at XIII International Congress of the Latin American Studies Association (LASA), Boston, MA, 23-25 October 1986.

3. Rumbo Centroamericano (Costa Rica) critical supplement, II, 71, 7-13 March 1986; La Nación (Costa Rica), 2 March 1986; La Nación (Costa Rica), 24 March 1986.

4. Francisco Rojas Aravena. "Costa Rica: entre la neutralidad y el conflict," in Heraldo Muñoz (ed.) América Latina y el Caribe: Políticas Exteriores para Sobrevivir. Buenos Aires, Argentina: Grupo Editor Latinoamericano, 1986.

5. Oscar Arias. " Presidential Message: 1986" (1 May 1986). San José, Costa Rica: Republic of Costa Rica, Imprenta Nacional: 25.

6. The last attempt to gain approval for a neutrality law was made a few days after the elections. Through a parliamentary maneuver, the project was quickly approved by a committee of the Legislative Assembly

(22 March 1986). Foreign Minister F. Vilio described the approval as a drum roll; however, in the full session the law failed to obtain the votes needed for ratification.

7. New York Times, 25 October 1986; Miami Herald, 25 October 1986.

8. La Nacíon (Costa Rica), 30 July 1986.

9. The statement that had more impact on the *contra* issue was an interview (on 21 February 1986) granted to the National Broadcasting Company (NBC), a US television network, which was published by *La Nación* on 2 March 1986. He claimed to be anti-Sandinista in an interview with the Spanish newspaper *El País* (published in its international edition of 24 March 1986).

10. Oscar Arias Sánchez inaugural message: "Una Alianza para la Libertad y la Democracia" (8 May 1986). San Jose, Costa Rica: Republic of Costa Rica, Imprenta Nacional: 7. The sentence used is the same used by the President of Costa Rica almost a century ago.

11. In other theoretical instances, this would not be a case of limited sovereignty but a sort of "illusion of sovereignty," given the vulnerability of the country on the one hand and the very fact of being located in the Caribbean Basin — an area where the continental hegemonic power applied its resources to the maximum.

12. La Nación (Costa Rica), 15 April 1986.

13. At the time, bilateral conversations depended on whether Nicaragua would make excuses for the Las Crucitas incident, which took place a few days later.

14. La República (Costa Rica), 4 February 1986.

15. Oscar Arias inaugural message (see note 10 above): 8.

16. *Ibid.*: 14.

17. Oscar Arias Sánchez. "Paz para Centroamérica: Libertad y Democracia para Cinco Pueblos." Speech before the XLI General Assembly of the United Nations, 24 September 1986: 2.

18. *Ibid.*: 3.

19. In this regard, see "América Central Frente a la Decada de los '80." Costa Rica: Universidad Nacional, International Relations School, Department of Publications, 1983; "Centroamérica: Condiciones para su Integración." San José, Costa Rica: Facultad Latinoamericana de Ciencias Sociales (FLACSO), 1982.

20. In addition, preliminary procedures were held so that the PLN's *Tribunal de Ética* could analyze the case.

21. For the results of the incident, see Francisco Rojas Aravena (*op. cit.* in note 4).

22, The text of the notes can be found in La Nación (Costa Rica), 14 February 1986.

23. Envío (Managua) 51, July 1985. Edén Pastora subsequently announced that he was leaving the armed struggle and requested (17 May 1986) political asylum in Costa Rica, which was granted.

24. La Nación (Costa Rica), 11 March 1986.

25. Costa Rica's Deputy Minister for Security left the meeting because the document was a premature version that was being signed hastily.

26. Statements made to NBC television network, in La Nación (Costa Rica), 2 March 1986.

27. La Prensa Libre (Costa Rica), 21 February 1986.

28. La Prensa Libre (Costa Rica), 6 March 1986.

29. *Ibid.*

30. The Nicaraguan ambassador pointed out that Daniel Ortega "was not invited."

31. Contadora Group. "Communiqué" (9 May 1986).

32. This could have been an additional reason for the failure of the mini-summit since, according to Costa Rican diplomats, Guatemala would not participate in any action or declaration that would have frustrated the Esquipulas meeting.

33. La Nación (Costa Rica, 23 May 1986.

34. Informative Letter (of SIECA) 295, May 1986.

35. At the end of the meeting, Arias pointed out that "Nicaragua is not a democracy since there is no respect for human rights, freedom of expression, right of assembly, etc;" but he avoided calling it a dictatorship at that time (La Nación [Costa Rica], 26 May 1986).

36. La Nación (Costa Rica), 1 June 1986.

37. Francisco Rojas Aravena. "Interes nacional y toma de decisiones: el caso de la neutralidad costarricense," in University of Costa Rica (ed.) Anuario de Estudios Centroamericano, Vol. II, Fase I. See also "La percepción de la crisis centroamericana y la neutralidad como estrategia internacional en la Administración Monge." Relaciones Internacionales 11 (2nd Quarter, 1985).

38. Letter from the Nicaraguan Foreign Minister to Rodrigo Madrigal Nieto, Foreign Minister of Costa Rica, 28 July 1986. San José, Costa Rica: Embassy of Nicaragua.

39. Communiqué (1 August 1986). Ministry of Foreign Relations of Costa Rica.

40. La Nación (Costa Rica), 30 July 1986.

41. La Nación (Costa Rica), 5 August 1986.

42. La Nación (Costa Rica, 11 August 1986.

43. Communiqué (12 August 1986). *Partido de Liberación Nacional* (PLN) of Costa Rica, General Secretariat.

44. La Nación (Costa Rica), 11 September 1986.

45. Francisco Rojas Aravena. "Costa Rica, the Regional Crisis, and Contadora," in Bruce Bagley (ed.) The Contadora Process, Vol. II. Boulder, CO: Westview Press (in press). Also Rojas Aravena chapter on Costa Rica in *op. cit* (note 4).

46. *Ibid.*

47. La Nación (Costa Rica), 10 June 1986.

48. Francisco Rojas Aravena. "Contadora ha muerto ... Viva Contadora." Cono Sur 4, 4, (August-September 1986). Santiago de Chile: Facultad Latinoamerica de Ciencias Sociales (FLACSO).

49. Letter from Rodrigo Madrigal Nieto to the Foreign Ministers of Contadora (15 July 1986). Ministry of Foreign Relations of Costa Rica.

50. Luis Alberto Monge. "Alianza de Europa y América Latina para la Democracia y la Paz." Speech at meeting on Democracy and Democratization: a Dialogue between Europe and Latin America, Strasbourg, France, June 1986.

51. Diario Las Américas (Miami), 29 October 1986.

52. La Nación (Costa Rica), 20 April 1986.

53. Costa Rica: Balance de la Situación, No. 1, 16 (June-July 1986). San José, Costa Rica: CEPAS.

54. La Nación (Costa Rica), 22 July 1986.

55. Francisco Rojas Aravena. "Costa Rica, the Regional Crisis, and Contadora." (*op. cit* in note 45).

56. Gregorio Selser. "Costa Rica: prosigue aceleradamente el proceso de militarización del país que no tiene ejército." El Día (Mexico), 15 June 1986.

57. José Joaquín Trejos. 8 Anos en la Política Costarricense. San José, Costa Rica: Ediciones Hombre y Sociedad, 1973.

NICARAGUA 1986: FOREIGN POLICY DILEMMAS IN THE FACE OF FOREIGN AGGRESSION

by BORIS YOPO H.

INTRODUCTION

THIS CHAPTER WILL ANALYZE some of Nicaragua's most important foreign policy actions through October 1986. Specifically, it will examine Sandinista state-to-state relations with those regions/countries towards which Nicaraguan diplomacy has been directing its principal initiatives over the past 12 months.

Foreign policy has been one of the fundamental axes in the Sandinista's survival strategy. Conceived as an "instrument of the revolution," according to Minister of the Interior Tomás Borge, Nicaraguan diplomacy is planned and controlled at the highest levels of government. That foreign relations play a leading role in setting the agenda for the Nicaraguan president and other high-ranking officials in the government is evidenced by the extensive international tours undertaken by Daniel Ortega and Vice-President Sergio Ramírez in 1986. Thus, when the Sandinistas cite the principal achievement of their revolution as "having survived" in the face of US pressure and hostility, this has been made possible, in large part, by an assertive, diversified foreign policy designed to foil efforts to isolate their regime internationally.

Boris Yopo H. is a Chilean specialist in international relations and researcher for PROSPEL.

Nevertheless, some of the government's decisions — such as strict application of the state of emergency when the "low-intensity war" intensified — have had a negative impact, such as causing some western countries to distance themselves from the regime at those times when US pressure increased and when Nicaragua needed, more than ever, the assurance that international assistance would continue in order to deal with its critical economic situation. [According to the latest report from the UN Economic Commission for Latin America (ECLA), in 1986 Nicaragua had an external debt of US$5 billion, a trade deficit of US$550 million, a gross national product (GNP) of -3%, inflation of 780%, and unemployment of 21.7%.]

Furthermore, various factors — such as growing *rapprochement* with the socialist bloc, increases in the military infrastructure, successive border clashes, and the perception of Nicaraguan intransigence toward Contadora mediation (in the September 1985-April 1986 period) — worked to nibble away at prevailing international support. Despite the fact that these measures were taken in the context of a policy designed to preserve the immediate physical survival of the revolution, they still created dilemmas for Nicaraguan foreign policy in 1986.

RELATIONS WITH THE UNITED STATES

NICARAGUA'S RELATIONS WITH the United States did not improve during 1986 nor was there any progress toward negotiation of differences. This was due to the insistence of the Reagan administration that Nicaragua's internal politics must be included in the negotiating agenda [whether multilateral or bilateral] (Yopo H., 1986a). Various statements by President Reagan and other high-ranking officials of his administration, as well as the US preference for military pressure as a negotiating tactic, testify to the fact the US objective was not to modify (or regulate) Nicaragua's external actions but, rather, to prevent the Sandinistas from consolidating their regime internally and, hopefully, to prevent a recurrence of the US experience with Cuba of 25 years ago.[1]

This strategy, which seeks to reverse the situation created by the revolution of 1979, transcends traditional ways of handling dispute and is a throwback to the "rollback" policy of Secretary of State John Foster Dulles in the 1950s, now being applied to the Third World (Time, 1986c; Miami Herald, 1986h). This US policy, now known as the "Reagan Doctrine," [2] aims at the destabilization of some revolutionary movements in the Periphery, of which Nicaragua serves as the most obvious example, to demonstrate its effectiveness and viability.[3] It is within the context of this policy, consequently, where efforts to resolve the political crisis have been marked by a series of failures, that the US Congress decided to back President Reagan's crusade against Nicaragua.

Already, by the end of 1985, tension between the two countries became even more strained after Congress approved the delivery of funds (US$27 million) to the Nicaraguan *contras*. Military escalation followed. In December 1985, insurgent groups shot down a Nicaraguan helicopter with one of the several SAM-7 ground-to-air missiles provided through a private network organized by the National Security Council.[4] As a sign of protest, Nicaragua temporarily withdrew its ambassador from Washington. According to news sources, this act violated an implied agreement between Washington and Managua not to provide such missiles to any rebel forces in Central America (US News, 1986a). On this occasion, President Daniel Ortega issued a strong protest to the US Congress and rejected the request, by 80 members of that body, that Nicaragua lift its state of emergency (New York Times, 1985).

At the beginning of January 1986, Ortega sent a letter to the Contadora Group proposing that bilateral dialogue with the United States be resumed at the ministerial level (Excelsior, 1986f). This new effort was consistent with Nicaragua's basic objective towards the United States, i.e. to seek an agreement (even implied) that would guarantee the Sandinista revolution would continue, setting limits to state-to-state relations between the two (Yopo, 1986a: 376).

In this regard, the Nicaraguan government also communicated to ex-President Carter, during his visit to Managua, its willingness to relax (but not to negotiate) internal political control and exceptional measures in exchange for a cessation of US hostility. In more than 12 hours of conversation, the Sandinista leadership told Carter that, if the United States would suspend aid to the *contras* and establish a ceasefire, the Nicaraguan government would lift the restrictions on public activities (including press censorship imposed on the opposition and the Church) and would permit all political parties to participate legally in the municipal elections set for 1987 (New York Times, 1986a).

Renewed debate in Congress on aid to the *contras* revealed, however, that the US administration would continue seeking to "resolve the problem" of Nicaragua unilaterally, insisting on recognition of, and negotiation with, the *contras* as a prerequisite to renewing discussions with the Sandinista government. On the other hand, the high priority which the US government accorded Nicaragua became even more apparent when President Reagan declared the Sandinistas to be his Number One foreign policy problem in 1986. When the US House of Representatives first rejected funds for the rebels (20 March 1986), the President met with the group, declaring his unconditional support (Los Angeles Times, 1986c; Washington Post, 1986m). Early in May 1986, Reagan granted the *contra* leaders a 30-minute interview; they were also granted interviews with Vice-President Bush and Secretary of State Shultz as well. At the same time, when Shultz met with French President Mitterand, the main topic of conversation was Nicaragua, with Shultz stating that coexistence with the Sandinistas was "unacceptable" to the Reagan administration (Mercurio, 1986l; Time, 1986b).

During the early months of 1986, various congressional delegations (both Democrats and Republicans, from both houses of Congress) visited Managua. The result of these visits was an exchange of views which served only to reinforce existing opinions on both sides as to the source of US-Nicaraguan differences. During a meeting with Nicaraguan Vice-President Sergio Ramírez, nine Republican congressmen recommended that his government negotiate with the rebels; Ramírez rejected this suggestion, replying that Nicaragua would deal only with the US government (Washington Post, 1986n). Another delegation of congressional Democrats reported, upon their return from Nicaragua, that Nicaragua had become "another Cuba" and that they were therefore willing to support the administration policy to support the *contras* (New York Times, 1986g).

President Reagan's ability to place before the Congress his conditions for resuming dialogue with Nicaragua, and the crystallization of an anti-Sandinista consensus in the Congress, led to Managua's downgrading of this item in its policy toward the United States. For example, President Ortega and Minister D'Escoto, who had previously waged a strong campaign to discourage congressional support of Reagan's policy, attended the funeral of Swedish leader Olof Palme just a few days before the Senate vote. Deputy Minister Victor Tinoco announced that the government had decided to adopt a "low profile" in the congressional debate since past efforts had proved ineffective and counterproductive. During those same weeks, the Nicaraguan president visited Cuba, and Commandante Bayardo Arce attended the Soviet Communist Party Congress in Moscow in spite of the impact such trips might have on US congressmen, especially in the days just prior to the vote. Tinoco disregarded possible criticism, indicating that Nicaragua's diplomatic decisions were not based on the opinion of the US Congress (Miami Herald, 1986i).

The Sandinistas' conviction that (1) President Peagan would continue his policy with or without Congressional support, and that (2) in the final analysis, the most effective argument to "force" the United States to accept the Nicaraguan revolution as an "irreversible reality" (Ortega, 1986d) was military defeat of the *contras*, led Vice-President Ramírez to declare that, in practical terms, the Senate vote was "irrelevant" (New York Times, 1986h). Thus it seemed that only by neutralizing the military options of the Washington policy, dismantling the *contra* option, and increasing the political cost of any direct intervention (Newsweek, 1986b; International Herald Tribune, 1985b) would conditions be created in which an agreement to coexist would come to be seen as the only viable way out of the impasse between the two countries.

As every day the US Congress adopted more and more of the administration view as to appropriate demands to be made of the Nicaraguan government (its "democratization" was to be a key issue in any bilateral discussion), relegating problems of security to second place, and despite the fact that the Sandinistas were willing to make important concessions in these areas, the prospects for some understanding grew increasingly less as the year advanced. Some days before the vote, in May, Senator

Richard Lugar, Chairman of the Foreign Relations Committee, suggested retaining the *contra* funds if the Sandinistas would negotiate with the *contras* and agree to "democratize" their country (New York Times, 1986i). A large number of Democrats no longer questioned assistance to the *contras* so much as the amount and purpose of the assistance (non-military, about US$30 million according to a proposal by Senator Sasser), as well as the sense of support for the rebels (as instruments of pressure and negotiation, or for the overthrow of the Sandinistas).[5]

Finally, a Senate majority of Republicans approved US$100 million in assistance at the end of March, while the administration stepped up its pressure on the Sandinistas on other fronts, renewing the economic embargo decreed in May 1985 and blocking new credit from the Interamerican Development Bank (IDB) to the tune of US$58 million (New York Times, 1986b). In April, President Reagan named a new special envoy to Central America, Philip Habib, to project an image of willingness to negotiate to the Congress and assure approval of funds in an upcoming vote in the House of Representatives. In the weeks that followed, Habib came up with a proposal for "calculated risks" before US congressional representatives and the countries of the Contadora Group, in which the Reagan administration proposed to cease its assistance to the *contras* if Nicaragua would sign the Contadora Agreement by 6 June (Washington Post, 1986h; International Herald Tribune, 1986e). This proposal was based on the supposition that the Sandinistas would continue to refuse to sign the Act, thus reinforcing the view of Nicaraguan intransigence to the Congress and the Contadora mediation process. Nevertheless, as administration officials recognized, the United States did not really plan on holding up aid to the *contras* even if Nicaragua did sign the Act, since, in that case, the White House would re-establish the requirements not for signatures, but for the *fulfillment* of all provisions contained in the Act, besides reinterpreting the Act to coincide with US interests [for example, insisting on negotiations with the *contras* when the Contadora Act contains only general principles that refer to national reconciliation and increasing democracy] (Miami Herald, 1986g).

Habib's proposal — originally supported by Vice-President George Bush, as mentioned by several Latin American statesmen in Costa Rica during Arias' inauguration (Inforpress Centro-americana, 1986b; Analisis Politico, 1986) — undoubtedly impressed members of the Contadora and the Support Groups, as well as those members of the US Congress who were wavering on the policy of the Reagan administration.

Worried that other Latin American countries would pressure Nicaragua to sign the Act without any corresponding US commitment to respect Nicaraguan security, President Ortega strongly denounced Habib, declaring that "he is trying to sell false positions to Latin American nations… his speech is cynical and demagogic" (Mercurio, 1986k). He also pointed out at the same time, in an attempt to convince observers of his (and his government's) flexibility, that Nicaragua stood ready to sign a mutual security pact with the United States which would convert Central America into a "neutral zone" outside the East-West conflict, as well as to discuss other topics of interest to the United States, such as the alleged Nicaraguan assistance to Salvadoran guerrillas (Wall Street Journal, 1986).

The debate on giving aid to the *contras* picked up during June, preparatory to the vote scheduled for the end of the month, which prompted Ortega to dismiss the vote as irrelevant to his country on the grounds that the Reagan administration was committed to providing such aid with or without the consent of Congress.[6] Ortega seized upon a meeting with 13 members of the Congress to reaffirm his contention that the main obstacle to resolving the regional crisis was the US insistence on trying to determine Nicaragua's internal politics, "…especially when important progress on security questions have been made" (Agencia IPS, 1986g).

In the weeks prior to the House vote, Nicaragua relaxed its position toward Contadora to the point that both the Nicaraguan president, as well as Foreign Minister D'Escoto, announced that the Sandinista government was prepared to sign the Contadora Agreement (i.e., to comply with Habib's original proposal) if the United States would renew discussions with Nicaragua (Inforpress Centroamericana, 1986b; Agencia IPS, 1986g; and D'Escoto, 1986). Nevertheless, the US House of Representatives voted (221-209) in favor of the White House request (US$100 million for the *contras*), an outcome which reflected the central role played by

Reagan, who used his personal influence to swing the critical number of votes needed for approval (International Herald Tribune, 1986d; Miami Herald, 1986d). Encouraged by his political victory in the Congress, the US leader stated a few days later that, if the Sandinistas refused to negotiate with the *contras*, "the only alternative for them would be to win and take power" (Excelsior, 1986d).

Early in August, President Ortega travelled to New York to address the United Nations, taking advantage of the visit to undertake a direct public relations campaign which involved many meetings with US politicians and social and religious leaders. Out of a meeting in Chicago with the Reverend Jesse Jackson and more than 1200 US social leaders on this tour, Ortega emerged with a proposal. Briefly, it recommended that (1) the United States comply with the findings of the International Court of Justice which declared US aid to the *contras* to be illegal; (2) the two countries sign a treaty of peace and friendship which would pledge respect for the legitimate security interests of each nation and to convert Central America into a demilitarized peace zone; and (3) President Reagan agree to visit Nicaragua (Pensamiento Propio, 1986).

Not only did the US dismiss the proposal as propaganda, but Reagan used his speech before the United Nations in September to reaffirm his strategy — first suggested in 1985 by Robert McFarland, chief of the National Security Council — to gain concessions from the Sandinistas by pressuring the Soviet Union to cut off its aid to Nicaragua.[7] For his part, the Secretary of State instructed US ambassadors in Europe to seek an end to European assistance to the Sandinista government and, in a meeting with Latin American statesmen, pressed them to cooperate in "imposing" democracy on Nicaragua (Washington Report, 1986).

By the end of 1986, it was difficult to foresee how the impasse between the present US administration and the Sandinista government would turn out. High-level officials of the United States had made it obvious that they planned to step up military pressure and to "liberate" some Nicaraguan territory (probably on the Atlantic coast) and then declare a provisional government which the US would immediately recognize. To forestall another "Bay of Pigs trauma," the United States would intervene to support the rebels and/or to prevent their total defeat.[8] President Reagan and US foreign policy advisers at the highest level compromised the credibility of US leadership in the world to resolve (presumably before 1988) the dilemma posed by the Sandinistas.[9]

Nevertheless, a number of factors combined to complicate the viability of this strategy. New opportunities (as well as risks) were created for Nicaraguan diplomacy (1) by the persistence of the "Vietnam syndrome" in US public opinion, in Congress, and in the Pentagon[10] (an analogy made more credible by the increased capability of the Sandinista army in both conventional and irregular warfare); (2) by Latin America's probable reaction to more direct intervention; (3) by the continuing problem of political-military credibility which the *contras* have in the United States itself; (4) by the Hasenfus case; (5) by the victory of the Democrats in the November congressional elections; and (6) by the Iran-*contra* crisis.[11]

The fore-mentioned developments are important for Managua because so much of the Reagan policy towards the Sandinistas has been conditioned by US domestic politics and desire to restore US hegemony in the world (primarily *vis-à-vis* the Soviet Union but also as a symbol of leadership among allied countries) than by the specific relationship between the two countries. This is what has frustrated conciliatory gestures by the Nicaraguan government in spite of the concessions offered by the Sandinistas and recognized as such by US officials.[12] Perhaps what is needed is a crisis in US domestic politics, such as is now taking place, in order for the US to revise its goals in Nicaragua, making it more acceptable to negotiate on issues defined around bilateral and regional security, rather than focus on the Nicaraguan internal political regime.

What is at stake in Nicaragua's relations with the United States is the willingness of the latter to accept some arrangement which allows coexistence with the Sandinista revolution. It is obvious that the Reagan administration refuses to concede this possibility, and, on the contrary, the Iran-*contra* situation might even function as a spur to more direct US intervention if it could be presented in terms acceptable to the general public, thus neutralizing the worst political crisis faced by the present administration so far. Thus, 1987 has become critical for the survival of the Nicaraguan government since, if the US president sees his strategy to destabilize the Sandinistas neutralized, it would be difficult for another president without Reagan's charisma to maintain that policy, given the existing restrictions on a military solution to the so-called Sandinista "problem." Therefore, US policy towards Nicaragua will be decided, in large part, more by domestic US politics than by Sandinista diplomacy. Nicaragua's efforts to negotiate could gain new success in the wake of such an internal debate if certain sectors in the US foreign policy apparatus would accept the viability of an understanding with the Sandinista regime in exchange for Managua's explicit pledge to recognize US security interests in the area. If Nicaragua could obtain such a pact, it would constitute the greatest success of Sandinista foreign policy in the 7 years of revolution.

LATIN AMERICA AND CONTADORA EFFORTS

AT THE END OF 1985, Nicaraguan relations with the other Latin American countries entered a critical phase, during which the United States increased its pressure on the Sandinista regime. Nicaragua had rejected the proposal which the Contadora Group had presented in September 1985 since its concessions were in the US interest which, in the Sandinista view, seriously affected Nicaraguan security requirements (El Día, 1985). In December, the Contadora countries (with the exception of Mexico) had prepared the text of a UN resolution on the Central American crisis that outlined the US role in the conflict. Although this resolution was not passed, it strengthened Nicaragua's apprehension that Contadora, in its zeal to accommodate US concerns, would increase its pressure to sign an agreement which the Sandinistas had already rejected (Envío, 1985). It was in this context then that Nicaragua hardened its position toward the mediating process, asking for a 6-month suspension so that it could study the Act for Peace and Cooperation in Central America (Mercurio, 1985a, 1985b, 1985c).

Nevertheless, January produced an important development affecting Nicaraguan interests in the form of the "Message of Caraballeda," drawn up by the foreign ministers of the countries in the Contadora and Support Groups. This document confirmed the main points of the Nicaraguan position, such as stopping outside support of the rebel forces (contras), suspension of foreign military maneuvers, reduction — and eventual elimination — of foreign advisors and military installations, and non-aggression pledges by the Central American countries. Fundamental for Nicaragua, moreover, was the fact that the *Mensaje de Caraballeda* included using its good offices to encourage discussion between the United States and Nicaragua, and to promote acts of national reconciliation (but) which conformed with the *legal framework then in force* in each country (Estados Unidos-Centroamérica, 1986: 3).

The foreign ministers from both Contadora and the Support Group subsequently met with Secretary of State George Shultz in Washington to present the Caraballeda proposal. During the meeting, the ministers presented him with a formula for "simultaneousness" whereby the United States would suspend assistance to the *contras* and Nicaragua would implement measures to liberalize its domestic policies at the same time (Washington Post, 1986o).

In Nicaragua, President Ortega took advantage of the new openings provided by Caraballeda to send a letter to the Contadora countries reaffirming his government's promise to grant unconditional amnesty to all opposition forces who would agree to participate legally in national politics. The Latin American foreign ministers presented this proposal to Shultz as a first indication of the willingness of the Sandinistas to negotiate (CIDE, 1986).

However, in April the Nicaragua-Contadora dialogue suffered a new setback following a joint meeting of Contadora with the Central American countries at which they drew up the so-called "Panama agreement." Foreign Minister D'Escoto charged that the agreement forced Nicaragua to disarm in the face of US aggression, while President Ortega announced that Nicaragua would sign the peace treaty scheduled for 6 June 1986 (the date set for all five countries to sign) only when and if the United States ceased its aggressive actions by that date (Los Angeles Times, 1986b; Washington Post, 1986i). Behind these developments, it was apparent that different views had emerged as to the most effective strategy for neutralizing US military escalation. At the time, Contadora's goal was to obtain Nicaragua's firm promise to sign on June 6th as a way to forestall Congress' support of the Reagan policy. However, the Sandinistas felt such a promise was too risky considering that, in 1985, Congress had approved funds for the *contras* despite the fact that Nicaragua had already accepted the first version of the Contadora Peace Act (September 1984). Even more important for Managua, a vote of Congress was no guarantee of an *effective end* to US hostilities since, in the past, the Reagan administration had continued its covert actions against Nicaragua despite restrictions imposed by that legislative body (Ortega, 1986c).

It was in this atmosphere that Foreign Minister D'Escoto pointed out that the April 6 agreement was not the same as that of Caraballeda, which, from the Nicaraguan viewpoint, was *the* major document for discussion in concluding the Peace Agreement, and which required the United States to cease effective aid to the *contras* as an indispensable factor for resumption of, and progress in, any peace negotiations (Los Angeles Times, 1986b). In an official communiqué of 12 April, the Nicaraguan government clarified its position, emphasizing, in essence, that Contadora had so revised the Agreement in response to US pressure that it was now unacceptable to Nicaragua. Nicaragua repeated its support of mediation as the only viable path to a negotiated solution, but said that did not imply, nor was linked to, its unconditional acceptance of a revised Agreement. It called for immediate resumption of negotiations to resolve the two aspects of the Agreement which were still pending (control and reduction of armaments and military maneuvers); it agreed to sign on the 6th of June if the United States had completely ceased its aggression and if the accord succeeded in including those aspects pending in the revised agreement. Thus everything was to be finally agreed upon within the framework of "simultaneousness" set forth in the *Mensaje de Caraballeda* (El Día, 1986b).

This way, the Sandinistas tried to avoid a situation in which the United States could achieve, through Contadora, the goals which it had not been able to achieve through its policy of direct pressure. Minister of Defense Humberto Ortega pointed out, for example, that the US government "is directly pressuring the Contadora and Support Groups...in order to transform the Peace Agreement into a means for crippling the Sandinistas through imperialism." Ortega concluded that the US strategy of imposing a negotiation bordering on intervention…is meant to isolate Nicaragua from its Latin American friends using the false argument that we are inflexible (Alasei, 1986a).

The Nicaraguan president also reaffirmed that his country would not agree to disarm in a situation in which the US Ambassador to the United Nations Vernon Walters "intends to establish a Latin American military force to be used to intervene in Nicaragua" (Mercurio, 1986i).

By the middle of April, the Contadora and Support Group countries showed signs of greater receptivity to the Nicaraguan position. Venezuelan Foreign Minister Simón Alberto Consalví declared that the Contadora Group "understands the immense difficulties which some countries, especially those who are opposed to Nicaragua, have in signing the Peace Act." The same month President Alan García (of Peru) and President Julio Sanguinetti (of Uruguay) sent a message to Daniel Ortega declaring it was important to have an agreement that guaranteed the security of all, and in which they repudiated foreign interference, the use of force in the region, and foreign support for guerrilla forces (Der Spiegel, 1986; Agencia IPS, 1986i). As May began, and in an effort to facilitate Nicaragua's signing of the Peace Agreement, the Contadora members issued a declaration in which "they asked countries outside the region to guarantee consolidation of the peace process, and, especially, to cease support of rebel forces operating within the region" (Agencia IPS,1986h).

This produced a new convergence of views in which Nicaragua proposed that the Central American countries sign the Peace Accord on June 6th and postpone discussion of the section on arms limitations into the months following. Here Managua proposed to set limits on offensive arms but to exclude defensive armaments from discussion (US News and World Report, 1986b; New York Times, 1986b). Nicaragua also accepted the proposal of Guatemala and Costa Rica to establish an inventory of armaments, but one which would allow each nation to decide for itself the kind of arms it wished to keep, and which would not limit the number of troops (Washington Post, 1986g).

The last version of the Peace Accord, presented by Contadora on 7 June in Panama, was actively supported by Nicaragua — with Foreign Minister D'Escoto declaring it the only instrument capable of achieving peace in Central America. He also announced that, as a step towards resolving pending issues, Nicaragua was prepared to deliver an inventory of all its heavy arms (Agencia IPS, 1986k; Nicaragua, 1986). Thus, consolidation of this third version of the treaty constituted a major victory for Nicaraguan diplomacy in the sense that the new Peace Accord included provisions considered necessary for Sandinista security: it forbids foreign military maneuvers; incorporates the concept of "a reasonable balance of forces" among Central American countries; indirectly defines the difference between offensive and defensive arms; and forbids (a) one national territory to be used as a base of aggression against another country, (b) membership in military alliances which threaten the security of countries in the region, and (c) support for irregular forces operating in Central America (Nicaragua, 1986). Contadora and the Support Group rejected the Costa Rican petition (supported by Honduras and El Salvador) to reopen discussion of the political section of the treaty. The United States and its allies wanted to include democratization as an issue, which would have focussed debate on Nicaragua's internal politics instead of on problems of security, both bilateral and regional (Monde Diplomatique, 1986b).

Nicaragua's negotiations with Contadora and the Support Group eventually enabled it to reconcile two objectives it considered important:

(1) to clarify definitions — introduced in the June 1986 proposal regarding the September 1985 Act — which guarantee certain aspects Nicaragua regards as essential to its security and stability;

(2) to prevent a break with the mediating countries (which also prevented the definite collapse of Contadora).

This was important as the Sandinistas considered that Contadora constituted a major obstacle to direct US intervention (Ramirez, 1986; Christian Science Monitor, 1986a).

The subsequent stalemate in the mediating process — caused by stepped-up US support of the *contras* and by the refusal of some countries (Costa Rica, El Salvador, and Honduras) to sign the new peace proposal, thus bearing the onus for its failure of ratification — does not diminish Contadora's importance for the Nicaraguan government. In November, the 8 Latin American foreign ministers addressed the United Nations, pointing out, among other things, that "Latin America does not want the principles of free determination and non-intervention to be sacrificed in the name of security or democracy" (Monde Diplomatique, 1986b).

Nicaragua has tried to improve its relations with Latin America, the primary region to provide basic support for the Sandinista survival strategy (Yopo, 1986a: 378-79). The close relations with Cuba (Nicaragua's principal ally in the region) were illustrated by President Ortega's visit to Havana, in February 1986, to attend the Cuban Communist Party Congress, the first time he had participated in such an event. In his speech to the Cuban Congress, Ortega described Nicaragua's relations with Cuba as "friendly, unchangeable and non-negotiable." [13] As part of the ongoing discussions between the two countries, Cuba advised the Sandinista leaders to sign the Contadora Act and thus made US plans regarding Nicaragua more difficult (Washington Post, 1986h). Fidel Castro confirmed that Cuba is granting Nicaragua all the assistance necessary so that US intervention would be "virtually impossible because of high costs" (Castro, 1986). As part of this support policy, in 1986 Cuba purchased a third of Nicaragua's sugar crop, paying 10¢ a pound above the world market price, for later resale to the Soviet Union (Newsweek, 1986e; Latin American Monitor, 1986).

Mexico and Peru jointly sponsored a UN resolution denouncing the US economic embargo against Nicaragua, calling for economic cooperation with that country instead (Envío, 1985).

By way of support, Peru also announced it would break diplomatic relations with the United States if the latter were to intervene in Nicaragua; it also agreed to refinance Nicaragua's debt to Peru. Subsequently, the US$7.5 million owed was extended over a 20-year period (with a 5-year grace period), and the annual interest rate was reduced from 9% to 3%. In addition, a new US$10 million line of credit was set up for Nicaragua's use in purchasing Peruvian products (Informe Latinoamericano, 1986h; Newsweek, 1986c). Brazil followed suit, making US$6.5 million available for Nicaragua to purchase Brazilian industrial equipment, despite the fact that negotiation of the Nicaraguan debt with Brazil (US$50 million) was still pending (Informe Latinoamericano, 1986i). In Uruguay, political parties initiated a financial campaign to help Nicaragua, as a way to offset US assistance to the *contras* (Agencia IPS, 1986c).

There have been other expressions of solidarity. For instance, the major political parties in Argentina have declared their support for Nicaragua, and the Latin American Parliament unanimously passed a resolution condemning US policy towards Nicaragua (El Día, 1986c; Mercurio, 1986o). In 1986, almost all the South American governments expressed their opposition (both publicly and privately) to US military and economic pressure against Nicaragua to representatives of the US government.[14] Because of these expressions of support, the Sandinista government values the maintenance of good relations with the rest of the hemisphere. The various regional trips taken by high Nicaraguan officials in 1986 testify to the importance of this view.[15] In an interview with a Uruguayan newspaper, President Ortega pointed out that although

> Reagan has been able to impose a hegemonic policy in the
> world,...in Latin America he has met with a resistance which
> I believe is more forceful than ever before in history...
> Contadora is a good example of this (Ortega, 1986b).

Nonetheless, beyond the present interest shared by Nicaragua and the countries of South America in preventing an escalation of hostilities and/or US military intervention (degrees of compromise vary), still tensions and differences on foreign policy priorities exist, and, upon occasion, limit Latin American support for the Sandinista regime. One indication of the caution with which some Latin American countries view the Sandinista revolution, or tend to isolate it — and a critical setback for Nicaraguan diplomacy — is illustrated by the opposition of Argentina, Bolivia, and Colombia to Nicaragua's designation as host to the next summit meeting of the Non-Aligned Movement, scheduled for 1990, despite the fact that Nicaragua actively lobbied for that nomination. Significantly, the Latin American opposition was a determinant in postponing the decision (generally decided unanimously) in spite of support from the African bloc and other Third World countries, and the good-will of Peru, the alternate candidate, which indicated that it would not contest Nicaragua's nomination (Hoy, 1986; Alasei, 1986b).

On the other hand, despite statements from President Alfonsín (and other Latin American leaders) regarding the need for Latin America to increase assistance to Nicaragua to prevent its "radicalization" (thus increasing its range of political options), thus far such initiatives have not been substantial enough to alleviate Nicaragua's serious economic crisis (Periodista, 1986). Argentina, Uruguay, and Venezuela have informed the Nicaraguan regime that, despite their disapproval of Reagan administration methods, they expect to see Nicaragua take firm steps towards democratization, particularly if the US relinquishes its hostility in the near future (Washington Times, 1986; El País, 1986c; Periodista, 1986).

Relations with Colombia were especially difficult in 1986, due primarily to events surrounding the attack on the Palace of Justice by the M-19 (*Movimiento del 19 de abril de 1970*) guerrilla group — as well as to US and right-wing Colombian efforts to implicate Nicaragua in the situation — which caused Colombia to withdraw its ambassador to Managua temporarily. Colombia finally accepted Nicaraguan explanations, confirmed at a meeting between presidents Betancur and Ortega which took place in Guatemala in January (Mercurio, 1986n). Later in the year, Nicaragua revived its dispute with Colombia over territory in the San Andrés and Providencia archipelago when Foreign Minister D'Escoto described the Esguerra-Barcenas treaty as "null and void due to irremediable defects," by virtue of the fact that it had been signed while Nicaragua was occupied by US troops at the turn of the century.[16] In July, the Colombian Foreign Minister criticized new domestic restrictions imposed by the Nicaraguan government on the grounds that they were incompatible with terms of the Contadora peace accords (Agencia IPS, 1986e).

In sum, an overall evaluation of 1986 indicates that Nicaragua made gains in its relations with Latin America, due largely to the Contadora process and other international fora in which the Latin American countries defended Nicaragua's right to self-determination and non-intervention. On the bilateral scene, however, some countries took steps to distance themselves from the Sandinista experience, even countries like Mexico which had traditionally exhibited solidarity with Nicaragua.[17] Various factors provoked this chill, among which were: the apparent exhaustion of the Contadora mediation process; the need some countries had to reduce their profile in resolving the Central American crisis in deference to more important issues in their relations with the United States; the impact of domestic measures implemented by the Nicaraguan Government in mid-1986 which some saw as signs of increased radicalization of the regime; Nicaragua's increasing *rapprochement* with the socialist camp; and, finally, strains of an essentially bilateral nature which led Nicaragua to suspend relations with Bolivia and break with Ecuador in 1985, plus its series of difficulties with Colombia in 1986.

Considering the importance of Latin America in Sandinista foreign policy, Nicaragua will continue its efforts to prevent any further deterioration in bilateral relations (not always in a consistent manner since it seems poor timing, for instance, to have challenged Colombia on maritime limits under the circumstances), taking advantage of any opportunities to form ties, especially with regional middle powers, as was evidenced by Nicaragua's expressions of support for Argentina when new differences regarding the Malvinas/Falklands surfaced between Argentina and Great Britain (Razón, 1986; Agencia IPS, 1986b). Nevertheless, unless something dramatic happens (US intervention or Nicaragua joining the Socialist bloc, which is quite unlikely), Nicaraguan/Latin American relations will tend to remain within existing parameters for the foreseeable future.

RELATIONS WITH NEIGHBORING COUNTRIES

AFTER A PERIOD OF TENSION and differences between Nicaragua and its neighbors in Central America (excepting Guatemala) during the last months of 1985 (Yopo, 1986a: 396-98), 1986 seemed to promise Nicaragua some improvement, in the sense of reaching some sort of *modus vivendi* in which the neighboring countries would accept the existence of the Sandinista revolution, thus preventing consolidation of any regional bloc bent on its isolation.

The newly elected heads of state (in Honduras, Costa Rica, and Guatemala) publicly expressed their opposition to *contra* activities (Estados Unidos, 1986; Mesoamerica, 1986c: 10; International Herald Tribune, 1986g). Even more significantly, President Arias (Costa Rica) declared coexistence with the Sandinistas was possible; President Cerezo (Guatemala) announced it was important not to isolate Nicaragua; and President Azcona (Honduras) told Nicaragua's Vice-President Ramírez that Honduras would look with favor on an agreement to eliminate border tensions between their two countries. [In fact, such an agreement never materialized due to pressure from the United States (Mesoamerica, 1986a: 2; Washington Post, 1986k)]. The first sign of relaxation was Daniel Ortega's attendance at Vinicio Cerezo's inauguration in Guatemala (on 15 January). The foreign ministers of the 5 Central American republics used the occasion of the ceremonies to agree to resume the Contadora negotiations and to support the Message of Caraballeda, which called for a renewal of US-Nicaraguan discussions (Washington Post, 1986p).

Costa Rica and Nicaragua took the next positive step by agreeing (on 15 February) to ask the Contadora Group to establish a border patrol to monitor existing tensions on their common border and to prevent new ones from developing (Estados Unidos, 1986). In a conciliatory gesture, President Ortega sent a message to the Costa Rican president in which the Sandinista army acknowledged its responsibility for the death of two Costa Rican guards, thus paving the way for subsequent normalization of relations between their two countries (Miami Herald, 1986l). In a similar demonstration of tact, President Ortega refrained from criticizing other Central American countries in his annual message to Congress (Miami Herald, 1986m; New York Times, 1986j).

Around the middle of March, while the US Congress was embroiled in debate over aid to the anti-Sandinista forces (thus increasing Central American vulnerability to pressures from the Reagan administration), relaxation of regional tensions began to experience its first setbacks, and, in the months that followed, a scenario much different from the beginning of the year began to develop. The Nicaraguan army entered Honduran territory in March in order to eliminate *contra* bases there. Although — initially — both Nicaragua and Honduras denied this ever took place, public condemnation by the Reagan administration finally impelled Honduras to issue a protest. In reply, President Ortega accused Honduras of having "forfeited its sovereignty" in the area.[18]

In the weeks that followed, a new phase of confrontation with, and isolation of, Nicaragua became increasingly apparent. For example, Costa Rica failed to include Nicaragua in a meeting of Central American vice-presidents which had been convened to analyze the regional economic crisis (Mesoamerica, 1986b:10; Agencia IPS, 1986m). On the other hand, although the deputy foreign ministers of Costa Rica and Nicaragua did meet in mid-March to negotiate the creation of the border commission, the first differences began to emerge when the Costa Rican president, correcting Nicaragua's version of the meeting, declared that "the two countries didn't sign any agreement" at the meeting (Estados Unidos, 1986; Agencia IPS, 1986j). Moreover, President Ortega was not invited to the ceremonies for Arias' inauguration in Costa Rica.

At the same time that prospects for a regional accord began to seem more remote, the other Central American countries (and Costa Rica in particular) began to renew their insistence that the key to the Central American crisis lay in the "problem of democratizing Nicaragua's internal politics." In this sense, then, President Arias' strategy, while not necessarily one of excluding the Sandinistas from the regional community *a priori*, was to put political pressure on Nicaragua — by means of various initiatives and existing regional fora — to condition acceptance of the legitimacy and permanence of the Nicaraguan government upon its adopting a series of internal reforms. In the same vein, the presidents of El Salvador and Honduras stated that there could be no solution to the Central American crisis while the problem of democracy within Nicaragua remained unaddressed (Agencia IPS, 1986j and 1986n; Inforpress Centroamericana, 1986e).

Even traditionally cordial relations with Guatemala began to deteriorate, in April 1986, when Nicaraguan officials became unusually critical of the new government of Vinicio Cerezo. Various developments seemed to indicate that the Guatemalan government might abandon its neutrality *vis-à-vis* the regional conflict. In the Contadora negotiations, the Cerezo government was considering the proposal of the Tegucigalpa Group (Honduras, Costa Rica and El Salvador) regarding foreign military maneuvers and disarmament measures; then, concurrently with a presidential summit meeting in Esquipulas, a meeting of

CONDECA (*Consejo para la Defensa Centromericana*) took place to discuss reactivating this organization in the event of a confrontation with Nicaragua. Cerezo's comments indicated that Guatemala differed with the methods, but not the objectives, of the Reagan administration toward Nicaragua. Finally, Guatemalan legislators who had originally condemned the Nicaraguan *contras* in the Latin American Parliament refused to ratify that condemnation just two weeks later at the meeting of the World Interparliamentary Union. Faced with this situation, Nicaragua's Deputy Foreign Minister Victor Tinoco publicly denounced the Guatemalan regime for adopting the position of the Tegucigalpa Group (Monde Diplomatique, 1986b; Barricada, 1986; Inforpress Centroamericana, 1986a; Mesoamerica, 1986a).

Nevertheless, high-level contacts between the two countries, plus Guatemala's positive reception of the most recent version of the Contadora Accord (acceptable to Nicaragua) generated a new *rapprochement.* This became evident in July when President Ortega (reversing his previous critical posture toward Guatemala) omitted Guatemala from his denunciation of Central American states receiving economic assistance from the United States. The Nicaraguan president made this even more explicit when he observed that "Guatemala respects our revolutionary process" (Mercurio, 1986g; Uno Más Uno, 1986b).

Although some countries had originally perceived the summit meeting of Central American presidents in Esquipulas as a chance to put joint, direct pressure on Nicaragua, it ultimately worked to the Sandinistas' advantage since proposals to force Nicaragua to negotiate its domestic situation did not fare well (Inforpress Centroamericana, 1986a), Nicaragua's isolation *vis-à-vis* the region was lessened, and new channels were opened for realization of Nicaraguan diplomatic objectives. During the course of the meeting, President Ortega proposed, in effect, to accept one of the points (arms control) pending in the Contadora discussions and was able to specify the type of arms which Nicaragua would agree to limit or regulate (Inforpress Centroamericana, 1986a; Mesoamerica, 1986a). In addition, the Sandinistas agreed to creation of a Central American Parliament by direct elections, thus weakening (at least temporarily) those trying to label Nicaragua a totalitarian state.[19] Finally, according to the Guatemalan president, all the presidents agreed to repudiate US support of the *contras*.[20]

In the eyes of the Sandinistas, the regional scene changed radically when the last version of the Contadora Act was rejected by Honduras, El Salvador, and Costa Rica, and — more important- ly — when the US Congress supported the Reagan administration policy. Nicaragua denounced Costa Rica and Honduras before the International Court of Justice, and the Nicaraguan president linked Central American inability to resist US pressure to the inability of the US Congress to resist White House policies, charging that congressional support of the *contras* drastically reduced the ability of Costa Rica and Honduras to come to some kind of agreement with Nicaragua (Ortega, 1986a; Newsweek, 1986f).

The purpose of the appeal to the International Court was (1) an attempt to call world attention to the aggression faced by Nicaragua, and (2) to force Honduras and Costa Rica to negotiate agreements which would limit activity on their joint borders — crucial since US military activity was intensifying and the Con- tadora efforts were becoming paralyzed. The Sandinistas sought to utilize the International Court as a means of negotiation at a time when the Honduran and Costa Rican vulnerability to the United States was being considerably increased. Such an inter- pretation seems confirmed by Nicaragua's subsequent proposal to Honduras and Costa Rica that it would withdraw its appeal to the Court if (a) Honduras would agree to demilitarize its borders with Nicaragua and (b) Costa Rica would create a border patrol to forestall any more border incidents (Agencia IPS, 1986b; Informe Latinoamericano, 1986a).

In sum, the situation in Central America seemed to be worsen- ing by the end of 1986: Nicaragua would not negotiate its internal policy; efforts to limit border tensions were not successful; and the *contras* were planning a strong offensive for the beginning of 1987 in order to establish their credibility as a fighting force with the US Congress. While the Central American countries nurtured a mutual interest in preventing all-out war in the region and had made clear their rejection of *contra* activity, this was not enough to reverse the course of the Sandinista revolution in the face of the "carrots and sticks" employed by the Reagan administration to block agreement among the Central American countries.

Despite the pull of common interests and willingness to be flexible which drew Nicaragua and the other Central American countries together, as well as Sandinista diplomatic initiatives toward normalizing bilateral relations within the framework of regional coexistence,[21] stabilization of the isthmus does not look promising in the short run. The Nicaraguan president recognized this situation when he said

> There is no strong desire for war or sympathy for US inter-vention among the governments and leaders of Central America; but what does exist is a strong, ongoing desire that the threats and the pressure cease ... what these govern-ments and officials do not understand is that, if they want peace, if they want a negotiated solution to the conflict, it is inevitable that there will have to be a day of reckoning with a US policy that wants the opposite. Without that day of reckoning, which up till now you have not been willing to face, peace is impossible (Ortega, 1986b).

RELATIONS WITH WESTERN EUROPE

DURING 1986, the principal emphasis of Nicaraguan foreign policy towards the European community was directed toward limiting the distance which some European countries had begun to place between themselves and the Sandinista revolution after the Nicaraguan government imposed new internal restrictions (like the state of emergency) in June after the US allocated new funds for the *contras*. Though this deterioration in its ties with the continent had begun some years ago (Yopo, 1986a: 390), it ac-celerated in 1986 due not only to the adoption of such measures as the above-mentioned, but also to the increase in its military buildup and to its closer relations with socialism, as a function of insuring the immediate survival of the 1979 revolution (the European attitude was also influenced by its perception that Nicaragua behaved with intransigence towards the Contadora process early in the year.)

Already in January, for example, the Ministry of Economic Cooperation of the Federal Republic of Germany (FRG) indicated that it would not grant new assistance to Nicaragua so long as it remained on the path of increasing its military strength and des-tabilizing the region (Excelsior, 1986g). A German foundation with close ties to the Bonn government recommended putting pressure on Nicaragua to institute internal reforms and pointed out that the *contras* could contribute to this objective (Inforpress Centroamericano, 1986d; Informe Latinoamericano, 1986g). The German Social Democrats, through several of its representatives who travelled to Managua, also criticized domestic Nicaraguan politics as managed by the Sandinistas (Inforpress Centro-americano, 1986c).

On the other hand, the foreign ministers of the European Community had delineated, at the multinational level, Europe's attitude toward the regional crisis in general, and the Sandinista revolution in particular, at a meeting with their Central American counterparts which was held in Luxemburg at the end of 1985. Foreign Minister D'Escoto praised the Luxemburg agreement which included Nicaragua in the new EEC agreement with Central America for 1986-1990, and in which the European Community spelled out the points on which it disagreed with US policy, especially regarding the origins of the regional conflict, rejection of the use of force, and the necessity to eliminate all foreign military presence. Nevertheless, the Luxemburg agreement, which Nicaragua signed, also called upon the Sandinista government to lift internal restrictions and to promote national reconciliation (Financial Times, 1985a; Washington Post, 1985).

Given the importance with which the Sandinistas viewed their political and economic ties with Europe,[22] Nicaragua tried to improve its relations with European governments (and other sectors) in 1986 in hopes of maintaining at least the existing level of relations with those countries that had given their "conditional support" to the Nicaraguan revolution. In January, for example, when the Spanish foreign minister, Fernández Ordóñez, met with President Ortega in Managua, he encouraged the Nicaraguan opposition to renew discussions with the Nicaraguan government. At the time, the president of the Nicaraguan National Assembly thanked Luis Cuervo, the Spanish ambassador, for his government's efforts to encourage such a dialogue (País, 1986d; Christian Science Monitor, 1986c).

On the other hand, as the US administration increased its efforts to isolate Nicaragua internationally, relations with Europe acquired new relevance for the Managua regime. While the US

Congress was debating whether or not to continue funding the *contras*, many European countries — Greece, Norway, Denmark, Spain, Austria, Switzerland and Sweden, among others — opposed sending aid to the anti-Sandinista forces. During this same time frame, delegations from both the Socialist International and the EEC visited Nicaragua to assess whether new aid should be granted to the country (Inforpress Centroamericana, 1986c; Mesoamérica, 1986b: 3). The Sandinistas, for their part, gave a high priority to regularizing payments to Europe on the foreign debt in 1986 since, in the wake of the US embargo, that continent represented 46% of the Nicaragua's export market (Informe Latinoamericano, 1986f).

During his visit to Sweden to attend the funeral of Olaf Palme, Spanish President Felipe González took the opportunity to invite President Ortega to a meeting at the Spanish embassy there as a way of expressing support. However, while Spain authorized, on the one hand, the opening of an office in Madrid by the UNO (*Unión Nacional Opositora*), an administrative organization for the Sandinista opposition, on the other hand, and at the same time, González severed all ties with Alfonso Robelo (a *contra* leader) to signal his socialist government's rejection of that group (International Herald Tribune, 1986h; Pais, 1986b). The Madrid government also approved, in May 1986, a new line of credit to Nicaragua of US$26 million designated for the acquisition of capital goods, spare parts, and manufactures from Spain (Informe Latinoamericano, 1986e).

However, new differences emerged in June between Nicaragua and some of the European countries in the wake of internal restrictions imposed by the Sandinista government. The Nicaraguan president, recognizing the adverse effects that these actions would have internationally, sent Vice-President Sergio Ramírez on a special mission to Europe to explain the extent and context of these measures, converting the issue into subject for discussion with European leaders (Ramirez, 1986; Brecha, 1986b).

In July, the Congress of the Socialist International, meeting in Lima, passed a resolution regarding Nicaragua in which it rejected the Reagan policy but also noted that the three main objectives of the Sandinista revolution (pluralism, mixed economy, and non-alignment) "have not yet been fulfilled" (Nueva Sociedad, 1986: 69). Flaminio Piccoli, the president of the Christian Democrat International, had a tense discussion with the Nicaraguan president in Managua in which, though recognizing certain signs of increasing internal dissension, he asked the Sandinista government to lift the restrictions imposed in June as soon as possible (Jornada, 1986a; Excelsior, 1986c).

The governments of both France and Germany also publicly aired their criticisms of Sandinista actions. The German Vice-Chancellor, Jürgen Mölleman, stated that "the region will not have peace as long as Nicaragua rejects all domestic and external openings." The French Secretary of State for External Affairs, Dedier Bariani, declared that "the direction taken by the Nicaraguan regime is perceived negatively all over the world... the Nicaraguan government is seen as an increasingly difficult negotiator." He concluded that, beginning in January 1987, his country would seek a "new balance" in its aid to Central America, revising the privileged position which Nicaragua had held up to then (Informe Latinoamericano, 1986d).

Additionally, the problem of European volunteers — assassinated or taken hostage by the *contras* — also complicated Nicaragua's relations with some European countries. Chancellor Kohl sent a letter to President Ortega in which he warned that relations between the two countries would be affected if German hostages came to any harm due to actions of the Sandinista army. Subsequently, three German volunteers did die in an ambush by the *contras*, and the German Deputy Minister complained that the Nicaraguan government had been warned not to permit foreigners to enter war zones (Miami Herald, 1986e; Washington Post, 1986e). In September, France, Germany, and Switzerland again pressed the Nicaraguan government to relocate their nationals from fighting areas. Even the Swiss government, traditionally the most receptive to Nicaragua's needs, threatened to suspend aid if the restrictions demanded were not adopted, although it did finally agree to complete delivery of the US$20 million in funds slated for 1986 (Washington Post, 1986b).

A review of 1986 suggests that Nicaragua's relations with Western Europe clearly suffered some deterioration, especially with those countries who carried the greatest weight on the continent, such as Germany, France, England, and, to some extent, Italy.[23] Even though this distancing may not necessarily translate into European support of the US policy, and Nicaragua has not been excluded from meetings (or aid) from the EEC to Central America, Nicaraguas's economic needs, especially at the bilateral level, no longer receive the special attention of the initial years of the revolution. Nevertheless, the Scandinavian countries, Spain, Austria, Switzerland and Greece, among others, remain fairly responsive to the problems faced by the Sandinistas and continue to deliver financial aid, increasingly important for the deteriorating Nicaraguan economy.[24]

In sum, in spite of the conditions imposed by the still unregenerate US influence in the region, which the European countries had no intention of replacing or questioning (which in itself set specific limits on their tolerance of Nicaragua), the direction of Europe's policy towards Nicaragua continued to depend on existing European perceptions regarding the evolution of the principal goals of the Nicaraguan revolution: political pluralism, non-alignment and a mixed economy.

As a result, Europe's initial interest in avoiding the isolation, and closing, of Nicaragua's international options was contained within these parameters. For this reason, the principal dilemma of the Sandinista government in 1986 *vis-à-vis* its European counterparts was that it had to tighten the restrictions and controls established by the 1982 State of Emergency decree in order to counter formation of an "internal front" capable of supporting the *contras* (as a basic counterpart to the low-intensity warfare underwritten by the United States),[25] even though this imposed major international costs.

Under the imperatives of war and immediate survival, the situation was dominated by domestic factors and the government's need to reassert its authority over those sectors of the opposition spectrum who were inclined to escalate the confrontation with the Sandinistas, encouraged by the support the *contras* were receiving from the Reagan administration. The relative lack of understanding, or appreciation, of these facts by certain European countries impelled the Sandinistas to take steps to moderate these negative impressions (the sending of Vice-President Sergio Ramírez, a civilian with a moderate image, as special envoy to tour Europe formed part of these efforts), but their effects were limited in those European countries which had been distancing themselves from the Sandinista experience for some time.

Thus the principal challenge for Nicaraguan diplomacy toward Europe in 1987 will be maintain its relations with the continent in an environment ever more adverse and complex.

RELATIONS WITH THE USSR AND SOCIALIST COUNTRIES

WHILE NICARAGUA FACED major international limitations on, and obstacles to, the survival of its revolution in 1986 (Europe being the most striking example), it developed new and important ties with the socialist bloc. For example, the socialist countries had already sent Nicaragua about US$330 million in credit and aid in 1985 (or about 25% of the total). In 1986, it is estimated that Nicaragua's trade with the socialist bloc will have reached 39% of the total (Newsweek, 1986e; Excelsior, 1986a).

This active, principled foreign policy emphasizes a variety of international ties, besides reflecting the needs dictated by immediate circumstances, which has caused Julio López, who is in charge of the international relations of the FSLN (*Frente Sandinista de Liberacion Nacional*) to state, at the last celebration of the anniversary of the Bolshevik Revolution, that "Nicaraguan friendship with the Soviet Union is non-negotiable" (with third parties).[26]

In the first months of 1986, Nicaragua's aid from, and commercial exchange with, the Soviet Union demonstrated its crucial importance to the Nicaraguan economy which was then in a critical state: Moscow sent 10,000 tons of rice (as part of a 25,000-ton agreement) to cover a serious shortage of this Nicaraguan foodstuff. The Sandinista government also signed a 3-way trade agreement with the Soviet Union and Cuba, in which those countries acquired 30% of Nicaragua's sugar exports in 1986, paying approximately three times the going price on the world market (Financial Times, 1986). Bulgaria helped Nicaragua to revive its production of zinc and acquired, in 1986, 18,000 tons for approximately US$10 million, paying 30% more than the market value for this metal (Central America Report, 1986).

Also in 1986, the Soviet Union became the only stable supplier of oil to Nicaragua (even though, in 1985, Mexico supplied the Sandinista government with 10% of its needs, and Libya and Iran had also sent oil to Nicaragua occasionally), according to reports from the *Petroleum Intelligence Weekly* of New York. This would suggest that, in 1986, the Soviet Union will exceed the 300,000 tons of petroleum sent in 1985, and it was estimated that the deliveries were in the form of a donation and/or long-term credits (Miami Herald, 1986b). In October 1986, the Soviet Union signed a new agreement for economic cooperation with Nicaragua of about US$250 million, thus assuring the vital supplies which Nicaragua hopes to obtain from that country in 1987 (Informe Latinoamericano, 1986c).

Nicaragua also obtained important political and military support from the socialist bloc at a time when the United States was intensifying its military pressure. For example, during the latest of a series of meetings between the State Department and the Soviet Minister of Foreign Relations regarding Central America, the Soviet delegate confirmed to his US counterparts that Moscow would maintain its support for the "just cause" of the Nicaraguan people, including military assistance (New York Times, 1986d). At the same time, the German Democratic Republic (GDR) promised Vice-President Sergio Ramírez, during an offical visit in June, that it would increase its support to the Nicaraguan government in its struggle against the "forces of counter-revolution" (Mercurio, 1986h). The Vice-President of Czechoslovakia, while in Nicaragua for the 7th anniversary of the Nicaraguan revolution, expressed the support of his country for the persecuted Sandinista government as well.[27]

Another indication of socialist bloc support for Nicaragua was its increase of military aid in 1986. The Sandinista Air Force received at least 15 new M-17 helicopters for troop transport as well as between 6 and 8 assault helicopters (MI-24 models, which are highly effective in counterinsurgency actions), doubling the number of helicopters in use in 1985. The Sandinistas also received new SA-3 ground-to-air missiles, more sophisticated and modern than the existing SA-7s. According to White House reports, the USSR also supplied an AN-30 plane for air reconnaissance to provide information on the location of guerrilla forces in the fighting areas (Los Angeles Times, 1986d; International Herald Tribune, 1986c; New York Times, 1986c).

Above all, Soviet commitments toward the Nicaraguan revolution remain limited and cautious. The socialist bloc increased assistance and support to the Sandinistas in 1986 to enable Nicaragua to survive, but avoided any special relationship which would involve a large economic investment or risk of US intervention (Yopo, 1986b: 36-43). Within the "policy of solidarity" with Nicaragua, assistance from the socialist bloc was designed to satisfy the most pressing needs of the Sandinista government and to neutralize the strategy of the present US administration towards the Managua regime.

Despite Sandinista efforts to strengthen ties with the socialist world (especially when other sources of international assistance are reducing their support),[28] it is likely that socialist support will remain within present limits in 1987. Among the priorities of Soviet foreign policy, Central America does not rank very high, and the policy of the Gorbachev regime is to limit the current Soviet profile in the Third World, especially towards regional conflicts which do not impact the immediate interests of Soviet leaders (Time, 1985b; McFarlane, 1985: 311; Katz, 1986).

THE THIRD WORLD AND THE NON-ALIGNED

NICARAGUA MAINTAINED close relations with other Third World countries and organizations in 1986, and such ties proved important in the face of Reagan administration efforts to isolate the Nicaraguan government.

Despite the difficulties in which Managua finds itself, Third World political support and economic exchanges helped expand the range of Nicaragua's diplomatic alternatives. For example, Algiers became a major purchaser of Nicaraguan sugar (one of its principal exports) in 1986, while Libya signed a US$15 million agreement with Nicaragua to send oil in exchange for traditional Nicaraguan exports such as coffee, cotton, and plantain (Financial Times, 1986; Latin American Commodities Report, 1986: 5). In recent years, Libya has provided Nicaragua with nearly

US$100 million in credit and aid, used primarily to acquire oil and develop agricultural projects. President Ortega returned the favor by supporting Libya following the US attacks on that country in April (New York Times, 1986e).

The People's Republic of China (PRC) also supported the Nicaraguan government, inviting President Ortega to Peking in September 1986. The Secretary-General of the Chinese Communist Party, Hu Yaobang, told Ortega that China would provide "friendly support to Nicaragua in its battle for sovereignty and independence," while Prime Minister Zhao Ziyang told him that "the Chinese people, who suffered long from foreign aggression and interference, profoundly understand the feelings of the Nicaraguan people" (Financiero, 1986; Mercurio, 1986d and 1986e). The visit resulted in China sending Nicaragua some US$20 million in interest-free aid for the immediate purchase of food, tools, and other consumer goods. However, no military aid was negotiated despite the presence of Joaquín Cuadra Lacayo, Deputy Minister of Defense, in the Ortega delegation, indicating Sandinista interest in this regard (Washington Post, 1986c; Mexico and Central America Report, 1986).

The Indian government also expressed support of Nicaragua when President Ortega visited New Delhi on his tour of Asia. Prime Minister Rajiv Gandhi told US newsmen that President Ortega had been elected "in one of the most honest elections ever held in Latin America." Condemning US assistance to the *contras*, the Indian prime minister said that the NAM (Non-Aligned Movement meeting at that time) was concerned only with the independence of the Third World countries *vis-à-vis* the power blocs, not with the internal politics of its members (International Herald Tribune, 1986i and 1986j). The Indian government granted new credits (of US$20 million) to Nicaragua and, in an address to the UN General Assembly, the Prime Minister endorsed "the right of Nicaragua to follow its national policies without external intimidation" (Sol de Mexico, 1986; Jornada, 1986b).

President Sinan Hasani, of Yugoslavia, roundly denounced "the brutal aggression toward, interference and intervention in, Nicaragua" and expressed Yugoslavia's solidarity with the Nicaraguan people. Yugoslavia sent aid and several million dollars worth of credits to Nicaragua, and President Ortega, on a recent trip there, also asked for Yugoslav support of Nicaragua's bid to be president of the Non-Aligned Movement (Agencia IPS, 1986a; and, on Yugoslavian aid to Nicaragua, Yopo, 1986a: 399).

To reaffirm Nicaraguan identification with the Third World, Sandinista diplomats made an effort to strengthen ties with countries of the south, as illustrated by President Ortega's tour of Africa in September 1986, in which he visited — and presumably strengthened relations with — the Congo, Ghana, and Burkina Fasso. At the FSLN anniversary celebrations in Managua, moreover, could be seen Ghana's Head of State, a representative of India's prime minister, and the president of Burkina Fasso (Uno Más Uno, 1986a; Clarín, 1986).

At the multilateral level and in international meetings, Third World support played an important role in legitimizing Nicaragua's position. During June and July when Congress approved funds for the *contras*, the NAM Bureau of Coordination called for two things: (1) condemning such assistance and (2) appealing to the United States to comply with arbitral decision of the International Court of Justice (Agencia Nueva Nicaragua, 1986c and 1986d). NAM support was a major determinant in passing the UN resolution (94-3 with 47 abstentions) demanding that the US respect the decision of the International Court. In yet another resolution (sponsored by Mexico, Peru, Algiers, the Congo, Democratic Yemen, and Zimbabwe), the UN General Assembly deplored the US trade embargo of Nicaragua (86-1 and 46 abstentions).

Nicaragua's most important Third World diplomatic initiative in 1986 was its bid to become president of the Non-Aligned Movement in 1990, since the position was slated to go to a Latin American country based on the NAM system of rotation. In the Sandinista view, winning the presidency would be a slap in the face to US policy while, at the same time, raising Nicaragua's own international prestige and non-aligned credentials. This aim explains, in large part, the reasons for Ortega's tour of Africa in September, and his attendance at the NAM Summit Meeting in Harare. Nicaragua's Deputy Minister Javier Chamorro also made a serious effort to lobby for Nicaragua by attending the assembly of the Organization of African Unity (OAU) in Addis Ababa in

August where he sought the support of the African countries (País, 1986a; New York Times, 1986l).

Although designating the seat of the next NAM conference (1990) was postponed in Harare due to the inability of the conference to reach a unanimous decision (paradoxically, it was opposition from some of the Latin American countries that blocked the Nicaraguan nomination), Nicaragua will continue to pursue this candidacy in 1987, since maintaining a high international profile constitutes one of the basic supports of the revolution, which the Sandinistas will continue maximizing in order to consolidate the process begun in 1979.

CONCLUSION

ON THE INTERNATIONAL LEVEL, 1986 was a difficult year for the Sandinista revolution, especially regarding its relations with the so-called western world. The situation with the United States became aggravated, especially when the Congress voted to support the Reagan administration policy towards Nicaragua. It also produced greater alienation on the part of some of the European countries, who perceived the internal restrictions imposed by the Sandinista government in 1985 and 1986 as indications of a "radicalizing" of the 1979 revolutionary process. In addition, multilateral organizations continued to block financial assistance to Nicaragua in 1986, despite efforts made by the Nicaraguan government in this regard.

The Contadora mediation process became paralyzed after Nicaragua agreed to sign the Act of June 1986, while tensions with neighboring states rose as a result of *contra* activities and the support they received from countries like Honduras, El Salvador and, to some extent, Costa Rica. Nevertheless, the Managua government obtained some diplomatic successes, such as (1) the International Court of Justice decision which declared aid to the *contras* to be illegal; and (2) support from the NAM, like that declared by the Harare conference in September, and the UN resolutions endorsing the International Court decision and condemning US renewal of its embargo of Nicaragua. Finally, the socialist bloc remained faithful in its support of the Sandinistas, though economic aid was circumscribed in the face of the serious deficiencies of the Nicaraguan economy.

The Nicaraguan government's dilemma in 1987 will be how to assure (within the context of increased US pressure) continued smooth relations with those countries that have supported *sandinismo*, while, at the same time, avoiding any deterioration in relations with those states with whom Nicaragua maintains important commercial ties and who oppose the Reagan administration strategy in Central America. This must be achieved, however, in the face of a probable escalation of regional tensions (a *contra* offensive is planned for the beginning of 1987), which will make the prospects for relaxation of internal restrictions more difficult.

Finally, complete collapse of the *contras* could pave the way for an agreement to coexist with the United States but could also raise the risk of direct intervention by the Reagan administration in order to salvage the "credibility" of its Third World policy. Thus, as the previous *Anuario* indicated, and all actors involved in Nicaragua's main conflict concur, 1987 promises to be a decisive year for the stabilization of the Sandinista government.

NOTES

1. About this so-called "Bay of Pigs syndrome" affecting the conservative leadership of the White House, see CIDE (1985: 38).

2. About the definitions and content of the "Reagan Doctrine," see Rosenfeld (1986: 699); NACLA (1986: 13); and US News and World Report (1986d).

3. The important role that Nicaragua plays in the global hegemonic restoration of the United States has been explained on several occasions by US leaders. Ex-National Security Advisor Robert McFarlane clearly expressed the Reagan Administration's perspectives regarding this point, and said

> it is central to sustaining credibility at any level to be able to define important interests... [Nicaragua] is a case that's being watched very closely in Moscow as a measure of whether the United States can sustain a strategy for dealing with Soviet efforts to dominate key developing countries. ...It is central to the East-West geostrategic balance in the next generation that we win one. ... We must focus on one area we can defend as an important US interest (which ought to be in this hemisphere) and win with whatever it takes to do it, ... making it work in Nicaragua, you will stand a better chance of garner-

ing support in other geostrategic locations. Winning one first
is very important (US News and World Report, 1986c: 28).

4. On sending SAM-7 missiles to the *contras*, see the International
Herald Tribune (1985c: 3) and Mesoamerica (1986d: 10).

5. The growing hostility of important sectors of the Democratic Party
towards the Sandinista Revolution and the *rapprochement* with the
"moderate" faction of the *contra* movement (Robelo, Cruz) became
evident in 1986. See, for example, the opinions of influential Democratic
leaders such as Les Aspin (chairman of the Congressional Armed Services
Committee) and Charles Robb (ex-governor of Virginia and president of
the Democratic Leadership Council). In addition, 51 Democratic congressmen supported President Reagan in the referendum on assistance
to the *contras* in June 1986. Finally, in a recent document of the
Democratic Party which explains the leadership goals in foreign policy
through the year 1988, all criticism of Reagan's policy regarding
Nicaragua is omitted (Time, 1986a; New York Times, 1986a; International
Herald Tribune, 1986a).

6. A high-ranking official of the US government confirmed that the
Reagan administration would continue to assist the *contras* in the
eventuality of a negative vote in Congress, and indicated, for example,
that a clause in the Foreign Assistance Act authorized the use of up to
US$250 million in funds without authorization from the US Congress
(Miami Herald, 1986f; US News and World Report, 1986b).

7. McFarlane's proposal means a request of the Soviet Union virtually
to abandon its Third World policy. According to this plan, a negotiating
process should be developed on three levels: (1) direct negotiations
between the Sandinista government and the *contras*; (2) parallel conversations between the United States and the Soviet Union to promote the
elimination of foreign military presence (that is, Soviet and Cuban); (3)
once an internal agreement is achieved, support for the participation of
these countries in the world economy (in other words, an end to the US
financial-trade blockade against Nicaragua) by renewing economic assistance (Universal, 1986; Time, 1985a).

8. In March 1986, the US Congressional Committee on Intelligence,
using a CIA report as source, pointed out that only the presence of US
troops would solve the "Sandinista problem," and the administration's
objective was to permit the *contras* to take a portion of Nicaraguan
territory, declaring a provisional government that the United States could
back. In August, Elliot Abrams and National Security Advisor John
Poindexter told Senator Jim Sasser that the United States would intervene
to support the military offensive that the *contras* will initiate at the
beginning of 1987 since President Reagan does not intend to leave his
administration without solving the dilemma created by the Sandinistas.
Finally, in November, Abrams told the Uruguayan chancellor of the
existence of this plan, providing details of all phases such as the recognition of a *contra* provisional government and consequent break in

relations with the Sandinistas (see Miami Herald, 1986k and 1986d; International Herald Tribune, 1986b; Washington Post, 1986d; Newsweek, 1986a; Brecha, 1986a).

9. The formation of the Nicaraguan case as a central problem of "credibility" for US hegemony in the world has been explicitly established by President Reagan, Secretary of State George Shultz, and other high administration officials (see, for example, Reagan, 1986; also statements by Secretary of State Shultz and US Ambassador to the United Nations Vernon Walters (Los Angeles Times, 1986a; Excelsior, 1986b).

10. All public opinion polls reveal that the US public was opposed to the direct intervention of its troops in Central America and also rejected assistance to the *contras*. The armed forces and Congress are also skeptical about the results of any intervention in Nicaragua (see, for example, Miami Herald, 1986j; International Herald Tribune, 1985d; US News and World Report, 1985).

11. As a result of the political crisis it is experiencing, the Reagan administration desperately needs to demonstrate that the *contras* are a valid alternative, since a dangerous escalation of the conflict is foreseeable in the first months of 1987 (see Agencia Nueva Nicaragua, 1986a).

12. Since 1983, the Sandinistas have sought a bilateral agreement with the Reagan administration which would guarantee US security requirements. Recently-resigned US Ambassador to Honduras John Ferch is said to have told the Department of State that the Sandinistas were willing to carry out important concessions if the Reagan administration renewed negotiations. However, these reports were never considered, thereby motivating the ambassador's resignation. [For more on this topic, see the chapter on "Nicaragua in Latin America and the Caribbean" in Yopo (1986a), as well as the Washington Post (1986f) and El Mercurio (1986f)].

13. For more details on the important backing Cuba gave to the Sandinistas, see Yopo (1986a: 385) and Excelsior (1986e).

14. See, for example, the statements of Uruguayan Chancellor Enrique Iglesias, Argentine President Raul Alfonsin, Peruvian Chancellor Allan Wagner, and the Secretary of Political Affairs of the Brazilian Chancellory, pointing out discrepancies in the Reagan strategy towards Nicaragua (El País,1986c; Washington Post, 1986j; Agencia IPS, 1986l; and Mercurio, 1986c).

15. In addition to the visits to Latin American countries by the president, vice president, and cabinet ministers from Nicaragua in 1986, other Sandinista leaders such as Tomas Borge, Bayardo Arce and Carlos Nuñez visited countries such as Argentina, Peru, and Brazil that same year (El Día, 1986a; Mercurio, 1986j).

16. The existence of oil in this area that could be exploited during the following decades (as shown in certain studies) could also be influencing Nicaraguan interest in reactivating this dispute (Mercurio, 1986l; Latin America Commodities Report, 1986).

17. The Mexican government has begun to criticize Sandinista actions and has totally suspended the delivery of oil in 1986 (Miami Herald, 1986b).

18. Nicaragua has maintained secret contacts with Honduras, informing Honduras of the offensives of the Sandinista army in Honduran territory to eliminate *contra* bases. This permanent dialogue among military officials of both countries has prevented an open armed conflict and reflects the interest of Honduras and Nicaragua in minimizing border friction, those that generally got initial publicity after the Reagan administration's denunciations rather than from the countries involved (see International Herald Tribune, 1986f; Newsweek, 1986d; Christian Science Monitor, 1986b; Washington Post, 1986l).

19. See statements of the President of the Nicaraguan National Assembly, Comandante Carlos Nuñez (Agencia Nueva Nicaragua, 1986e).

20. According to the description of President Cerezo, the Central American presidents gathered in Esquipulas were unanimous in opposing US policy: 5 to 0 (see Inforpress Centroamericana, 1986a).

21. Since 1982, for example, Nicaragua has carried out multiple proposals to establish agreements to reduce border tensions. On this, see the chapter on Nicaragua in *Las Políticas Exteriores Latino-americanas frente a la Crisis* (Muñoz, 1985).

22. Nicaragua is the Latin American country which has received most assistance from the European Community during the 1979-1985 period (see Journal of Commerce, 1985; EEC, 1985: 9).

23. France and Germany, together with Spain, are Nicaragua's greatest trade partners in Europe. Nevertheless, the new French government, together with Germany and England, are the most bitter critics of *sandinismo* in Europe (on Nicaraguan trade in the EEC, see IRELA, 1986: 49; on high-level criticism by Germany, France, and England of the Nicaraguan government, see Informe Latinoamericano, 1986d; Business Week, 1985; Excelsior, 1985a and 1985b).

24. It is estimated that the European Community will provide Nicaragua with nearly US$100 million in credits during 1986. Nicaragua's Minister of External Cooperation Henry Ruiz visited Sweden around the middle of the year and received a warm reception and confirmation of assistance for US$18 million for 1986. Finland will give Nicaragua economic assistance of 70 million marks in the 1985-1989 period (Excelsior, 1985c; Financial Times, 1985b; Latin American Monitor, 1986; Miami Herald, 1986a).

25. On the importance of the formation of an "internal front" for the destabilization of the Sandinistas (defined by US analysts as the "fourth front"), see Time (1986a).

26. Comandante Bayardo Arce represented the FSLN in the Soviet Party Congress held in 1986; on the statements of Julio López, see Envío (1985).

27. Vice President of the Counsel of Ministers of the Soviet Union, Vladimir Kamentsev, on the other hand, was present at the anniversary of the FSLN in November 1986 (Clarín, 1986; Miami Herald, 1986c).

28. The appointment in 1985 of Henry Ruiz as new Minister of External Cooperation is significant in this regard since Ruiz has been responsible for all negotiations with eastern countries during the 1980-1985 period. In 1985 Minister Ruiz indicated the interest of the Sandinista government in participating in the bimonthly COMECON plan for 1986-1990 (International Herald Tribune, 1985a; Informe Latinoamericano, 1985: 526-527; Excelsior, 1985d).

REFERENCES

Agencia IPS (1986a) cable, 3 September.

———— (1986b) cable, San José, 29 August.

———— (1986c) 6 August.

———— (1986d) 28 July.

———— (1986e) 10 July.

———— (1986f) 30 June.

———— (1986g) cable 3 June.

———— (1986h) 8 May.

———— (1986i) 12 April.

———— (1986j) 17 March.

———— (1986k) 21 June (Managua).

———— (1986l) 22 August.

———— (1986m) 17 April.

———— (1986n) 31 July (cable).

Agencia Nueva Nicaragua (1986a) 9 December.

———— (1986b) 4 November.

———— (1986c) cable 28 July.

———— (1986d) cable 30 June.

———— (1986e) 9 May.

ALASEI (1986a) May AL-MEX-291-86 67.

———— (1986b) AL-RCMEX-499-86 83.

Análisis Político (Guatemala) (1986) 15 May.

Barricada (Managua) (1986) 22 May.

Brecha (Montevideo) (1986a) 7 November:7.

______ (1986b) 17 July.

Business Week (1985) 29 July: 45.

CASTRO, F. (1986) Interview. London (Sunday) Times (22 June).

Central America Report (1986) 16 May: 141.

Centro de Investigación y Docencia Económicas (CIDE) (1986) Carta de Política Exterior Mexicana. No. 1 (enero-marzo): 30.

______ (1985) Estados Unidos Perspectiva Latinoamericana (April). México, DF, México: CIDE.

Christian Science Monitor (1986a) 26 June.

______ (1986b) 13 May.

______ (1986c) 20 February.

Clarín (Buenos Aires) (1986) 9 November: 6.

D'ESCOTO, M. (1986) Interview with Nicaraguan minister. Brecha (Montevideo) (13 June): 32.

(El) Día (Mexico) (1986a) 30 November.

______ (1986b) 13 April.

______ (1986c) 6 April.

______ (1985) 13 December: 15.

Envío (Managua) (1985) No. 54 (December): 10-A.

Estados Unidos-Centroamerica (1986) CINAS 9 (July-August):3-4.

Excelsior (1986a) 30 September: 2.

______ (1986b) 27 September: 1.

______ (1986c) 26 September: 2.

______ (1986d) 15 August.

______ (1986e) 6 February: 14.

______ (1986f) 11 January: a-A.

______ (1986g) 6 January: 2-A.

______ (1985a) 30 May: 1-A.

_______ (1985b) 20 May: 1-A.

_______ (1985c) 18 May: 10-A.

------ (1985d) 15 May: 10-A.

European Economic Community (EEC) (1985) European Community Cooperation for Development. Santiago de Chile: EEC.

Financial Times (1986) 8 January.

_______ (1985a) 13 November.

_______ (1985b) 14 May.

(El) Financiero (Mexico) (1986) 18 September.

Hoy (Santiago) (1986) No. 477 (14 September).

Informe Latinoamericano (1986a) No. 12-86-48 (11 December).

_______ (1986b) 8 November: 526-527.

_______ (1986c) 15 October: 470.

_______ (1986d) 11 September: IL-86-35.

_______ (1986e) 11 April: 168.

_______ (1986f) 2 May.

_______ (1986g) 21 March: 138.

_______ (1986h) 16 May: 223.

_______ (1986i) 24 July: 336.

_______ (1985) 8 November: 526-7.

Inforpress Centroamericana (Guatemala) (1986a) 29 May.

_______ (1986b) 22 May.

_______ (1986c) 3 April.

_______ (1986d) 6 March.

_______ (1986e) 29 May.

Instituto de Relaciones Europeas-Latinoamericans (IRELA) (1986) Cronología de las Relaciones entre Europa Occidental y América Latina: 1985 (Working Paper 2). Madrid, Spain: IRELA.

International Herald Tribune (1986a) 22 September: 6.

_______ (1986b) 12 August.

_______ (1986c) 11 July: 3.

________ (1986d) 27 June: 1.

________ (1986e) 21 May: 1.

________ (1986f) 31 March: 3.

________ (1986g) 3 March: 2.

________ (1986h) 19 March.

________ (1986i) 14 September.

________ (1986j) 13 September.

________ (1985a) 28 October.

________ (1985b) 22 October.

________ (1985c) 14 August: 3.

________ (1985d) 1 July: 3.

(La) Jornada (Mexico) (1986a) 29 September: 15.

________ (1986b) 27 September: 20.

Journal of Commerce (1985) 24 April.

KATZ, M. (1986) "The Soviet Union and the Third World." Current History
    (October): 329-333.

Latin American Commodities Report (1986) No. CR-86-14 (24 July): 5.

Latin American Monitor (1986) August: 321.

Los Angeles Times (1986a) 14 April.

________ (1986b) 8 April.

________ (1986c) 8 March.

________ (1986d) 30 October.

McFARLANE, N. (1985) "The Soviet Conception of Regional Security."
    World Politics (April).

(El) Mercurio (1986a) 22 November: A-8.

________ (1986b) 4 November: A-7.

________ (1986c) 28 October.

________ (1986d) 15 September: A-7.

________ (1986e) 14 September: A-9.

________ (1986f) 26 July: A-7.

________ (1986g) 13 July: A-9.

________ (1986h) 17 June: A-6.

________ (1986i) 12 May: A-9.

________ (1986j) 5 May.

________ (1986k) 26 April.

________ (1986l) 7 April.

________ (1986m) 22 March: A-7.

________ (1986n) 15 January: A-2.

________ (1986o) 6 August.

———— (1985a) 12 December.

________ (1985b) 9 December.

________ (1985c) 6 December.

Mesoamérica (1986a) June: 3-4.

________ (1986b) April: 10 and 3.

________ (1986c) February: 10 and 2.

________ (1986d) January: 10.

Mexico and Central America Regional Report (Mex/CA RR) (1986) 25 September: 8.

Miami Herald (1986a) 25 September

________ (1986b) 22 July.

________ (1986c) 20 July.

________ (1986d) 27 June.

________ (1986e) 9 June.

________ (1986f) 25 May: 3-A, 7-A, 10-A.

________ (1986g) 16 May.

________ (1986h) 12 May.

________ (1986i) 11 May.

________ (1986j) 12 April.

________ (1986k) 13 March.

________ (1986l) 25 February.

________ (1986m) 22 February.

(Le) Monde Diplomatique (español) (1986a) November (No.93): 2.

______ (1986b) June: 27.

MUÑOZ, H. (ed.) (1985) Las Políticas Exteriores Latinoamericanas frente a la Crisis. Buenos Aires, Argentina: Grupo Editor Latinoamericano.

New York Times (1986a) 7 July: A-20.

______ (1986b) 22 June.

______ (1986c) 12 June.

______ (1986d) 22 May.

______ (1986e) 20 April.

______ (1986f) 13 April.

______ (1986g) 6 April.

______ (1986h) 19 March.

______ (1986i) 16 March.

______ (1986j) 22 February.

______ (1986k) 12 February.

______ (1986l) 23 August.

______ (1985) December.

Newsweek (1986a) 3 November: 16.

______ (1986b) 1 July: 56.

______ (1986c) 2 June: 41.

______ (1986d) 5 May: 9.

______ (1986e) 31 March: 13.

______ (1986f) 11 August: 52.

Nicaragua. (1986) Comunicado del Ministerio del Exterior, 20 June. Managua, Nicaragua.

North American Congress on Latin America (NACLA) (1986) NACLA Report on the Americas 20, 4 (July-August): 13.

Nueva Sociedad (Caracas) (1986) "XVII Congreso de la Internacional Socialista: Resolucion sobre America Latina y el Caribe." Vol. 85 (September-October): 67-70.

ORTEGA, D. (1986a) Interview. Time (11 August): 9.

______ (1986b) Interview. Brecha (Montevideo) (17 July).

______ (1986c) Interview. US News and World Report (2 June): 27.

______ (1986d) Interview. Time (31 March): 9.

(El) País (Madrid) (1986a) 4 August: 2.

______ (1986b) 26 May.

______ (1986c) 3 March.

______ (1986d) 20 January.

Pensamiento Propio (Managua) (1986) No. 35 (August).

(El) Periodista (Buenos Aires) (1986) 21 August: 7.

RAMIREZ, S. (1986) Interview with Nicaragua's vice-president. Washington Post (17 June).

(La) Razón (Buenos Aires) (1986) 12 November.

ROSENFELD, S. (1986) "The Guns of July." Foreign Affairs 64, 4 (Spring): 698-714.

(El) Sol de México (1986) 21 September: 7.

(Der) Spiegel (Hamburg) (1986) No. 4 (April).

Time (1986a) 21 April: 29-30.

______ (1986b) 24 March: 16.

______ (1986c) 10 March: 35.

______ (1985a) 4 November: 13.

______ (1985b) 9 September: 5.

(El) Universal (Mexico) (1986) 23 September: 1.

Uno Más Uno (Mexico) (1986a) 21 September: 18.

______ (1986b) 26 July: 17.

US News and World Report (1986a) 16 December: 43.

______ (1986b) 2 June: 27.

______ (1986c) 7 April: 28.

______ (1986d) 27 January.

______ (1985) 3 June: 28.

Wall Street Journal (1986) 18 April: A-9.

Washington Post (1986a) 13 November.

______ (1986b) 21 September.

______ (1986c) 15 September.

______ (1986d) 14 August.

______ (1986e) 30 July.

______ (1986f) 25 July.

______ (1986g) 22 June.

______ (1986h) 13 May.

______ (1986i) 13 April.

______ (1986j) 10 April.

______ (1986k) 28 March.

______ (1986l) 27 March.

______ (1986m) 22 March.

______ (1986n) 16 March.

______ (1986o) 11-16 February.

______ (1986p) 16 January.

______ (1985) 13 November.

Washington Report on Latin America and the Caribbean (1986) Vol. I, No. 12: 1-5.

Washington Times (1986) 28 January.

YOPO H, B. (1986a) "Nicaragua 1985: la Política Exterior como Estrategia de Sobrevivencia," pp. 365-378 in Heraldo Muñoz (ed.) América Latina y El Caribe: Políticas Exteriores para Sobrevivir. Buenos Aires, Argentina: Grupo Editor Latinoamericano.

______ (1986b) La Unión Soviética y la Crisis Centroamericana (Working Paper 6, July). Santiago de Chile: PROSPEL.

PANAMA: GROWING TENSIONS WITH THE UNITED STATES

by RICARDO URRUTIA

As HAPPENS WITH ALL COUNTRIES that make up the Central American isthmus, Panama's foreign policy is strongly affected by its relationship with the United States. As a result, Panamanian foreign policy is exquisitely sensitive to every fluctuation in the US attitude toward Panama and/or its policy involving the Canal country.[1]

In 1986 Panama was very active in the foreign policy area, reflecting its concern — particularly by its leaders — with those US actions which carried the potential for destabilization and, by implication, for the future return of the Canal to Panamanian jurisdiction. This perception strongly colored all of Panama's international relations and influenced changes in its foreign policy agenda and attitudes.

The issue of the Canal returned to become a number one foreign policy priority after some years of being downplayed in deference to other more pressing interests. At the same time, Panama strongly supported a negotiated solution to the Central American conflict. It also demonstrated its desire to subject the hottest issues in its relations with the United States — particularly joint government discussions on implementation of the Torrijos-Carter Treaty — to forums of international opinion, thus broadening the country's international view after a period of relative withdrawal during the 1980s compared to the preceding decade.

Ricardo Urrutia is a scholar and researcher with the *Programa de Seguimiento de las Políticas Exteriores Latinoamericanas* (PROSPEL) in Santiago de Chile.

PANAMA-UNITED STATES: THE DETERIORATION OF RELATIONS

As THE DATE APPROACHES when the US will finally relinquish control of the Canal area to Panama (31 December 1999), US-Panamanian relations have begun to show signs of deterioration. This development alters the bilateral relationship, which is, theoretically, the most appropriate level at which to work out compliance with the Canal treaties and to create the best climate for agreement on key issues between them with a minimum of political friction.

During 1985-1986, the greatest source of bilateral tension originated from public comments in the United States critical of various aspects of domestic Panamanian society, such as the human rights situation, the narcotraffic, and the country's political stability. The US Congress and media fed each other information on the so-called "Panamanian Case." Although the Reagan administration displayed a certain ambivalence toward charges made in the Senate and carried by the press, it was clear that the administration was not disposed to downplay either the allegations regarding Panama's domestic situation nor their implications for US national security.

In November 1985, Norman Bailey, former Special Assistant for National Security Affairs to President Reagan, took a grave view of recent political developments in Panama, indicating that the United States, together with other democracies in the hemisphere, needed to be concerned about events in Panama which, in his opinion, threatened Panama's democratic process (Los Angeles Times, 1985). By that time, the US had made abundantly clear its disgust at the abrupt termination (in September 1985) of the mandate of President Nicolas Ardito Barletta, which Washington attributed to intervention by the Panamanian military. To express its displeasure, the White House canceled the flow of US financial assistance from both the US Agency for International Development (AID), as well as from the Inter-American Development Bank (IDB). Elliot Abrams, Assistant Secretary of State for Interamerican Affairs, expressed the official US position of "strong opposition to the forced resignation" of President Barletta (Excelsior 1985).

Towards the end of 1985, US media publicized a story that the Panamanian Army had forced Barletta to resign in an effort to defuse the scandal arising from charges that it (the Army) was involved in the assassination of Panamanian physician-guerrilla Hugo Spadafora, a staunch critic of General Manuel Antonio Noriega, Commander-in-Chief of the Armed Forces (New York Times, 1985). During the months that followed, this allegation gained momentum within the United States. The gravity of the charge, the personality of the victim, and the ghastly circumstances of the crime combined to make the Panamanian government anxious to clear up the tragedy, as well as to make it of constant concern in US/Panamanian relations in 1986.

It is certainly true that Washington viewed the Barletta administration with favor. A graduate in economics from the University of Chicago and former vice-president for Latin America of the World Bank, Barletta focussed his attention on the country's domestic economy, implementing a policy designed to stabilize public finances through a series of measures which meshed well with the "structural adjustment" policy advocated by the White House. During his tenure, Panama's foreign policy shifted away from the issues of the Canal and Central America (issues which Washington found sensitive and disturbing) and toward international financial negotiations.

Under the new Panamanian government headed by Erick Arturo Del Valle, who had been Vice-President of the republic up till Barletta's departure, US/Panamanian relations became marked by controversy. The first discordant note was supplied early in February 1986 when Arthur Davis, the newly-appointed US ambassador to Panama (replacing Everett Briggs), made statements which the Del Valle government viewed as constituting a clear intervention in its internal affairs.

Even before his appointment had been accepted by the Panamanian government, Ambassador Davis — adviser to the State Department for Latin American Affairs and former US ambassador to Paraguay (Miami Herald, 1986b) — had expressed concern regarding Panama's freedom of the press and the Spadafora killing to the Senate Subcommittee for Western Hemisphere Affairs. This statement sparked sufficient resentment within Panama that its government dispatched Foreign Minister

Jorge Abadía Arias to the United States to ask for clarification of Davis' opinions (La Prensa, 1986r). US reassurances were such that the Panamanian administration was subsequently able to state that it was "clearly established that neither the government of the United States nor Mr. Davis had any intention of intervening in the internal affairs of Panama" (Alasei, 1986d). Though weak, the explanation mollified Panamanian officials, who then downplayed the incident (Miami Herald, 1986a).

However, as the months went by it became apparent that resolution of the diplomatic impasse provoked by Davis' remarks had been merely a *pro forma* gesture on the part of the US State Department in order to secure Panama's approval of its representative. In any event, Davis' statements provided Panamanian officials with a good index of US attitudes and future policy towards Panama.

A second discordant note was introduced on 21 March 1986 when the Panamanian government denied a Reagan administration request to accept Ferdinand Marcos, deposed dictator of the Philippines, as a permanent resident.[2] Influenced more by the wealth of the erring former president than by any strict humanitarian motives, the Panamanian government had initially been disposed to grant the asylum (La Tercera, 1986b). Its refusal was motivated by the desire to safeguard its relations with the Philippine state, which threatened to break off diplomatic relations if Panama granted the asylum (El Mercurio, 1986e). At this point, the US government dropped its request.

Only a month later (21 April), Senator Jesse Helms opened a hearing before the Subcommittee for Hemispheric Affairs to investigate the situation in Panama, at which high-level officials of the Reagan administration testified on various aspects of Panama's domestic policies. In general, Elliot Abrams' statements created the greatest turmoil, constituting a message directed both to the Panamanian government as well as to its military. In particular, Abrams questioned the nature of the Panamanian regime, saying: "We are not willing to consider Panama as a democracy." He also expressed concern over "persistent rumors" of official corruption and criticized the overwhelming influence of the military over the civilian government. He went on to criticize the fact that the armed forces did not depend exclusively on public funds as the main source of its operational costs, stating that "it is not clear if these activities (commercial) are consistent with Panamanian law." Abrams deplored the fact that "the investigation of the Spadafora case was closed without solving the crime." In conclusion, he stressed that the US interest could be served only through the development of a viable, democratic, civilian government functioning within a constitutional framework (La Prensa, 1986q).

During the same hearing, an official of the US Drug Enforcement Administration (DEA) testified that Panamanian authorities had failed to cooperate with the DEA in tracing money-laundering operations between the drug traffickers and the Central Bank of Panama (IPS, 1986k). Throughout all of 1986, the Del Valle administration resisted continuing pressure from the United States to change Panamanian banking legislation to enable US officials to obtain information about the deposits of suspected drug traffickers. In the US view, the drug issue was directly linked to Panamanian laws then in force, particularly the one allowing secret bank accounts.

Within Panama, political opposition groups capitalized on the US information and gave it ample coverage in the opposition press. On the other hand, Panamanian authorities across the whole official spectrum reacted with indignation, immediately denouncing this as a campaign against the nation. In the words of President Del Valle, speaking from the seat of government, this was a campaign promoted by "a minority of bad Panamanians" who, "in unacknowledged complicity," were attempting to create a climate of confusion "with the most lamentable consequences for our country" (La República, 1986). General Noriega seized the opportunity to deliver into the hands of the president some documents collected by Panamanian intelligence which purported to be a plan to destabilize the country, explaining that the purpose of the plan was to prevent the Panama Canal from "fulfilling the mission of all Panamanians" (El Matutino, 1986j).

On 7 May, the Panamanian foreign minister expressed the displeasure of his government to Ambassador Davis at the "suspicious insistence" with which Senator Helms manipulated the hearings on Panama's domestic situation before the Senate Subcommittee. The official statement protested that the hearings constituted an "unacceptable intrusion" into affairs which were exclusively Panamanian (El Matutino, 1986i). On 10 May, after attending the inauguration of the new Costa Rican president, Oscar Arias, Abrams himself travelled to Panama for an interview with President Del Valle, ostensibly to soothe his ruffled feelings. Despite his Senate testimony, Abrams used the occasion to declare publicly that relations between Panama and the United States were "very good" and that one did not need "to better them, but to strengthen them." He also declared that the Reagan administration had "great respect for the Panamanian government and its leaders, both civilian and military " (IPS, 1986j). Although describing relations with the United States as "good," Del Valle, for his part, continued to deplore the attitude of Senator Helms, sponsor of the hearings on Panama but declared that "the improper conduct" of the senator would not be allowed to alter relations between the two countries (La Hora de Guatemala, 1986c).

At the same time, Panama instructed its ambassador to the United States, Dominador Kaiser Bazán, to explain to the US public (1) that Panama had a civilian government, (2) that the military did not influence the government though "contacts" between them did exist, and (3) that a *coup* had not taken place in September (1985) but, rather, a constitutional succession brought about by the resignation of the president. Kaiser Bazán further maintained that Panama "enjoys broad freedom of the press, has no guerrillas, and terrorism does not exist" (La Prensa, 1986p). Through such official statements, the Panamanian government attempted to counteract the negative image portrayed in the US media. Meanwhile, the Helms subcommittee continued to hold closed sessions in which it heard testimony on Panama from US officials, including representatives from the Central Intelligence Agency (CIA), Pentagon intelligence, Customs, and the DEA.

On 12 June, the *New York Times* returned Panama to the front-page in an exposé of General Noriega. Quoting sources within the US government, the *Times* linked Noriega to the traffic in both drugs and arms, to money-laundering, and to the assassination of Spadafora. It also alleged that Noriega had served as a kind of double agent: acting as informant to Cuba regarding US activities in Panama on the one hand, and, at the same time, reporting to the CIA on events in both Cuba and Nicaragua (New York Times, 1986c). During the weeks that followed, major news media in the US gave prominent coverage to the charges against the Panamanian general.

The US government immediately expressed its concern. Referring to the *Times* article, Secretary of State George Shultz commented, "I have seen the reports, and allegations of this kind are obviously of importance and concern to us" (Prensa Libre, 1986d).

The Panamanian government also responded immediately and with unusual vigor, expressing support for Noriega as Commander-in-Chief of the Armed Forces and warning that it would not tolerate slander of the country's name, government, armed forces and General Noriega, through innuendo and calumny (La Hora de Guatemala, 1986b). The Minister of Foreign Relations called upon Ambassador Davis to provide a full, detailed explanation of the charges (Prensa Libre, 1986c). Four days later (16 June), the US government sent a note of explanation to the Minister, who announced to the press that the response was "positive" (Prensa Libre, 1986b). In reality, a good part of the note only reiterated US concern over the drug issue, making clear that the Reagan government "was interested" in the articles on Panama which had appeared in the press but did not wish "to speculate" on them. [3] The US statement seemed to satisfy the Panamanian authorities — curious, considering that it was US officials who had initiated the incriminating charges and provided the evidence cited in the reports — who later maintained that only "some (US) sectors" wanted to destabilize the country.

In reality, the US government found itself in a delicate situation in which it was necessary to tread lightly, adopting as conciliatory an approach as possible if it wished to keep relations with Panama from deteriorating into a (probably) risky extreme. From then on, the White House attempted to contain public criticism of the Panamanian regime as much as possible. In fact, James Michel, US Assistant Undersecretary for Inter-American Affairs, stated before the House Select Committee on Drugs that "we do not believe that our interests are well served by adding to public speculation in this area" (La Prensa, 1986o), and US officials began to sidestep the subject of the Senate hearings on Noriega. [4] As further evidence, John Gusack, Chairman of the Select Committee on Drugs, put forth that intelligence reports "neither confirm nor deny" the charges against the general (La Prensa, 1986o).

Nevertheless, Senator Helms continued his crusade against Noriega, whom he characterized as "the Number One trafficker in the Western hemisphere" and "a business associate of the president of Cuba, Fidel Castro" (La Prensa, 1986n). At the end of June, Castro himself entered the ring to defend Noriega by declaring that the accusations constituted "a dirty war against Panama," designed to destabilize the country in order to avoid compliance with the Panama Canal treaties. And he denied absolutely the charge that the Panamanian military man had served as a double agent for both the United States and Cuba (Alasei, 1986b).

Panamanian diplomats promptly seized the initiative by seeking out opportunities to garner significant international support before its bilateral relationship with the US deteriorated further. Panama took the position that accusations against the Panamanian leadership were a form of reprisal for independence exhibited in its foreign policy,[5] while, at the same time, they pursued a course of denigrating the peace efforts of the Contadora Group and, especially, complying with the Panama Canal accords.[6] At the same time, it was clear that the US power structure had decided to set distinct parameters to the relationship, with a view to distancing the Reagan administration from the center of the destabilizing impetus. By the same token, Noriega himself, in an interview granted to the Spanish publication *El País*, stated that

> one cannot speak about the United States in general. US society has political groups with conservative attitudes, and it is to them that we refer (El Pais, 1986).

In the month following (18 July), Leonardo Kam, Panama's Ambassador to the United Nations, met with Natarajan Krishnan, President of the Non-Aligned Movement (NAM) and the Coordination Bureau and informed him of the campaign of "international isolation and political instability," whose objective, he explained, was to facilitate US non-compliance with the 1977 Panama Canal Treaty (El Mercurio, 1986c). On 30 July, President Del Valle himself repeated the same idea in a letter to the Secretary-General of the UN, and, at the same time, "strongly" rejected the "calumny" against his country and against the Commander-in-Chief of its Armed Forces, emphasizing that "none of the attacks have been proved with evidence of any kind, nor have there been any specific charges complete with facts or circumstances" (El Mercurio, 1986b).

Early in August, Helms made a speech before the Senate in which he characterized the Panamanian diplomatic offensive as a "a campaign of propaganda and falsehoods" intended to "convince people that I seek to destabilize Panama and take over control of the Canal." He further declared that his concern with respect to the Canal was the possibility that, in 1999, "it would revert to a bunch of corrupt drug traffickers," in which case "a grave threat to the security of the United States would exist." He assured his audience that his continued interest in Panama was inspired by concern for the "political and economic stability" of that country (La Prensa, 1986i).

Meanwhile, the government of Panama continued to use international fora to denounce US factions who wanted to destabilize the country. One such was the Organization of American States (OAS), whose Permanent Council met at the end of August to discuss institutional aspects of the war on drugs (Prensa Libre, 1986a). During the early days of September, the Del Valle government lobbied at the 8th Summit Meeting of the Non-Aligned Movement (NAM) — held in Harare, Zimbabwe — and obtained the whole-hearted support of that Third World organization when that body approved a resolution recognizing the validity of the Panamanian allegations.[7] This demonstration of solidarity was further reinforced by the election of Ambassador Kam as vice-president of the Political Commission of the Summit Meeting (La Estrella de Panama, 1986b).

On his side, Del Valle appeared before the 41st General Assembly of the United Nations the same month to charge that "reactionary forces" were conspiring to weave a tissue of "infamous lies" against the image of the Contadora governments, in a backlash to the objective which had presumably inspired the accusations against the Panamanian general (La Prensa, 1986e). The Committee for Latin America and the Caribbean of the Socialist International (SI), meeting in Panama at the end of September, also recognized Panamanian claims and expressed its solidarity with that government against the United States. Moreover, the *Partido Revolucionario Democrático* (PRD), leader of the government coalition, received the support of that organization in its efforts to develop and maintain a foreign policy of neutrality, non-alignment, and cordial relation with all the nations of the world (El Matutino, 1986c).

In spite of the enormous efforts which both governments certainly put forth in order to extend, at least in appearance, their diplomatic relations, a new episode took place in Washington which came to cloud Panamanian-US relations even more. In short, on 24 September, the US Senate approved (by 53 to 46) a Helms-sponsored resolution that the CIA investigate whether or not the Armed Forces of Panama were trafficking in drugs and arms, and whether or not they were linked to violations of human rights (New York Times, 1986a).[8]

Minister Abadía immediately protested to the US government that this Congressional resolution constituted "unacceptable intervention" in the internal affairs of Panama. The Panamanian government issued an official statement that it was "incomprehensible and cause for concern" that a US Senator had such "unusual power" to influence "dangerously the friendly, productive, and mutually beneficial relations which had taken so much effort to consolidate" (El Matutino, 1986a). The Senate action aroused profound uneasiness among Panamanian authorities. So much so that the entire cabinet fully supported the protest sent to the US government (El Matutino, 1986b).

But if the US Ambassador to the United Nations, Vernon Walters, rose to the occasion by telling a Panamanian official that the Senate action did not represent official US foreign policy (La Prensa, 1986d), it was clear that Reagan Administration feelings toward Panama were not substantially incompatible with the position of the Congress. The Panamanian government responded by enumerating the most important items on the bilateral agenda and by increasing its efforts at vindication. While it repudiated the act as one of US interventionism, it took care not to implicate the Reagan administration officially and to reassure those outside the country of its adherence to a policy of non-alignment.

THE CANAL

THE PANAMA CANAL has always dominated the life of the country and, without any doubt, constitutes the one subject which most symbolizes its foreign policy. Panamanian elites have always held the conviction that it is the country's most important resource and the one on which the viability of its future independence, in great measure, rests.

However, if it has been some years since the Canal has been an issue in Panama's relations with the United States, it should come as no surprise that the root of the present tension between the two countries is the Canal, which has returned to center stage in the country's situation and its foreign policy.

Two factors have combined to mobilize Panamanian international diplomacy around the Canal issue. The first flows from the dynamics of the criticism which has characterized its relations with the United States, originating from the afore-mentioned Senate hearings and denunciations of Noriega in the press. The second flows from the dissension — frustrating to Panama — which arose at bilateral negotiations on the Canal during meetings with the Board of Directors of the Panama Canal Commission (PCC), and which persisted throughout the year whenever Panama set forth its priority interests in any definitive way.

Uncertainty over the Canal situation began to be openly expressed in January (1986) at ceremonies commemorating the "9th of January 1964," the date on which 22 Panamanians and 4 Americans lost their lives in one of the worst incidents in recent bilateral history. During the ceremonies, various government spokesmen denounced the "continuous and multiple violations of the Torrijos-Carter Treaties" (Rumbo Centroamericano, 1986).

In May, following the April Board of Directors meeting of the CPC, at which Panama apparently failed to obtain any major concessions, President Del Valle renewed his request that the US speed up implementation of the treaties. He also raised issues of interest to Panama, such as: (1) an increase in the number of Panamanians in executive positions; (2) the "exclusive" responsibility of the US Government to improve Canal infrastructure; and (3) cessation of "waste and mismanagement" by the Canal Commission. [9]

In July, the US majority on the Commission rejected the request of Panama's Ministry of Finance to conduct an audit of Canal finances on the grounds that the PCC belonged to the US government and permitting such a procedure would violate US sovereignty (El Matutino, 1986g). This decision was announced at one of the most hostile meetings in the history of the Commission's Board of Directors.[10] At the same meeting, US officials also rejected Panama's contention that the PCC owed the country $54 million dollars in surplus revenues from Canal operations (La Prensa, 1986m). The Panamanians then accused the Commission of employing dubious accounting practices in order to withhold these millions from the country (El Mercurio, 1986d). In reality, the Canal Commission has found itself under continuing Panamanian criticism because it is controlled by the US government. Panama maintains that this organization ought "to operate as a bi-national corporation and not as a federal agency of the United States" (Alasei, 1986c).

After evaluating these negotiations, the Del Valle government decided to internationalize the Canal issue again (El Matutino, 1986f). The apparent heart of this effort was a denunciation of (US) Public Law 96-70,[11] to which was added the task of persuading the countries of Europe and the NAM to guarantee the neutrality of the Panama Canal (Informe Latinoamericano, 1986a).

The government's strategy was based on the premise that the country was, in large part, the target of a determined effort to destabilize it, spearheaded by US conservatives bent upon nullifying Panama's efforts to assert its sovereignty. The Panamanian strategy was directed primarily toward the Third World, which had a special bias towards supporting causes — like that of Panama *vis-à-vis* the Canal — which bore clear hallmarks of anticolonial struggle. In fact, the Non-Aligned Movement was reassessed as a way for the country to reinforce its international position at a time when tension with the United States was increasing. The nature of Panama's participation at the Zimbabwe summit meeting (in September) left no doubt as to the direction of the country's foreign policy in that regard. It is a matter of record that, on that occasion, Panama was represented by a high-level mission headed by Vice-President Roderick Esquivel, accompanied by Vice-Minister José Cabrera, Ambassador to the United Nations

Leonardo Kam, PRD Secretary-General Carlos Azores, and Mayor Luis Carlos Samudio (Boletín del Gobierno de Panama, 1986a). The Panamanian government succeeded in obtaining the full support of that Third World organization (a) in the form of a policy resolution backing the Panamanian demands, and (b) in the fact that the summit conference unanimously elected Panamanian Ambassador Kam as Vice-President of its Political Commission (La Estrella de Panama, 1986b).

Besides PL 96-70, another major subject addressed in the 1986 US-Panama discussions on the Canal was that of increasing Panamanian participation in administration of the Canal, a subject expressly contemplated by the 1977 agreements. Panamanian authorities maintained that the only increase in employment of their nationals had been in low-level positions and that they continued to be under-represented at the executive level. The Panamanian response to this situation was expressed by the Minister of Economic Planning and Policy, Ricaurte Vásquez, in August when he said that this situation demonstrated that US efforts toward the transfer of the interocean waterway were "limited and unsatisfactory" (Alasei, 1986a).

Maintenance and improvement of Canal facilities was another item of intergovernmental debate that proved especially controversial. Panama's position has always been that, according to the treaties, the United States is obligated to hand over, in the year 2000, a navigable waterway in perfect operating condition. At the beginning of October, Foreign Minister Abadía declared to the Legislative Assembly that the interocean Canal was "undeniably inefficient," and he warned that if the United States did not deliver it in good condition it would be guilty of a "universal fraud" (La Prensa, 1986b).

Panama's main concern in this matter was the need to widen approximately 15 kilometers in a section of the Canal called the Culebra Cut. Widening of the Cut would increase the flow of traffic significantly. Panama argued that the financing of this operation — variously estimated at US$320-380 million (Boletín del Gobierno de Panama, 1986b) — should be borne by the US government *in toto*, and that the work should be completed before the year 2000 (La Prensa, 1986f). However, though technical studies on the widening may have been completed, up to that moment the financing had not been secured (La Prensa, 1986h). Nevertheless, Panama's position was firm. At October's end, Chancellor Abadía repeated his position that this was the exclusive responsibility of the United States (La Prensa, 1986a). From the Panamanian point of view, carrying out this project constitutes the only way possible to assure continued functioning of the Canal under satisfactory conditions.

In sum, Panama has turned its attention to the Canal once again and has determined to solicit international support to advance implementation of the Canal treaties (until recently, the preference had been to handle this bilaterally). At the same time, Panama has presented its demands to its United States counterparts in a more critical way than has been heard in recent years (Castillo, 1985; Urrutia, 1986).

THE CENTRAL AMERICAN CRISIS

THE CENTRAL AMERICAN CRISIS is an important point of reference in Panama's foreign policy, as the result of objective concerns. On the one hand, geographic proximity to the conflict carries a potential threat to the country's stability; on the other, there is concern that prolonged instability in the region would maintain (or intensify) the important presence the United States has acquired in the region, thus making implementation of the Torrijos-Carter Treaties even more difficult. In the face of such threats, Panama found it imperative to try to defuse the tension in the troubled region, with the result that, over the last 4 years, the country has tried to serve as a mediator in the peace effort, together with Mexico, Venezuela, and Colombia, in the Contadora Group.

During the period under discussion, Panama's position as a country negotiator and arbitrator with Contadora has been much in evidence. This is due to the particularly critical circumstances in which the Latin American peace initiative developed. A situation which — as we know — was generated by the great US hostility towards Nicaragua, reflected by its decision to give material assistance to the so-called *contras*, who seek to destabilize the Managua government.

On different occasions during the year, Panama manifested its objection, in principle, to all outside supply of "any group of irregular forces whatever in the area" (IPS, 1986n; IPS, 1986d) and insisted that the "lack of confidence" between the United States and Nicaragua impeded resolution of the conflict. At the same time, Panama reiterated its call to both countries to resume the discussions suspended in January 1985 (IPS, 1986m). The Panamanian government at all times expressed its confidence in dialogue and political negotiation as the only way to achieve peace in the region. It also defended its position that any discussion of the Central American conflict must involve Contadora. In August, Vice-President Roderick Esquivel rejected the possible transfer of peace negotiations to the Organization of the American States on the grounds the "influential" presence of the United States in that forum made that option "impractical" (IPS, 1986c).

On the other hand, the aggressive US attitude towards Nicaragua, together with the highly negative atmosphere in which the regional peace process was being debated, plus Panama's interest in safeguarding its own connection to the peace discussions led the Del Valle government to declare — at various times — its desire to deny the US government the advantage of using the military infrastructure of the Canal Zone for its undertakings in Central America. In fact, in August, when rumors surfaced in Washington that the United States was planning to initiate a training program for the anti-Sandinista forces in October (New York Times, 1986b), Vice-Minister of Foreign Relations José Cabrera declared that Panama would oppose such an action and would permit the use of US military installations only for the purposes of defense and protection of the canal zone as stipulated in the Canal treaties (IPS, 1986b). This position was later repeated by Panama's Head of State himself (IPS, 1986a) and confirmed again, at the end of August, by Minister Abadía, in response to a spokesman of the US Southern Command (SOUTHCOM) who argued that the sense of the 1977 treaties permitted the United States "to train Latin American military personnel" at bases in the Canal Zone (La Prensa, 1986g). Nevertheless, at the end of September the Southern Command saw the need to announce that it had nothing to do with the *contras* and that they were not being trained (La Prensa, 1986c).

An interesting aspect of Panamanian relations in the Central American crisis has been the significant diplomatic insertion maintained by the Panamanian military hierarchy in this conflict. The participation of the Armed Forces has been justified on the grounds, on the one hand, that the Contadora peace effort requires consideration of the military situation in the region, and, on the other, that it is facilitated by the strong personal ties which General Noriega maintains with the principal Central American political and military figures. In fact, in 1985 the Panamanian military chief played an active role in negotiating various difficulties which arose in the region: in April, he served as mediator between Honduras and Nicaragua; in August, he helped to mediate between Costa Rica and Nicaragua; in October, he took part in the negotiations to free the daughter of President José Napoleón Duarte (of El Salvador) from the Salvadoran guerrillas who had kidnapped her in September and held her hostage (Urrutia, 1986: 413-416). In 1986, General Noriega reiterated the position of the military that the Contadora peace efforts required the assistance of the military and stressed the importance of his diplomatic role.[12] In the latter capacity, for example, Noriega was a catalyst in bringing about the September meeting, in Panama, between representatives of the government of El Salvador and members of the *Frente Farabundo Martí de Liberación Nacional/Frente Democrático Revolucionario* (FMLN-FDR).[13]

To sum up, it has been Panama's policy to emphasize the principle of non-intervention in the Central American crisis and to express this concern by rejecting any possibility that the United States would use the Canal's defense infrastructure to intervene in the region.

THE FOREIGN DEBT

DURING THE LAST FEW YEARS, Panama, as a debtor country, has had to confront the stringent conditions imposed by international lending organizations, a circumstance which has had significant domestic political repercussions. It is a matter of record that the resignation of President Ardito Barletta was related to differences over matters of foreign economic policy (Urrutia, 1986: 409-410). In the period under analysis, the debt problem exhibited two contradictory aspects. On the one hand, it affected all the Latin American countries, as was reflected in the increasingly critical discussions of the subject and in the interest in convening a summit meeting of Latin American presidents in Panama to analyze the worldwide problem. On the other hand, the Del Valle government continued its strict adherence to the conditions imposed by the international lending institutions. The only way in which the new government differentiated itself from its predecessor was in adopting a more political approach, such as instituting price-fixing measures and decreasing the prices of some popular consumer goods in an effort to counteract the more restrictive consequences of economic stabilization.[14]

At the beginning of 1986, the head of the Panamanian Defense Force (PDF) strongly condemned the "economic terrorism" directed against the developing countries and declared that 1986 should be a year "of economic revolution, the year in which to expose and confront the white-collar terrorist." The military leader seized the moment to praise the decision of Peruvian President Alán García to challenge foreign interests who were "strangling" the economy of that Andean country (Alasei, 1986e). In April, Panama officially renewed its offer to host a Latin American presidential summit meeting to analyze the debt problem (IPS, 1986l). In May, the Ministry took an important step in that direction. An official mission, headed by Minister of Foreign Relations Jorge Abadía, travelled to Lima to extend to President García a personal invitation from President Del Valle to visit Panama (Boletín del Gobierno de Panama, 1986c). The idea was that the two presidents would meet in advance to draw up plans for a meeting on the debt to take place sometime during 1986 (IPS, 1986h). Panama's Minister of Justice Rodolfo Chiari, who also took part in the mission, declared that only if the region presented a united front could they bring about "fairer treatment regarding the interest paid on the foreign debt or longer terms for repayment" (IPS, 1986g).

Towards the end of the same month (May), Alán García announced his decision to postpone his trip to Panama due to domestic problems (IPS, 1986f). The presidential summit initiative did not fare well in 1986. The US Senate hearings on Panama, the denunciations of Noriega in the US press, as well as the sharpening of the Central American politico-military conflict, combined to create a climate of instability in Panama and in the subregion, which augured poorly for an event of such magnitude to take place. Nevertheless, the Panamanian government did not modify its stand on the subject, subsequently incorporating it into its discussion of the "anti-Panama campaign" in international fora (La Estrella de Panama, 1986a).

The government's continued strict observance of foreign financial requirements became apparent early on. In September 1985, a few days after being confirmed in his position as Minister of Economic Planning and Policy, Ricaurte Vásquez informed the creditor banks that Panama would continue to follow "the economic and financial programs negotiated at the beginning of the year" (Informe Latinoamericano, 1985).[15] In addition, the 1986 national budget (approved at the end of December 1985), which estimated total expenses at $1,551.6 million dollars, allotted $633.7 million to service the foreign debt — or 42% of the total expenses authorized (Inforpress Centroamericano, 1986c).

In March, despite pressure from labor and business,[16] the Del Valle administration approved three important economic laws:

    (1) a law to stimulate and develop national industry and exports;

    (2) a law to foster agroindustry; and

    (3) reforms of the labor law (Inforpress Centroamericano, 1986b).

The legal changes responded to requirements of the stabilization program and were prerequisites both for the World Bank to grant new loans and for the ability of the country to reschedule its foreign debt — which rose to approximately $4,710 million dollars in 1986 (Análisis Económico, 1986). Meanwhile, the government continued to reduce the prices of primary goods with the obvious intention of forestalling demonstrations of popular unrest (Boletín del Gobierno de Panama, 1986c).

By mid-year, the government was operating well within the parameters of its financial agreements with the international lending agencies. According to these agreements, the International Monetary Fund (IMF) would grant Panama a total of US$44 million in 1986, and the private banks would grant credits of US$60 million (IPS, 1986e). In compliance with these measures, at the beginning of August the government announced the sale of state property valued at US$13 million (El Matutino, 1986d). This move toward privatization was viewed as another indication that it was complying with conditions imposed by the IMF and the World Bank (La Prensa, 1986j).[17]

Certainly, the domestic atmosphere was upset by the adjustment measures imposed by external economic pressure, but it did not reach the level of crisis which had contributed to Barletta's downfall. The fact that the Del Valle government was also experiencing foreign political pressure at the same time created a feeling of nationalism which kept demonstrations of domestic differences within bounds. Nevertheless, the high external financial obligation continues to threaten Panama's social peace and, for that reason, constitutes a source of tension capable of affecting the transfer of the Canal.

SUMMARY

CERTAINLY, THE MOST OUTSTANDING ISSUE in Panama's foreign relations during the period under consideration was its bilateral relationship with the United States. US doubts about the future stability of the Panamanian regime, in which country the US has developed and acquired vital security interests, have formed the basis of the serious accusations directed against General Noriega, perhaps the most serious of any that can be recalled against any head of the armed forces of a country "friendly" to the United States. This fact, particularly in light of the importance of the military in the Panamanian power structure, determined the sensitive changes in the priorities on its agenda in the emphases of its foreign policy. This situation also suggests that the Panamanian national interest has been redefined to include closer, more vigorous ties with the Third World, as well as a stronger espousal of the international policy of non-alignment. Tensions with the United States are also linked to differences between the two countries regarding the Central American conflict. Finally, Panama's external debt demonstrated the limits and vulnerabilities which beset developing countries, such as Panama.

NOTES

1. The foreign policy of those countries has been characterized as "reactive" (Eguizábal, 1985).

2. The note from the presidential press secretary stated that the government had decided that "it is not favorable for Panama presently to accept the presence of Mr. Marcos in our country" (La Tercera, 1986a: 17).

3. See complete text of the US official response in *El Matutino* (1986h).

4. US officials subsequently stated privately that "substantial evidence" had been gathered to support the accusations in the press, but that the US Government had decided to keep quiet because "to discuss it openly would endanger important US interests in the region" (La Hora de Guatemala, 1986a).

5. On 9 July, Leonardo Kam, Panama's Ambassador to the United Nations, stated in New York that the attacks sought "in vain for us Panamanians to abandon our non-aligned independent Latin American foreign policy." He ended saying that what was intended was to "destabilize our country" (El Matutino, 1986g)..

6. Ambassador Bazán wrote a letter to the *New York Times* which interpreted the allegations against the Panamanian military chief as an intention to destabilize the country (La Prensa, 1986l).

7. The political document recognizes and condemns

> the defamation campaign against the Republic of Panama and high level authorities of that country, organized by ultra-conservative sectors of the United States in alliance with the reactionary elements of the opposition, intending to destabilize the country, block the process of returning the property and control of the Panama Canal to Panamanians as well as its participation in the Contadora Group and discredit its international banking center (Política Internacional, 1986:68).

8. The Helms Amendment was subsequently added to the budget law of the CIA after joint consideration by both houses of Congress. In this amended form, the director of the CIA is asked to "provide all information concerning this topic for the intelligence committees" of Congress (El Mercurio, 1986a).

9. The controversy over "waste and mismanagement " arose from Panama's bitter objections to privileges granted the 1,800 US citizens who work for the Canal Commission by the US majority on the Board of Directors in 1983. The privileges functioned as subsidies to the United States for the costs of housing, electricity, telephones, drinking water and other services, as well as for education and vacation expenses for their families. Panama felt that the privileges affected the annual fiscal

superávit (residual) which it had been granted by the 1977 treaties (IPS, 1986i).

10. Dennis McAuliffe, US Canal executive, characterized the meeting as "contentious;" on the other hand, a close PDF source described it as "hostile and explosive" (La Prensa, 1986k).

11. PL 96-70 (also known as Murphy's Law) was approved by the US Congress on 27 September 1979. It establishes, unilaterally, the norms by which the US government must fulfill obligations contracted through the signing of the 1977 treaties.

12. At the beginning of 1986, Noriega declared that the greater "realism" of the military and the fact that in the Central American conflict had overridden the purely political and diplomatic aspects made it necessary for Contadora to include "military integration" in the peace negotiations (Excelsior, 1986).

13. PRD leader José Blandón affirmed that the military chief in Panama had been "the nerve" of that meeting, since he "maintains tight relations with the Salvadoran armed forces and with the church, and political relations with the country's guerrillas" (El Salvador Proceso, 1986: 13).

14. In its first months, the Del Valle administration lowered the prices of various basic consumer goods (Inforpress Centroamericano, 1986a).

15. Del Valle's economic ministers and advisers continued practically the same, with Ricaurte Vásquez serving as principal negotiator on the debt; the only change came when Arturo Melo was replaced (by Hector Alexander) as Minister of Finance and the Treasury (Rumbo Centroamericano, 1985).

16. On 10 March, the workers went on strike to protest the proposed reform of worker legislation, and, on 17th March, the Association of Industrialists of Panama (SIP) closed some industries to support the labor action (Informe Latinoamericano, 1986b: 144).

17. The *Frente de Servidores Públicos* (of the PRD) put out a statement that the action to privatize was signed "within the present juncture of pressures and internal and external blackmail" used to weaken the Panamanian state and government (El Matutino, 1986e).

REFERENCES

Alasei (1986a) August.

_______ (1986b) 30 June.

_______ (1986c) June.

_______ (1986d) March.

_______ (1986e) January.

Análisis Económico (Guatemala) (1986) 24 April.

Boletín del Gobierno de Panama (1986a) 27 August.

———— (1986b) 12 June.

———— (1986c) 14 May.

CASTILLO, M. (1985) "Después del Canal: Nuevos desafíos en la política exterior de Panama," in H. Muñoz (ed.) Las Políticas Exteriores Latinoamericanas Frente a la Crisis. Buenos Aires, Argentina: Grupo Editor Latinoamericano.

EGUIZABAL, C. (1985) "Determinantes Internos y Perspectivas de una Política Exterior Autónoma para Centroamerica: Elementos para la Discusión." Preliminary version of a paper prepared for the international seminar on Domestic Determinants and Perspectives of an Autonomous Foreign Policy for Central America, Confederación Universitaria Centroamericana (CSUCA), 15-18 May.

El Salvador Proceso (1986) (255) September:13.

(La) Estrella de Panama (1986a) 6 September.

———— (1986b) 2 September.

Excelsior (1986) 9 January.

———— (1985) 5 October: 2-A.

(La) Hora de Guatemala (1986a) 8 July.

———— (1986b) 13 June.

———— (1986c) 10 May.

Informe Latinoamericano (1986a) 16 October: 471.

———— (1986b) 21 March: 144.

———— (1986c) 11 October: 470.

Inforpress Centroamericano (1986a) 14 November.

———— (1986b) 10 April.

———— (1986c) 30 January.

IPS (1986a) 23 August.

———— (1986b) 22 August.

———— (1986c) 20 August.

———— (1986d) 8 July.

________ (1986e) 2 July.

________ (1986f) 23 May.

________ (1986g) 16 May.

________ (1986h) 14 May.

________ (1986i) 13 May.

________ (1986j) 10 May.

________ (1986k) 21 April.

________ (1986l) 5 April.

________ (1986m) 1 April.

________ (1986n) 27 March.

Los Angeles Times (1985) 1 November.

(El) Matutino (1986a) 5 October.

________ (1986b) 1 October.

________ (1986c) 27 September.

________ (1986d) 9 August.

________ (1986e) 19 July.

________ (1986f) 15 July.

________ (1986g) 11 July.

________ (1986h) 18 June.

________ (1986i) 9 May.

________ (1986j) 25 April.

(El) Mercurio (1986a) 3 October.

________ (1986b) 31 July.

________ (1986c) 19 July.

________ (1986d) 17 July.

________ (1986e) 22 March: A-17.

Miami Herald (1986a) 2 March.

________ (1986b) 7 February.

New York Times (1986a) 25 September.

________ (1986b) 21 August.

________ (1986c) 12 June.

________ (1985) 2 October.

(El) País (International Edition) (1986) 28 July.

Política Internacional (Belgrade) (1986) (875) 20 November: 68

(La) Prensa (1986a) 28 October.

________ (1986b) 3 October.

________ (1986c) 1 October.

________ (1986d) 28 September.

________ (1986e) 25 September.

________ (1986f) 19 September.

________ (1986g) 31 August.

________ (1986h) 10 August.

________ (1986i) 6 August.

________ (1986j) 27 July.

________ (1986k) 24 July.

________ (1986l) 16 July.

________ (1986m) 11 July.

________ (1986n) 23 June.

________ (1986o) 22 June.

________ (1986p) 11 May.

________ (1986q) 23 April.

________ (1986r) 25 February.

Prensa Libre (Guatemala) (1986a) 28 August.

________ (1986b) 18 June.

________ (1986c) 14 June.

________ (1986d) 13 June.

(La) República (1986) 27 April.

Rumbo Centroamericano (1986) 24 January.

________ (1985) 13 November.

(La) Tercera (1986a) 22 March: 17.

———— (1986b) 21 March: 18.

URRUTIA, R. (1986) "Presiones internas y externas en la política exterior de Panama," in H. Munoz (ed.) America Latina y el Caribe: Politicas Exteriores para Sobrevivir. Buenos Aires, Argentina: Grupo Editor Latinoamericano.

URETA, E. (1980). Prácticas de inseminación artificial y profilaxis respecto de la paratifoidea en H. Hinnuleus. *Anales de Instituto de C. … de Toluca*. Buenos Aires: Comisión … Latinoamericano.

A "STATUS APART:" INTERNATIONAL RELATIONS IN THE CARIBBEAN 1985-1986

by JORGE HEINE

PERHAPS NOTHING illustrates the present situation of the Caribbean better than the "status apart" which Aruba assumed at the stroke of midnight 31 December 1985. As 1986 dawned, this small island off the Venezuelan coast (population 67,000) entered into a new phase of existence as its political status metamorphosed from that of Dutch territory into the legally innovative "status apart." This new definition implies that Aruba will enjoy a substantial increase in autonomy, its own currency, and control over all of its affairs except defense and foreign relations — which will continue under control of The Hague until 1996 when the island will become fully independent.[1]

At first glance, the progress of decolonization in a region which has been described as having the greatest concentration of colonial territories in the world is nothing special; after all, for many years the Dutch government itself has been encouraging the Dutch Antilles to begin taking the necessary steps leading to full sovereignty. Most revealing, however, and illustrative of the difficult dilemmas that Caribbean territories confront when entering the hazardous world of international relations, is the extreme ambiguity with which the Arubans view this new arrangement and the distinctive circumstances which surrounded the development.

Jorge Heine is Associate Professor of Political Science at the University of Puerto Rico, Mayaguez.

The path which led up to Aruba's eventual independence was begun and directed by a young political leader, Benito Croes, and his political party, the *Movimiento Electoral di Pueblo* (MEP). One of the most controversial aspects of this movement was the decision to separate Aruba from the rest of the Federation of the Netherlands Antilles (which include the islands of Curaçao, Bonaire, Saba, St. Martin, and St. Eustasius) which did not share the urge for independence exhibited by Creos and his followers. Though the two largest islands within the Federation (Aruba and Curaçao) had always displayed a certain rivalry with one another, few thought that the move towards independence would lead to fragmentation of the Netherlands Antilles — whose islands are among the smallest, most deficient in natural resources, in the Caribbean. To emphasize the extreme vulnerability of these tiny economies to decisions made far away, by metropolitan governments and multinational corporations, just 9 months before Aruba raised its new flag (a red star on a blue ground) in March 1985, Exxon decided to close its refinery on the island, the mainstay of the economy and principal source of jobs and income. This closing of the refinery — after 60 years of operation — left 1,500 Arubans unemployed and wiped out 40% of government revenue, a total of $50 million.

Aruba suddenly discovered it had embarked upon a road of no return, for the Hague had been firm in its insistence that, once the island opted for an independence (even by stages) that separated it from the rest of the Federation, there would be no possibility of return to the status of Dutch colony — thus a substantial part of its resources were snatched away without consideration or prior notice. The Aruban reaction was immediate: far from demonstrating their confidence in Benito Croes and conferring upon him and his party a new mandate permitting them to head up the island government during the first years of the "status apart," on 22 November 1985 the citizenry voted against the MEP and in favor of the 4-party opposition coalition headed by Henry Eman, who formed the new government of Aruba.[2]

The decolonization impulse, growing fragmentation of the region, ambivalence toward the colonial relationship, enormous vulnerability of Caribbean economies, as well as the effect of the drop in the world price of oil on the region, were all dramatically illustrated by the happenings in Aruba, setting the stage for the way the 1985-86 year would shape up in the Caribbean. During this time it again became evident that the deep crisis affecting the region is not so much the consequence particular world circumstances as simply a natural reflection of the structural situation of Caribbean economies in a post-plantation period, a period in which many characteristics of the plantation economy still persist, a means of production that defined the Caribbean economies for almost 3 centuries, perpetuating their underdevelopment.[3]

MANIFESTATIONS OF POST-PLANTATION ECONOMIES

THE CARIBBEAN PRODUCT *par excellence* has, of course, been sugar, much more than petroleum. The economic difficulties of the region's major sugar producers — Cuba, the Dominican Republic, Guyana and Jamaica — are due, at least in part, to long-range trends in the world sugar market which have lessened their ability to dispose of this commodity in the markets of the central economies, leading, in turn, to reduced foreign exchange earnings and concomitant negative impact on their economies — highly open and dependent on imports for a great many of their necessities.[4]

Although the Caribbean produces only 10% of the world's sugar (about 10 million out of a total world production of 95-97 million tons), this accounts for a third of the world's sugar exports, thus the region is a major player in the international trade of this commodity. Compared to the situation that obtains in markets for other raw material, sugar market relations, rather than consisting of a free market between producers and importers, exhibit a mercantile tendency, with various Caribbean countries locked into a system of quota agreements and preferential pricing with a major importing country or group, such as the United States (for the Dominican Republic, Jamaica, Guyana, Barbados, and Trinidad and Tobago), the European Common Market (for Barbados, Jamaica, Guyana, St. Kitts-Nevis, and Trinidad and Tobago), and the socialist bloc countries of eastern Europe and China (for Cuba).[5]

In general, the quota has guaranteed the producer countries a price well above that of the free market (for example, over the last few years the United States has commonly paid 18¢ per pound although the world market price sunk to a low of 5-6¢ per pound). Nevertheless, this situation is inherently unstable because of certain trends in consumption and production patterns in the developed economies which forecast a bleak future for producers in the Caribbean. In the United States, sugar consumption has dropped considerably, from 89.2 pounds per capita (in 1975) to 67.2 pounds per capita (in 1984). On the other hand, corn-based sweeteners — which have almost totally replaced sugar in carbonated drinks like Coca-Cola and Pepsi-Cola, for example — have increased their share of the sweetener market from 4% (in 1975) to 23% (in 1984). As a consequence, producers in the Caribbean Basin have seen their exports to the United States drop from an annual average of 1.6 million tons (1977-1981) to a mere 594,000 tons (in 1984), with an accompanying fall in revenue from an annual average of $680 million (1977-1981) to only $250 million (in 1985).[6]

In Europe, for somewhat different reasons, the situation is hardly more hopeful. Within the European Economic Community (EEC), sugar beet production increased so dramatically — from 8 million tons a year in 1975 to 13 million in 1985 — that the EEC was forced to re-export a great part of the 1.3 million tons of sugarcane it imports from the ACP (African, Caribbean, Pacific) countries. Under these circumstances, the major Caribbean producers of sugar have basically oriented the conduct of their foreign economic policies toward trying to avoid any further reduction in the quotas which favored them in the past, primarily through the multilateral ACP/EEC forum set up by the Lomé Convention, and through a somewhat informal lobby composed of the Dominican Republic and the CARICOM (Caribbean Community) countries toward the US government.

The relative inefficiency of this lobby in the face of pressure from US producers of sugar and corn (who view Caribbean sugar as a direct competitor of corn-fructose sweeteners) became apparent when the US announced its new 1985-86 sugar import quotas in September 1985. As Table 1 shows, the new quotas imply a cutback of about 30% for most Caribbean countries and

TABLE 1

UNITED STATES SUGAR QUOTAS

(in tons)

Guyana	20,592 (--32.4%)
Jamaica	18,876 (--32.4%)
Belice	18,876 (--32.4%)
San Cristobal	12,500 ----
Barbados	12,012 (--32.4%)
Trinidad-Tobago	12,012 (--32.4%)
Republica Dominicana	216,000 (--43.6%)

Source: Latin American Monitor, Caribbean Regional Report,
        October 1985.

more than 40% for the Dominican Republic. It is perhaps symptomatic of the weakness of the position of Caribbean producers that some viewed these reductions as a kind of partial victory since they had expected the cuts to be much greater, more than 50%. Another of the ironies of the quota reduction is that it took place just when many Caribbean producers had increased their production compared to previous years.

CARICOM and OAS (Organization of American States) requests that the Reagan administration reconsider the reductions fell on deaf ears for a variety of reasons, mostly an adverse combination of factors — the fore-mentioned pressure by domestic US producers, US budget difficulties aggravated by requirements of the Gramm-Rudman amendment, and the US growing trade deficit — which forecast that additional reductions might be forthcoming in 1986-87 as well.

However, international market difficulties were not a prerogative of sugar alone. Bauxite, another major Caribbean commodity (produced by Jamaica, Guyana and Suriname), was also in trouble due to a drop in price: which fell from $125 a ton to only $80 per ton between September 1984 and September 1985. The impact of this trend of falling prices was devastating, particularly in Jamaica, which had to close 3 producing plants between August 1984 and September 1985. In 1985, bauxite production was 30% lower than 1984 levels (totalling 6.14 million tons), and alumina exports were 7% less than the previous year. Jamaica's net profits from the industry were estimated as not over $150 million for 1985 compared to the $220 million earned the preceding year, in 1984. Two of the industry's major companies — Reynolds and Alcoa — with investments in Jamaica have closed their plants there in the last 2 years.[7]

The 1985-86 year witnessed a somewhat better situation for producers of bananas, a key product for many Eastern Caribbean economies. In 1985, the value of Eastern Caribbean banana exports rose 22.8% over that of 1984 (for a total of $31 million) due partly to an increase in volume (up 9.5%) and partly to an increase in price (up 12%).

However, the Eastern Caribbean producing countries became increasingly concerned over possible competition from Nicaraguan bananas which, when displaced from the US market by that country's embargo (instituted at the beginning of 1985), began to find a ready market in England and other European countries, which consider them to be a better product selling at a lower price.[8]

Finally, the falling price of oil, though initially benefiting the majority of non-oil-exporting Caribbean countries, had negative repercussions far beyond the violent economic contraction it provoked in Trinidad and Tobago, which owed its economic strength of the 1970s and early 1980s directly to the high price of oil. To the closing of the Exxon refinery in Aruba must be added that of the Shell refinery in Curaçao, both plants which played a key role in local economies, as did that of the Chevron refinery in Freeport (The Bahamas) which closed in September 1985.[10] Cuba, on the other hand, although it produces only 20,000 barrels daily and depends for the rest of its petroleum needs on purchases at a subsidized price from the Soviet Union, has come to depend heavily on the re-export of a quarter of the Soviet oil in order to obtain about $500 million a year, a sum equal to the value of all Cuban exports to the advanced capitalist countries. And finally, Trinidad, which owed 80% of its exports (valued at $2.5 million) to petroleum in 1984 and which estimated that it lost $500 million in 1985 due to the drop in the price of oil, had come to be the principal market in the region for the products of the other CARICOM members — so its sudden economic contraction was keenly felt by them.[11]

Thus 1985-1986 was a year which made it unmistakably clear that the post-plantation economies of the Antilles were in the midst of a profound crisis. This crisis was triggered by long-term trends in the world economy which undermine the very foundations of regional economies, which have traditionally rested on quotas and mechanisms of preferential access to the markets of the central powers more than on the ability of their products to compete in terms of price and quality. Traditional products, like sugar, thus facing an ever more restrictive market — 3 plants in Jamaica closed during the period under study — while manufactured products (like textiles, clothing, and shoes) are generally in such an early stage of development that it is difficult for them to compete in major world markets without some kind of preferential access, which up till now both the United States and Canada, despite their numerous expressions of good will toward the region, have refused to grant.

PUBLIC DISSATISFACTION AND POLITICAL CHANGE

THE MAJOR CRISIS in which the Caribbean finds itself has affected not only those countries with a long history of economic difficulty, like Haiti and Guyana, but also those whose economic performance has historically been relatively satisfactory, like Trinidad, Barbados, and Suriname among others (and embraces the socialist countries, like Cuba, as well as capitalist ones like the Dominican Republic, those who have been independent for several decades, like Jamaica, and others that are still under metropolitan control, like the Netherlands Antilles) and has translated into the growing dissatisfaction of Caribbean electorates with the governments in power.

During the 25-month period of November 1984-1986, citizens displayed their unhappiness with governments in power by switching majority support to parties in the opposition. This process began with the November 1984 elections in Puerto Rico, in which Rafael Hernández Colón and his Popular Democratic Party (PPD) defeated incumbent Governor Carlos Romero Barceló and his New Progressive Party (PNP), passing through the May 1986 elections in Barbados, in which Errol Barrow and his Democratic Labor Party (DLP) overwhelmingly defeated Bernard St. John and the Barbados Labor Party (BLP), and culminating with the December 1986 elections in Trinidad and Tobago. The trend has been clear. It is important to emphasize that this series of reverses for governments in power goes far beyond the usual pattern of mere alternation of power typical of representative democracies that are fairly well established. The defeat of George Price and his People's United Party (PUP) in Belize and his replacement by Manuel Esquivel and his United Democratic Party (UDP), for example, brought 30 years of uninterrupted PUP rule to a close; at the same time, the fall of Jean-Claude Duvalier in Haiti (February 1986) ended 3 decades of Duvalierist dictatorship in the second most populous country in the Caribbean. On the other hand, the 30-year government of the People's National Movement (PNM) in Trinidad-Tobago — first under its founder Eric Williams (1956-1981) and later under his successor, George Chambers — came to an end in the general elections of 15 December 1986, in which the United Front of the opposition, with the significant name of National Alliance for Reconstruction and headed by A. N. R. Robinson, obtained a resounding victory.

These results do not reflect so much a consistent pattern of Caribbean electorates rejecting either the Left or the Right, nor being either for or against recent US policies toward the region, as much as a pragmatic attitude of rejecting those government teams which have demonstrated an inability to confront the challenges that have emerged from the profound crisis that affecting the region, and that includes the great majority of them. Thus in May 1986, 4 months after the Haitian people made continuation of the Duvalierist dictatorship untenable, voters in the presidential elections in the neighboring Dominican Republic gave a comparative majority to Joaquín Balaguer, the great representative of *neotrujillismo* whose *dictablanda* (1966-1978) was considered by many as a stage in Dominican political development that has never been surpassed. The sad truth is that the administrations of

Antonio Guzmán (1978-1982) and Salvador Jorge Blanco (1982-1986) of the *Partido Revolucionario Dominicano* (PRD) had demonstrated extreme incompetence in managing the Dominican economy, bringing the country to the brink of bankruptcy, a situation which contrasted sharply with the great economic growth experience by the country during the greater part of Balaguer's first three (4-year) terms in office.[12]

Not all governments who faced the voters during this period were forced to bite the dust of defeat; those incumbents who succeeded in maintaining a fairly reasonable rhythm of growth in their countries managed to survive, as was the case of John Swan in Bermuda and Eugenia Charles in Dominica. Those elections held in Grenada in December 1984 (which brought the victory of Herbert Blaize and his New National Party) and those in Guyana in December 1985 (marked by the victory of Forbes Burnham's successor, Desmond Hoyte, and his People's National Congress) took place under circumstances so special that they fall into a separate category.[13] However, the central point is that the Caribbean people appeared increasingly ill-disposed to place their confidence in those leaders, parties, and movements incapable of providing alternatives and/or solutions to the crisis which affected the region at the time.

VULNERABILITY AND REGIONAL SECURITY

IF THE SEVERITY AND SYMPTOMS of the crisis are obvious, reflecting themselves in such indicators as (1) unemployment that fluctuates between 25-40% in the majority of countries; (2) massive waves of emigrants from the region, of which the most dramatic example is the thousands of Dominicans who risk their lives crossing the Mona Channel in fragile boats in search of a better future in Puerto Rico; (3) the continuing closings of refineries, mining installations, and sugar mills up and down the entire archipelago of the Antilles; as well as (4) the paradox that Guyana, the country with the region's most extensive territory, lowest population density, and wealth of natural resources, is unable to provide sufficient *bread* to feed its own capital city, Georgetown — the responses have varied considerably.

One response has been the region's growing militarization, particularly through the Regional Security System (RSS) in which the English-speaking Caribbean, traditionally only marginal to the inter-American military system, have been increasingly incorporated into the Pentagon's regional military operations and exercises.[14] At the same time, the United Kingdom has been developing its own Rapid Deployment Force, using troops from the 5th Air Brigade and the 3rd Commando Brigade, which total some 10,000 soldiers. While US military aid to the Eastern Caribbean was set at $10.8 million, this was increased to $8.3 million for Jamaica and $10.8 million for the Dominican Republic.[15]

In September 1985, military exercises with the code-name "Operation Exotic Palm" were held at the Vieux Fort promontory in St. Lucia, in which some 500 US troops took part along with those of St. Lucia, Grenada, Dominica, St. Kitts-Nevis, Antigua, Jamaica, and Barbados, under the command of Colonel Wayne Topp, Deputy Commander-in-Chief of US forces in the Caribbean, and Brigadier Rudyard Lewis of the Barbados Defense Force (BDF) and RSS coordinator. Along the same lines, in November 1985 Antigua granted use of the naval facilities at Coolidge to the United States as a training center for its military personnel in the Caribbean, followed in December by the holding of military exercises ("High Key") in Antigua, in which both US troops and Antiguan military personnel took part. These various exercises culminated in the "Ocean Adventure 1986" military maneuvers which were held in the Caribbean and the Atlantic from 24 April–10 May 1986, together with the forces of those same Caribbean countries who had participated in "Operation Exotic Palm."

Despite the considerable impetus which the United States and several Caribbean countries (particularly Barbados, Jamaica, and Dominica) have given to the RSS in recent years, several factors — such as (1) the March 1985 death of the Barbados Prime Minister Tom Adams, a major promoter of the RSS (as well as of the October 1983 invasion of Grenada which was the catalyst for creating the RSS); (2) the defeat of his party, the Barbados Labour Party (BLP), in the May 1986 elections; (3) the return of the less-militaristic Errol Barrow as Prime Minister of Barbados; and (4) the critical attitude which countries like St. Vincent and Trinidad have shown toward it — indicate that militarization, as a response to the regional crisis, is far from receiving the unanimous support of the governments of the English-speaking countries. In fact, Errol Barrow's open hostility toward the RSS, given Barbados' central role, raises serious doubts as to its viability in the near future, at least in its present form and structure.[16]

RESTRUCTURING, LIBERALIZATION AND THE CHALLENGE OF THE CBI

ANOTHER RESPONSE to the crisis, similar to the previous one, was provided by President Reagan through the Caribbean Basin Initiative (CBI), which was announced in February 1982 and came into force in January 1984. Basically, through unilateral establishment of a free trade zone between the United States and certain designated countries in the Caribbean Basin, the United States departed from its previous practice of avoiding the establishment of preferential trade zones in developing countries of the region.[17]

As the heads of CARICOM countries made clear (in a letter to President Reagan dated August 1985), the CBI raised expectations throughout the region, expectations which have generally remained unmet, either in terms of investor response or in significantly increasing trade between the US and the Caribbean. Over the last 5 years (as Table 2 shows), Caribbean Basin exports to the United States have either remained the same or exhibited a downward trend; in 1985 total exports (amounting to $7.29 billion) of Basin countries to the United States declined dramatically: by 23%.

It is this downward trend of Caribbean exports to the US market which has roused strong protests on the part of regional leaders, some of whom have identified themselves completely with Reagan's Caribbean policies, which have so far not succeeded in translating themselves into concrete economic benefits for these countries. Among the complaints most frequently heard within the Caribbean regarding US economic policies are (1) that the cuts in sugar quotas have meant a drastic drop in income of many Caribbean countries; (2) that the refusal to allow free entry of certain products — textiles, clothing, leather goods, and shoes — represents a powerful constraint on the ability of the region's manufacturing sector to expand; and (3) that congressional

TABLE 2

EXPORTS FROM CBI BENEFICIARY COUNTRIES TO THE UNITED STATES
(in thousands of millions of dollars)

1981	10.0
1982	8.2
1983	9.2
1984	9.3
1985	7.2

Source: Latin American Monitor, Caribbean Regional Report,
         December 1985.

refusal to approve tax benefits for US investors in the region has meant that many of them continue to prefer investing in the Far East.[18] On the strictly political level, the US response has been to throw the blame back on the Caribbean countries themselves: at the annual conference on the Caribbean (held in Miami 17-21 November 1985), Vice-President George Bush declared that lack of investment in the region was due to the existence of duties that were too high, trade barriers of every kind, and a bureaucracy that obstructs the plans of foreign investors. However, Commerce Department specialists did not hesitate to admit that, up till now, the CBI has failed to achieve the anticipated results for reasons which are often beyond the control of the Caribbean countries themselves.

They emphasize, nevertheless, that the drop in exports to the United States is basically due to the decrease in commodity prices (of oil, sugar, and bauxite) and point out that if one dis-aggregates the non-traditional exports, the picture is quite different. During the first six months of 1986, for example, those exports increased 15.4% (reaching $1.59 billion). Excluding petroleum, the exports of CBI beneficiaries to the United States rose 6.4% during the first half of 1986, for a value of $2.65 billion.[19]

A way to overcome the CBI limitations in matters of textile and clothing imports has been through joint venture agreements, by which cloth produced and cut in the United States is sent to the Caribbean for the more labor-intensive work of garment construction. Those products are then able to enter the US market at a very low rate of duty. The major beneficiaries of this arrangement were the Dominican Republic, whose exports in this category rose 22% in 1985 (reaching $111 million) and Jamaica, whose exports rose 83% (to $44 million) during the first half of 1986.

The US Department of Commerce, according to the CBI, has introduced 285 new investment projects that have come into force since 1 January 1984, creating 35,000 new jobs. However, the sad reality is that, for the remaining years of this century, the bulk of Caribbean country exports will continue to be of the traditional type. As long as prices of these products continue to be subject to the abrupt fluctuations experienced in the past, and as long as the Caribbean continues losing the comparative advantages it has enjoyed not only in the production of sugar, but also in the production of alumina (production of which is increasingly being transferred to countries which not only have bauxite but also cheap sources of energy for processing the alumina, like Australia and Brazil), and in the refining of oil (due to changes in the international petroleum market which have made obsolete the great majority of the refining plants located in the Caribbean), the Caribbean will continue to face serious difficulties in its foreign trade.

Another type of response to the obvious need to restructure the Caribbean economies has been that of the International Monetary Fund (IMF), which played a particularly prominent role in Jamaica and the Dominican Republic in recent years. The fascinating point about *both* cases is that the usual IMF-imposed conditions for loans (reduced public spending, tax increases, elimination of subsidies, consumer price increases, etc.) not only did *not* help solve, at least minimally, the most pressing problems of both economies, but ended by being denounced by such government *conservatives* as Prime Minister Edward Seaga and President Joaquín Balaguer, whose economic policies could be expected to coincide wholly with the philosophy and objectives of the Fund.[20] In countries with the level of development of the Caribbean countries (even the most advanced among them), one of the fundamental problems is specifically the lack of an adequate infrastructure as well as an adequate production capability in many areas of the economy, which often can only be provided by the state. One cannot have an economic policy of extreme orthodoxy and austerity without perpetuating that situation with the result that it becomes self-defeating.

THE CARIBBEAN AND THE UNITED STATES

IT IS WITHIN the context of this deepening Caribbean crisis that the US-Caribbean relationship of 1985-86 must be analyzed. And perhaps the best way of describing the US Caribbean policy would be by saying that, little by little, the Reagan administration has been changing its Caribbean policy from one of high priority on its agenda — expressed most dramatically by the 1983 invasion of Grenada and the 1984 implementation of the CBI — to one of secondary importance. This does not mean that the Caribbean has disappeared from the map in its effect on the White House or the US Department of State, as seems to have happened over a long period in the past, from the end of the 1960s to the mid-1970s. President Reagan's visit to Grenada (February 1986) for a meeting with the leaders of the English-speaking Caribbean demonstrates that he is far from forgetting that the invasion of Grenada gave him what some commentators have called the greatest foreign policy achievement of his presidency.

But it means that US Caribbean policy has entered a stage of institutionalization and consolidation, more than of great innovations. Illustrative of this process are such developments as (1) the unquestionable follow-up of the CBI; (2) the final decision not to change Section 936 which allows US corporations a federal tax exemption on their multi-million dollar investments in Puerto Rico; (3) the continued support for development of the Regional Security System (RSS); and (4) sponsoring the creation of a Caribbean Democratic Union, founded in Jamaica in February 1986 (at the instigation of the Republican Party in the United States) which brings together the conservative parties of the English-speaking

Caribbean.[21] Washington is carrying out a strategy designed to develop a vast and solid network of political, economic, and military ties between the United States and the Caribbean.[22] Although the Latin Caribbean — particularly Puerto Rico, the Dominican Republic, and Haiti (and, Cuba immediately before the revolution) — has traditionally been very entwined in the US military-political system, this has been much less true of the English-speaking Caribbean, whose colonial ties with the United Kingdom have historically kept them at a certain distance from Washington's diplomacy in the region. To remedy this situation has been one of the fundamental objectives of US foreign policy in the Antilles.

As Table 3 shows, the level of US economic aid to the Caribbean, though substantially less than that provided to Central America, is relatively high in *per capita* terms in comparison with aid granted to other countries (like Peru and Bolivia, for example). In absolute terms, certain grants of aid stand out, such as that received by Jamaica ($124.4 million in economic aid and $8.27 in military aid) and by the Dominican Republic ($111.8 million in economic aid and $10.8 million in military aid), although on a *per capita* basis, aid granted to the Eastern Caribbean micro-states is even greater.

Although military aid figures for the English-speaking Caribbean remain quite small in absolute terms, they have increased enormously in recent years. In 1980, the amount was scarcely US$ 217,000; in 1986, it rose to US$ 18,825 million, a 9,000% increase.

WASHINGTON, DICTATORSHIPS, AND THE CASE OF HAITI

THE POPULAR REVOLT which put an end to 29 years of Duvalier dictatorship in Haiti provided, at the same time, an occasion for the Reagan administration to demonstrate that an important change had been taking place in Washington's policy toward dictatorships in the Third World.[24]

Although originally viewed through a lens which looked at dictatorships, both military and personalist, with great sympathy (a sympathy based on distinguishing between governments that were "totalitarian" and others simply "authoritarian" which

TABLE 3

US FOREIGN AID TO LATIN AMERICA AND THE CARIBBEAN
FY 1986
(in millions of dollars)

	ECONOMIC				MILITARY			
	ESF	DA	PL 480	TOTAL	MAP	FMS	IMET	TOTAL
Centroamerica	600.5	268.6	110.8	979.9	235.9	14.0	4.25	254.95
Zona Andina	70.0	57.4	50.6	186.0	24.35	35.0	3.0	62.350
Caribe	160.0	110.1	87.9	358.3	24.5	4.0	2.15	30.65
Las Bahamas	0	0	0	0	0	0	.05	.05
Republica Dominicana	50.0	30.0	31.8	111.8	6.0	4.0	.800	10.800
Caribe Oriental	35.0	31.1	0	66.1	10.0	0.0	.400	10.400
Guyana	0	0	0	0	0	0	.050	.05
Haiti	5.3	25.0	25.7	56.0	0.5	0	.475	.975
Jamaica	70.0	24.0	30.4	124.4	8.0	0	.275	8.275
Surinam	0	0	0	0	0	0	.050	.050
Trinidad and Tobago	0	0	0	0	0	0	.050	.050
Otros	2.2	24.8	0	27.0	0	2.5	7.3	9.8
TOTAL	833.0	460.9	257.3	1,551.2	284.75	55.5	16.575	356.95

ESF = Economic Support Funds; DA = Development Aid; MAP = Military Assistance Program;
FMS = Foreign Military Sales; IMET = International Military Education and Training
Source: Caribbean Insight, VIII, 7 (July 1985).

Jeane J. Kirkpatrick dusted from the shelves of the Cold War), political reality and the difficulty of publicly rationalizing a foreign policy which aggressively denounced the lack of liberty in Eastern Europe on the one hand, while simultaneously singing the praises of dictators in the Western Hemisphere on the other, led to a change of focus. Particularly in a period like that of the 1980s, marked by the process of redemocratization with popular forces on the offensive throughout Latin America, a gradual but firm turn in this policy became an imperative. This led to a gradual distancing of Washington from these traditional dictatorships, reaching, in practice, a position not too different from that of the Carter Administration with its whole emphasis on human rights, although with a quite different rhetoric and focus.

The characteristics of this policy (as well as its considerable limitations) were highly visible in the case of Haiti. Despite the attempts of US government officials and various sectors of the press, it was a gross distortion of the truth to declare that the principal actor responsible for Duvalier's downfall was the Reagan administration (nor was it in the case of the downfall of Ferdinand Marcos in the Philippines). The sequence of events which led to the fall of Jean-Claude Duvalier show something very different. After 5 years of a relatively close relationship between the United States and Port-au-Prince, during which the major focus of US attention was on establishing ways to stop undocumented Haitians from flowing from the coast of Haiti to the beaches of Florida, it was not until a popular insurrection began in Gonaïves and in Cape Haitien (but soon extended to the rest of the country) that Washington began to re-examine seriously its policy toward Haiti. And the series of measures taken by Washington at that time doubtlessly accelerated and considerably facilitated resolution of the *impasse* in which the country found itself — among other things, because, unlike his father François, Jean-Claude Duvalier had increasingly come to depend on a coalition of interests, including a mulatto bourgeoisie, for whom the "US connection" was indispensable to carry on their economic activities, which were basically tied to the import-export trade.[24]

The announcement by the US State Department (29 January 1986) that the annual certification of the human rights situation in Haiti could not be granted owing to their violation of same became the first sign of this distancing, which was quickly followed by a statement of Secretary of State George Shultz himself (31 January 1986) that Haiti needed an elected, democratic government, and, finally, on the same day, White House spokesman Larry Speakes announced that Duvalier had left Haiti, which was not true but which made the position of the Reagan administration very clear. It was, of course, in a US government plane (which subsequently made a stop at the US base of Roosevelt Roads in Puerto Rico) that Jean-Claude Duvalier and members of his family finally left Port-au-Prince for France.

The major point that emerges from the fall of Duvalier based on these facts, is that indeed the United States is no longer willing (as it was in the past) to give its unconditional support to any dictator simply because he has anti-communist credentials. This does not mean that the United States has embarked on a global crusade against dictators of the Right nor that it is going to assume a leading role in putting an end to such dictatorships. It does imply that in those situations in which the popular forces take the offensive and make it impossible, through a variety of ways and means, for a dictator to continue in power, the United States has no trouble in helping to hasten his departure. This still remains an important factor, but is not anything decisive *unless* there is a correlation of forces completely unfavorable to the dictatorship, a correlation which should not only encompass all of civil society but should include the armed forces as well. Just as in the Philippines, in which the withdrawal of support by General Juan Ponce Enrile and General Fidel Ramos was decisive in the process of isolating Ferdinand Marcos after open fraud in the presidential elections, so in Haiti, in which the refusal of the officers to order their troops to fire on demonstrators in anti-government protests indicated that Duvalier's hours were numbered, this was amply demonstrated.

THE REGIONAL ALTERNATIVE

IF THE CBI HAS not brought about the dramatic increase in Caribbean exports to the US market which many expected, the regional market of the Caribbean Community (CARICOM) has continued to contract mainly due to the economic difficulties of

TABLE 4

CARICOM Intra-Regional Trade
(in millions of dollars)

1981	636
1982	555
1983	481
1984	444

Source: Latin American Monitor, Caribbean Regional Report,
          November, 1985

Trinidad and Tobago, whose foreign exchange earnings have fallen drastically owing to the drop in the world price of oil.

As Table 4 indicates, the total volume of regional trade has been progressively declining in recent years, creating serious difficulties for many Caribbean producers. The closing of the Regional Credit Facility, made bankrupt when Guyana found it impossible to pay its debt of around $80 million, mainly to Trinidad but also to other countries, like Barbados, came to constitute a major obstacle to the development of regional trade.

The lack of government solutions to this critical situation was made as clear in the 6th Summit Meeting of CARICOM Heads of State (held in Barbados in July 1985) as it was in the 7th Summit Meeting (held in Georgetown, Guyana, in July 1986). The Georgetown Declaration, which emerged from the latter, made reference mainly to the need (1) to broaden and deepen CARICOM, (2) to broaden regional trade, (3) to increase agricultural production in member countries, (4) to establish mechanisms for financial cooperation, and (5) to prevent the possibility of nuclear plant accidents in the region. And one of the major decisions of the meeting was the establishment of an Export Credit Facility to facilitate regional trade. None of these measures, however, suggests a real willingness to give decided impetus to regional integration.[26]

Of all regional initiatives, however, the most promising may have been that of Puerto Rico (discussed by Juan M. García-Passalacqua in his chapter on the foreign policy of Governor Rafael Hernández Colón). A measure of the potential of this new Puerto Rican policy is given by the fact that the Government of Puerto Rico has stated that up to $700 million could be used for the promotion of twin plants located in Puerto Rico and other Caribbean territories, which is almost twice the total of all US aid to the Caribbean in 1986. The nature of the project is not without some complications, one of which is the close degree of cooperation required between the government of Puerto Rico, foreign investors, and governments in the rest of the region. This implies a considerable challenge in and of itself.

What is not visible anywhere, however, is a consciousness that overcoming the present Caribbean crisis can succeed only through a genuine, major reorganization of regional economies. To throw off at once the weight of economic institutions appropriate to the post-plantation period and to allow themselves to enter the 21st century under conditions that begin to resolve the many socio-economic problems of the Antilles is the key task, but nonetheless one largely ignored by the region's governing elites.

NOTES

1. For an analysis of Aruba's situation upon entering this new stage, see George J. Cvejanovich, "Future Aruba: Can It Make It Alone?" in Caribbean Review 14 (Summer 1985): 18-20 and 42-43.

2. Tragically, Croes not only lost his political power before the "status apart" took place, but he was seriously injured in a car accident a few hours before New Year of 1986, never regained consciousness, and died (27 November 1986) in Utrecht, Holland.

3. The classic formulation of the characteristics of the plantation economy is found in Kari Levitt and Lloyd Best, "Characteristics of Caribbean Economy," pp. 34-60 in George Beckford (ed.) Caribbean Economy (Mona, Jamaica: ISER, 1975). George Beckford has another important book on the subject: Persistent Poverty (London, England: Zed Press, 1983).

4. For an excellent historical analysis of the development of the sugar industry, see Sidney W. Mintz's Sweetness and Power (New York: Viking Press, 1985). For a study of the problems that Caribbean sugar producers face with the numerous substitutes that are taking over an important share of the market, see Clive Y. Thomas: "Sugar Threat or Challenge: An Assessment of the Impact of Technological Developments in the High-Fructose Corn Syrup and Sucrochemicals Industry" (Ottawa: IDRC, 1985).

5. For an analysis of the international political economy of sugar, see G.B. Hagelberg, "Sugar in the Caribbean: Turning Sunshine into Money," pp. 85-126 in Sidney W. Mintz and Sally Price (eds.) Caribbean Contours (Baltimore: Johns Hopkins University Press, 1985).

6. Figures from Latin American Monitor-Caribbean Regional Report, October 1985 (from now on cited as LAM-CRR).

7. LAM-CRR, January-February 1986.

8. LAM-CRR, March 1986.

9. For the reasons for the failure of the development strategy adopted by Trinidad and Tobago to utilize their petrodollars, see the Trevor Farrell article entitled "Why a T & T Crisis?" in Caribbean Contact 13 (February 1986): 8. For a recent book on the political and economic development of Trinidad, see Scott McDonald's Trinidad and Tobago: Democracy and Development in the Caribbean (New York: Praeger, 1986).

10. For an analysis of the political economy of petroleum in the CARICOM countries, see Trevor Farrell's "Oil and Political Economy in the Caribbean Commonwealth," in Jorge Heine and Leslie Manigat (eds.) The Caribbean and World Politics: Cross Currents and Cleavages (New York: Holmes & Meier, 1987).

11. Statistics from LAM-CRR, May 1986.

12. For an introduction to the political situation in the Dominican Republic, see Jan Knippers Black's The Dominican Republic: Politics and Development in an Unsovereign State (Winchester, MA: Allen and Unwin, 1986).

13. For an analysis of elections in Guyana and the fraud committed, see "An Absurdity" by C.M. Hope in Caribbean Contact 13 (January 1986). For a recent book on the political system in Guyana, see Colin Baber and Henry Jeffrey: Guyana: Politics, Economics and Society (London: Frances Pinter, 1985).

14. A useful collection of essays on the militarization of the Caribbean is Alma Young and Dion Phillips (eds.) Militarization in the non-Hispanic Caribbean (Boulder, CO: Lynne Rienner, 1986).

15. Caribbean Insight (July 1985): 7. In the words of then-British Defense Minister Richard Heseltine: "We must be prepared to share the responsibility of protecting trade routes and promoting peace and stability in those areas where local conflicts could be extended, thus risking a broader East-West confrontation" (*Ibid.*: 7).

16. For an analysis of the security problems of mini-states in the modern world, see the interesting report of the Secretary of the British Commonwealth: "Vulnerability: Small States in the Global Society" (London, 1985).

17. On the CBI, see Richard Feinberg: "The Caribbean Basin Initiative: First Steps Toward Implementation," CISCLA Working Paper 22 (San Germán, PR: Interamerican University, 1986).

18. Caribbean Insight 8 (November 1985): 5.

19. Statistics from Kal Wagenheim's "Caribbean Basin Exports Show Healthy Increase," p.6 of the San Juan Star (12 October 1986).

20. For a good analysis of the problems faced by Michael Manley with the IMF program, see pp. 199-250, Chapter 6 in John and Evelyn Stephens book entitled Democratic Socialism in Jamaica (Princeton: Princeton University Press, 1986). For a somewhat different perspective, see Michael Kaufman's Jamaica Under Manley (London: Zed Press, 1985). For a discussion of the political economy of Seaga (after he became disillusioned with the IMF), see "Seaga Defies the IMF with an Expansionary Budget" in Caribbean Insight 9 (May 1986). One of the first measures taken by Balaguer once he returned to the presidency was to plan a vast program of public works (something completely opposed to the orthodox policy of the IMF), stating that he would not remain tied to IMF prescriptions.

21. In the meeting held in Kingston (February 1986), the Caribbean Democratic Union (CDU) elected Prime Minister Edward Seaga as its first president. The 3 vice-presidents elected were the Prime Minister of Grenada, Herbert Blaize; that of St. Kitts-Nevis, Kennedy Simmonds; and that of Belize, Manuel Esquivel. The founding parties of the CDU are the Jamaica Labor Party, the People's Action Movement of St. Kitts-Nevis, the United Democratic Party of Belize, the New National Party of Grenada, the Dominican Party of Liberty of Dominica, the People's Action Movement of Monserrat, the United Workers Party of St. Lucia, and the New Democratic Party of St. Vincent. Although parties invited from Barbados, Trinidad and Tobago, and Antigua refused to participate, the fact that the 8 founding parties are government parties is a significant indication of the strength of the conservative movement in the English-speaking Caribbean at the moment; see Caribbean Insight 9 (February 1986). Frank Fahrenkopf, president of the US Republican Party, attended the Kingston meeting. The CDU is also sponsored by the Konrad Adenauer Foundation of Federal German Republic (FRG or West Germany). For an analysis of the role of the United States in the creation of the CDU, see Catherine Sunshine's "CDU's Roots in Washington," Caribbean Contact 14 (August 1986): 13.

22. For a review of this process, see the special issue of NACLA Report on the Americas, "Mare Nostrum: U.S. Security Policy in the English-speaking Caribbean," Vol.14, No. 4 (July-August 1985).

23. For an analysis of this change, see Tamar Jacoby, "The Reagan Turnaround on Human Rights," in Foreign Affairs 64, 5 (Summer 1986).

24. For two relatively brief, but very sharp, analyses of the changes that have taken place in the Haitian political system under Jean-Claude Duvalier (1971-1986) see David Nicholls, "The Haitian Predicament," CISCLA Working Paper 18 (San Germán, PR: Interamerican University, 1986) and "Haiti: Family Business" (London, England: Latin American Bureau, 1985). For a good anthology of the social and economic changes that have occurred during this period in Haiti, see Charles Foster and Albert Valdman (eds.) Haiti Today and Tomorrow (Washington, DC: University Press of America, 1984).

25. See Caribbean Contact 14 (August 1986).

THE FOREIGN POLICY OF PUERTO RICO IN 1985-1986

by JUAN M. GARCIA-PASSALACQUA

ITS STATUS AS A COLONY of the United States ever since 1898 has prevented the Caribbean island of Puerto Rico from having its own foreign policy.[1] Nevertheless, during the time it was a colony of Spain, as well as under the hegemony of the United States, the island has played a relevant role in the history of the Caribbean and the Americas.[2]

As Jorge Heine has pointed out in this *Anuario*, there is a close correlation between the priority which Washington gives to the Caribbean at any moment and the extent of Puerto Rico's international activism in the region. During the last ten years, revolutions in both Granada and Nicaragua have drawn US attention to the area and, for this reason, stimulated more international involvement by Puerto Rico.[3] Ever since 2 January 1985, the government of the Associated Free State of Puerto Rico has intensified its international activity.[4] This has been amply reported, but its results remain to be seen.[5]

BASES OF INTERNATIONAL ACTIVITY

THE GOVERNMENT OF the *Partido Popular Democrático* (PPD) and of its leader, Governor Rafael Hernández Colón, took the following international initiatives in 1985, which have been continued in 1986:

Juan M. García-Passalacqua is a Puerto Rican political scientist and journalist and has served as adviser to former governors of Puerto Rico Luis Muñoz Marín and Roberto Sánchez Vilella.

- to assume a leadership role in fulfilling objectives of the Caribbean Basin Initiative (CBI) of President Ronald Reagan;

- to offer use of US$700 million deposited by multinationals in Puerto Rico for the promotion of manufacturing in the Caribbean;

- to develop a program of twin plants (*maquiladoras*) between Puerto Rico and neighboring countries of the region;

- to promote Puerto Rico's membership and participation in SELA (*Sistema Económico Latinoamericano*), ECLA (Economic Commission for Latin America), ACIC and the Caribbean Development Bank;

- to open up contact at the diplomatic level with Venezuela, Costa Rica, the Dominican Republic, the English Caribbean (Barbados, Grenada, Dominica, Jamaica), other Central American countries (Panama, El Salvador, Guatemala) and the rest of the world (Spain, Argentina, Ecuador, Peru, Mexico, Great Britain and Japan);

- "to expand Puerto Rico's borders" in order to carry out international activity in sports, banking, political and trade affairs;

- to promote the island's participation in the Latin American parliament and to sponsor the creation of the Caribbean Parliament;

- specifically to exclude any international activity/relations with Cuba, Nicaragua or UNESCO (United Nations Economic and Social Council).

In all these initiatives, the Hernández Colón administration received firm public support from the White House in the United States.

However, from the outset this unusual international activism was incompatible with Puerto Rico's present political status as a colony. In 1986, this incompatibility generated a crisis and provoked a major debate to clarify Puerto Rico's future course in the Caribbean.

In his State Address (3 February 1986), the governor announced additional initiatives in the Caribbean: an annual conference on goods and services in the region, a free trade zone, consolidation of area transport facilities and the creation of a regional Center for Applied Technology to be located on the island. Meanwhile, all the 1985 initiatives remained in effect and their activities expanded in three areas:

1. The International Offensive.

In the areas of culture, finance, trade, tourism, and the war on crime, Puerto Rico continued to stand out in the Caribbean:

- The island made plans to hold the 5th meeting of the National Commission for the 500th Anniversary of the Discovery of America in San Juan in May 1987, with the endorsement of Costa Rica, Spain, Chile, Peru, Mexico, Bolivia and the Dominican Republic, and with the possible participation of the King of Spain.

- The Federation of Latin American Tourist Organizations (*Confederación de Organizaciones Turísticas Latinoamericanas* or COTAL) agreed to make an effort — with Puerto Rico's strong support — to draw more visitors to the region.

- The island's Department of Commerce sponsored an aggressive program to promote the twin-plants concept by sending trade missions to the Dominican Republic, Aruba, Curaçao, Costa Rica, Panama, Antigua, St. Lucia, Mexico, Venezuela and Ecuador.

- The port of San Juan opened its Free Zone (27 February), declaring its intention to convert the island into the "trading center of the Caribbean."

- Puerto Rico was recommended as a location for the Caribbean headquarters of INTERPOL's general information network on the drug traffic, illegal funds, stolen vehicles, and international terrorism, and the site of its 1988 regional meeting.

- Legislation was approved to convert Puerto Rico's Government Bank for Development into a promoter (as a lender) of twin industrial plants in the Caribbean.

- Puerto Rico bestowed the title of "General Delegate" on its official representatives to European and regional capitals.

- At the suggestion of the United States, the Organization of American States (OAS) held a technical conference, attended by 30 delegates, in San Juan in July to discuss the importance of private investment in helping to resolve the economic problems of Latin America and the Caribbean. Meanwhile, the countries participating insisted on discussing tariffs and the foreign debt, and representatives from Barbados, Grenada, and Trinidad-Tobago were conspicuous by their absence.

- In August, the island's government announced its intention to request admittance to the Caribbean Economic Community (CARICOM), despite failure of a previous attempt 10 years ago.

2. Bilateral Relations.

In the first 9 months of the year, the government of Puerto Rico was active in its relations with various foreign governments:

- It signed a trade agreement with Costa Rica.

- Governor Rafael Hernández Colón paid an official visit to Spain (in March) to foster cooperation in the fields of telephone technology, industry, trade, restoration of cultural ties; and he attended a food fair in Barcelona.

- Puerto Rico's Undersecretary of State presented a paper at a forum sponsored by the Committee on Foreign Relations of the Venezuelan Chamber of Deputies on the topic of Puerto Rico as a "Latin American and Caribbean country."

- A delegation from the *Asociación de Exportadores de Venezuelas* (AVEX) and the banking sector (FINEXPO) visited San Juan (in April) to discuss areas of cooperation, lines of credit, and possible exports to Puerto Rico.

- After officials from Puerto Rico's Departments of State, Economic Development and the island's Electric Energy Authority visited Venezuela, they drew up a preliminary agreement with the Ministry of Energy and Mines to purchase part of the island's oil requirements from that country.

- Other agreements with Venezuela (in March-April) included: a plan to combat crime; joint programs in health, education and sports; meetings between legislators of both countries, joint acts to promote tourism and an intensive program for cultural exchange.

- In July, the president of El Salvador, José Napoleón Duarte, announced his upcoming visit to Puerto Rico.

- A delegation of Puerto Rican officials met (in March) with the presidents of Costa Rica and Guatemala to plan joint projects between their countries and Puerto Rico in construction, pharmaceuticals, and clothing.

- During a state visit to Puerto Rico (on July 25), the president of the Dominican Republic signed an agreement with the governor to develop projects in the economic, trade, cultural, and tourism areas and honored Puerto Rico Secretary of State Héctor Luis Acevedo for his dedication to furthering relations between the two countries.

- The Vice-President of the Dominican Republic, Carlos Morales Troncoso, visited Puerto Rico after his election "to strengthen industrial and commercial ties."

3. The Caribbean Basin Initiative (CBI).

During 1985-1986, Puerto Rico emphasized its role in the US-sponsored CBI in its foreign relations:

- A US Department of Commerce official was appointed to coordinate the efforts of the "CBI Task Force" in Washington with the government of Puerto Rico.

- As part of the US tax review program, the US Congress approved the Puerto Rican government's plan for twin plants in the Caribbean after a "regional battle" to preserve Section 936 of the US Internal Revenue Code which allows an exemption on this kind of investment.

- On 21 March, the Puerto Rican government and Citibank cosponsored a conference in San Juan, attended by a thousand people from the region, whose purpose was to "pressure" those multinational corporations holding more than US\$ 12 billion in exempt funds on deposit in Puerto Rico to invest those funds in the Caribbean. Several heads of state participated: Vinicio Cerezo of Guatemala, Edward Seaga of Jamaica and Eugenia Charles of Dominica. Cerezo stated that "Puerto Rico is a nation with a special character … a kind of doorway to the United States and a kind of doorway for the United States to the countries of South America."

- Nine complementary twin plants began to select land and construct facilities in Grenada, Costa Rica, the Dominican Republic and Antigua; 24 multinational corporations drew up plans for projects in St. Kitts-Nevis, Dominica, Guatemala, and Jamaica.

- The Chase-Manhattan Bank announced it would serve as coordinator for several economic projects in the region, using as its slogan: "In the world of finance, Puerto Rico is not an island."

- The First Regional Conference of the Caribbean, attended by more than 500 investors and businessmen, was held at the beginning of September for the purpose of enabling the private sector in Puerto Rico and those of the Caribbean and Central American region to become better acquainted with one another.

- Parts of President Ronald Reagan's speech on Grenada, in which he endorsed Puerto Rico's role in developing the CBI, were re-broadcast over Puerto Rican television on 17 March.

THE OPPOSITION COUNTERATTACK

IN THE FIRST 6 MONTHS of 1986, the international offensive of the Puerto Rican government met with strong domestic opposition, which led to a confrontation with the US Congress.

In January, the *Partido Nuevo Progresista* (PNP), which favored annexation with the United States, attacked the government of Rafael Hernández Colón for initiating measures "secretly designed to place Puerto Rico on the road to independence." At the same time, it also argued that Puerto Rico "by means of its twin plants, will exploit the economic inferiority of the Caribbean countries in colonial fashion."

The local annexation movement focussed its strategy on bringing this allegation before the congressional Committee of the Interior and Island Affairs. US Representative Robert Lagomarsino (R-CA), acting as spokesman for the group, objected to Puerto Rico's international activity and demanded that the US Department of State withdraw its authorization. The White House, confronted with a conflict between its own political party and its regional interests, claimed "executive privilege" in refusing to discuss its policy on Puerto Rico before the committee.

In April, the US State Department issued an official declaration that the international accord between Puerto Rico and Costa Rica (signed on 21 October 1985) was "absolutely valid" and that it "favored Puerto Rican efforts in the region within the context of the Caribbean Basin Initiative."

The House Committee on Interior and Island Affairs held hearings (on 22 May and 17 July 1986) to clarify the situation. In an extensive paper, Michael G. Kozak, State Department Legal Advisor, stated that at the moment Puerto Rico was a territory (or commonwealth) and, as such, was limited in the exercise of foreign policy. However, he added that by opting for the status of Associated Republic (or "free associated state"), like Micronesia, "it would have the ability to conduct its own foreign affairs."[6]

In this way the White House made clear something forecast many years ago: that its geopolitical interests would promote a change in Puerto Rico's political status that would steer the territory towards independence.

CARIBBEAN OBJECTIONS

IN 1986, many voices were raised in the Caribbean objecting to the US strategy of using Puerto Rico as its client-state in the region.

In July, Jamaica's PNP (People's National Party) criticized an agreement with Puerto Rico to construct housing on the island on the grounds that it threatened Jamaica's own construction industry and jobs. In June, Prime Minister Errol Barrow (Barbados) criticized the twin-plants strategy on the grounds that it did not help the countries of the eastern Caribbean become self-sufficient, pointing out that the problems of the Caribbean "would not be resolved by making Reagan the Santa Claus of the Caribbean." Political observers on Martinique criticized the proposal as one designed to convert Puerto Rico into the "US base" of a Caribbean Reagan Plan, making it, more than ever, into a *Mare Americanum*.[7]

These reactions caused veteran Caribbean watcher Harold Lidin to point out that Puerto Rico was in serious danger of becoming a propagandist for the expansion of the multinationals and for Reagonomics, a "hustler" rejected by the rest of the Caribbean.

OTHER ASPECTS OF THE NEW ROLE

PUERTO RICO'S NEW ROLE in the Caribbean, begun in 1985 and expanded in 1986, has four other major aspects: (1) the military aspect, (2) that of the international community, (3) the island's internal political aspect, and (4) that of Puerto Rican public opinion.

The Military Aspect

A basic element of Puerto Rico's new role is its military activism in the region. In June, military forces from the Dominican Republic and Jamaica trained with Puerto Rico's National Guard at their summer camp in what was called part of a "military-cultural exchange." During the year, the US Navy invested $62 million in modernizing its Roosevelt Roads base in Puerto Rico. In August, UNITAS held joint maneuvers in which 7 ships from the Venezuelan fleet took part (at the base), along with forces from Brazil, Argentina, Peru, Chile and Colombia. When the Venezuelan ship Simón Bolívar visited San Juan for the maneuvers, US Admiral William J.M. O'Connor joined with Governor Rafael Hernández Colón in conducting the public ceremony.

The International Community

The Puerto Rican case, debated annually before the UN Committee on Decolonization, received major attention during the year. The government of Puerto Rico sent Under-Secretary of State Barbara Sanfiorenzo before the Committee "to clear up any doubt" about the island. At the beginning of the hearings, Venezuela presented the Committee with a resolution (seconded by Cuba) declaring the right of a people "to independence and self-determination." Venezuelan Ambassador Andrés Aguiler declared:

> We all know that Puerto Rican people have had the opportunity to demonstrate their preference for different plans but, as we have said on many occasions, the exercise of the right to self-determination is not dissipated by choosing limited autonomy.[8]

The international press gave the mission's work on Puerto Rico's "limited" autonomy prominent coverage. The resolution was approved without amendments.

The Internal Political Aspect

A dialectical tension over the issue of Puerto Rican power exists between the geopolitical interests of the United States and the electoral interests of the party. Governor Hernández Colón stated (in a major interview with the Spanish news agency EFE) that "there is no desire for independence" on the island and that its present colonial status as an "Associated Free State" (or commonwealth) is, in his opinion, "permanent." He added: "Here we are integrated economically, politically, demographically. It is a firm attachment." And he postponed all discussion of political change til 1988. As Dr. Aída Montilla shrewdly pointed out, the US "*voluntad*" to grant an Associated Republic status that is truly free comes up against (in the words of José Ortega y Gasset) the "*noluntad*" of the political leadership in Puerto Rico.

Public Opinion on the Island

The US determination to steer Puerto Rico towards the political status of an Associated Republic has generated widespread debate on the island. At the very least, hundreds of articles on this subject have been published by the 5 newspapers in the country over the last 16 months.

Meanwhile, polls taken on the island show that Governor Rafael Hernández Colón still maintains his slight 4% lead over the opposition; it has not diminished in any way.

CONCLUSION: THE FUTURE AGENDA

PUERTO RICAN PUBLIC OPINION has responded favorably to the initiatives of Governor Rafael Hernández Colón during his first two years in office, nor, more specifically, has any significant opposition arisen to challenge his policy for the "Caribbeanization and Latinamericanization" of Puerto Rico.

Nevertheless, the course of US geopolitical interests and Puerto Rican internationalization in the region pose a serious question: Puerto Rico's role in the Caribbean cannot be clearly defined while the island retains its status as a colony of the United States.

This position — as we have already pointed out — was made clear in the sight of the House Committee on Interior and Island Affairs. It has also been discussed in influential political studies.

In mid-1986, the Puerto Rico Research Institute (in Washington) circulated a very candid, factual, 50-page evaluation of Puerto Rico's present and future situation. The title sums up its thesis: "Puerto Rico and the Caribbean Basin Initiative: The Complexities of Interdependence."[9]

The introduction puts the matter bluntly. The text reads:

> The Caribbean Basin Initiative (CBI) announced by President Reagan in 1982 and approved by Congress in 1984 has provoked substantial debate and analysis in both the United States and the Caribbean. The basic question has been whether the CBI can be successful in its declared objective: to bring economic development to this strategically important region. To describe the issue in this way is to lose sight of CBI objectives in one important aspect. The CBI was inspired by a renewed emphasis on the geostrategic importance of the Caribbean Basin and has as its objective, above all else, the comprehensive redesign of the international relations model within the region. Moreover, this is to be

achieved, not indirectly or piecemeal, but through developing and applying a cohesive, directed regional policy.

In sum, since 1982 the United States has had a new foreign
policy for the entire Caribbean, directed by the National Security
Council. It is within that policy that one must consider Puerto Rico.

The US analysts go on to say:

> The relationship between the CBI and Puerto Rico provides
> a useful case study for a broader spectrum of questions, such
> as the nature of regional economic development, security
> plans for the region, and comparative strategies for economic
> development. Underlining this set of issues is the future of
> Puerto Rico's relations with the United States.

First, the need for the CBI is examined from the standpoint of
its historical determinants. And it points out that the Initiative is,
more than anything else, an "attitude" that determines a broad
band of government programs, encouraging officials to focus
greater attention on, and resources to, the region. Furthermore,
the Caribbean Basin is a very recent US geopolitical concept,
determined by a new strategy for the security of the United States
to protect "its southern flank." At the same time, this strategy has
been determined by 6 important factors: (1) the independence of
new mini-states over the past 20 years, (2) the regional economic
crisis, (3) the internationalization of that crisis, (4) increasing
nationalism and political violence, (5) the imperatives of energy,
trade, and raw materials for the United States in the area, and (6)
the human interpenetration caused by migration to the United
States. For these reasons, the Basin is a priority in US strategic
planning.

Second, the domestic factors which have influenced the form
the CBI has taken all followed the W.A. Lewis design of "industrialization by invitation."

Third, the analysis compares the CBI to other programs for
international development, such as the case of Taiwan and that of
the Lomé Treaty as it affects the former French colonies. It con-
cludes that the purpose of the CBI is to integrate the development
of the region into the US economy, using Puerto Rico as a model.

Fourth, the US analysts deal with how the Puerto Rican
experience shaped the CBI. And they pose a serious problem:
which of the two resulting Puerto Ricos will be used? Will it be an

economically powerful Puerto Rico, with the highest *per cápita* income in the region, with manufacturing, banking, finance, housing, construction, and other developed businesses? Or will it be a Puerto Rico with a precarious, unbalanced economy, based on federal aid and tax exemptions, burdened with an enormous financial deficit, and with chronic unemployment running at more than 20%? And the answer is candid: at the moment there are only two models for development, the *boricua* (Puerto Rican) or the Cuban. And ideological polarization "has reduced the political flexibility."

Even so, the *boricua* model contains a major defect: migration to the continent. And one must limit this also through the creation of a "second border" in the Caribbean. For this and other reasons, one must "reexamine" the *boricua* model of modernization-by-industrialization and make agriculture the firm base for development in Puerto Rico and the Caribbean. Never before has the voice of imperialism spoken so clearly.

Fifth, the analysts deal with how the CBI affects Puerto Rico. They say, logically, that the island had only a peripheral relevance to the original geostrategic policy for the Caribbean. In 1981, the White House had created an Inter-Agency Committee on the island, which succeeded in pinpointing the difficulties that the CBI would create. In November 1981, it deliberated on the matter in secret (an important meeting in which Puerto Rico was defined as a "profligate environment that we must get rid of"). And following the congressional held hearings on the CBI in 1982, the question of Puerto Rico came to be considered crucial.

Analysts describe how the *Partido Nuevo Progresista* (PNP) fought the CBI because it alienated the island from "statehood" and how it convinced the *Partido Popular Democrático* (PPD), who were opposed, that it coincided with the the their leader's New Thesis for a "special relationship" with the United States. And here the study reached its logical conclusion. It said:

> A notable effort to expand this terrain can be found in suggestions which have been circulating in Puerto Rico recently that, in the final analysis, the most viable model for Puerto Rico may be that of an Associated Republic based on the model of Micronesia. Despite the fact that this model has stimulated some provocative academic debate, it has had

little impact on the level of an operating policy and even less on the ideas, and implementation, of economic planning.

The US analysts went on: "There can be no doubt that the question of Puerto Rico's political status will surface with new dimensions, as the new US Caribbean policy acquires a higher profile." And they added further: "The increased autonomy which this could give to Puerto Rico, in its trade policy and diplomatic relations, would help Puerto Rico move to a new status of free association."

The **sixth** point of this significant US analysis is precisely that "new model" for Puerto Rico as a way to achieve the goals of the CBI. Thus, they say, Puerto Rico will be a substitute for the colonial empires of Holland, Great Britain and France in the Caribbean. This is the White House policy for Puerto Rico: in the "future logic" of an Associated Republic, "it would play the role of a middle power" in the region, becoming the "entrepôt" of the Caribbean.[10]

The ideal of an Antilles federation has a profound significance and great following in the Caribbean. Many of our leaders and people subscribe to it.[11] However, that ideal can only be achieved by a free people.

NOTES

1. For an introduction to the topic of Puerto Rican foreign relations with the United States, see Jorge Heine and Juan M. García-Passalacqua (eds.) The Puerto Rican Question. New York, NY: Foreign Policy Association (Headline Series 266, November/December 1983).

2. For Puerto Rico's political history, see García-Passalacqua: Puerto Rico: Equality and Freedom At Issue (Hoover Institution Series on Politics in Latin America). New York, NY: Praeger Publishers, 1984.

3. For an evaluation of the important changes that have occurred since 1982, see J. García-Passalacqua article, "Intertwined Futures: Puerto Rico, The United States, The Caribbean Basin, and Central America." The Fletcher Forum (Summer 1985): 269-294.

4. See Jorge Heine, "Puerto Rico y su 'politica exterior:' aproximación teórica y análisis de 1985," in Heraldo Muñoz (ed.) América Latina y El Caribe: Políticas Exteriores para Sobrevivir (Buenos Aires: Grupo Editor Latinoamericano, 1986); see also García-Passalacqua essay in Abraham

F. Lowenthal (ed.) Latin America and Caribbean Contemporary Record 1985-86, Vol. V (New York, NY: Holmes and Meier, 1986).

5. Unless otherwise indicated, the principal sources for this review are Puerto Rico's 4 major daily newspapers: El Nuevo Día, El Mundo, El Reportero, and The San Juan Star, and the following weeklies: Caribbean Business and Claridad.

6. Statement of Michael G. Kozak, Deputy Legal Adviser to the Department of State, before the House Committee on Interior and Insular Affairs, regarding International Activities of US Territories and Commonwealths (Thursday, 17 July 1986): 1.

7. Bruno Marin, "Le 'Plan Reagan pour la Caraibe:' Port Rico la base americaine." La Tribune de L'economie (Port-de-France) 338, 16 April 1986.

8. El Mundo (14 August 1986): 2.

9. Sara Grusky & Richard Ruth, "Puerto Rico and the Caribbean Basin Initiative: The Complexities of Interdependence" (Occasional Papers Series). Washington, DC: Puerto Rico Research Institute, May 1986.

10. On the necessity of a new paradigm in the Puerto Rico-United States relationship, see García-Passalacqua essay, pp. 141-162 in Richard J. Bloomfield (ed.) Puerto Rico: The Search for a National Policy (Boulder, CO: Westview Press, 1985).

11. Ramón de Armas, "El ideal antillanista de nuestros libertadores." Claridad (2-10 January 1986): 12-29.

CUBA'S FOREIGN POLICY IN 1986: CONTINUITY IN THE FACE OF INTERNAL AND EXTERNAL CHALLENGES

by BORIS YOPO H.

INTRODUCTION

DURING 1985-1986, a major reorganization of Cuba's internal decisionmaking apparatus took place. Not only were leaders replaced at the highest echelon, but various ministers and hundreds of mid-level officers in industry, the ministries, and the party were affected as well. For example, at the Third Congress of the Cuban Communist Party (CCP), held in February 1986, some 37% of the members of the Central Committee were replaced, reflecting the magnitude of the internal reforms set in motion by Fidel Castro since the end of 1984. Fundamental reasons behind this crisis have to do with the administration of the economy and its internal effects (social and political) on domestic Cuban society.

Given that Cuba's political stability has been linked to Cuban involvement on the international scene since the early days of the revolution (and conversely: domestic stability has allowed the Cuban regime to project its influence at the world level), whatever happens in Cuba's foreign policy will not only bear the stamp of these domestic changes (still going on), but their success or failure will also will have a significant impact on Cuba's ability to maintain its high profile in global diplomacy. Thus, any changes in Cuban foreign policy over the last few years must be understood as a

Boris Yopo H. is a Chilean specialist in international relations and a researcher for PROSPEL.

consequence of both the domestic demands on the Cuban government as well as of the challenges actually confronting Cuba (in its particular role) on the world scene. The following sections analyze Cuban diplomacy by regions, with special attention paid to some of the problems, changes in objectives, and reevaluation of operating tactics which characterize the present style of Cuban foreign policy.

RELATIONS WITH LATIN AMERICA

THE LAST *Anuario* (1985) mentioned that a major Cuban foreign policy success of the last few years had been its growing *rapprochement* with a majority of the Latin American democracies. In 1986, this process grew and deepened, to the point that it is now possible to state unequivocally that Cuba has ended its isolation from the region. Cuban foreign policymakers feel that this new level of relations with Latin America is due primarily to changes in the region itself: democratization, crisis of the interamerican system, more autonomous foreign policies, an increased interest in promoting intra-Latin American relations, and so on. Nevertheless, *rapprochement* was also facilitated by Cuba's emphasis on state-to-state relations as its preferred mode of dealing with Latin America.[1]

On the bilateral level, January saw Flavio Bravo, president of the Cuban General Assembly, visiting Peru to dramatize the cordial relationship now existing between the two countries — despite their 1985 differences over the foreign debt.[2] He was followed by Carlos Rafael Rodríguez, Vice-President of Cuba, who visited Lima in May. Subsequent to these visits, Cuba extended its loan of two fishing boats to Peru for six more months without charge. In September, the Cuban leader twice met with President Alan García during the Non-Aligned conference in Zimbabwe.[3]

Despite ideological differences, Cuba's relations with the government of President Febres Cordero of Ecuador remained friendly. In January 1986, a parliamentary delegation from Ecuador, headed by its president, visited Havana; Cuba's Vice-Minister Antonio Nuñez then reciprocated with his own visit to Quito where he met with Minister Edgar Terán. Significantly, and demonstrating the pragmatism which currently characterizes

Cuba's Latin American diplomacy, Havana came out in support of President Febres Cordero when the latter confronted an attempt at insurrection by General Frank Vargas of the Ecuadoran Air Force.[4]

Following a period of tension in 1985, Cuba and Bolivia regularized their relationship in 1986, which was confirmed when Bolivia's Minister Guillermo Bedregal made an official, 5-day state visit to Havana in October, during which he met with President Castro and characterized his visit to the island (the first by a Bolivian Minister) as "historic." Cuba and Bolivia signed three agreements of bilateral cooperation, in which the Cuban government agreed to provide Bolivia with aid in the areas of health, technology, and sugar-cane processing.[5]

Despite the absence of formal diplomatic relations, Cuba also maintained a friendly relationship with Colombia, as demonstrated by Flavio Bravo, president of the Cuban General Assembly, attending the inauguration of the new Colombian president, Virgílio Barco. While the new Colombian leader renewed a pledge that his government would study — "in detail" — the possibility of restoring diplomatic relations with Cuba, nevertheless the veto of the Colombian military still stands, since Colombia's intelligence service continues to hold the Cuban government responsible for organizing a continental conference of guerrilla groups, including some from Colombia.[6]

At the same time, relations with Uruguay received a boost when Cuban Vice-President Carlos Rafael Rodríguez visited Montevideo in 1986. The Cuban vice-president was given a high-level reception, meeting with President Sanguinetti and addressing the Uruguayan parliament as an honored guest.[7] In his meeting with Carlos Rafael Rodríguez, the Uruguayan president indicated that the conversations about Central America were very interesting and the points of agreement were greater than we had previously imagined.[8]

Cuba and Uruguay did sign a couple of agreements. One was an agreement in which each granted the other most-favored-nation status in matters of trade. The Uruguayan Chamber of Commerce signed another which provided for joint production of products to be sold to other areas of the Third World.[9]

1986 marked a significant increase in Cuba's ties with Argentina. Early in June, the Cuban Vice-President went to Buenos Aires where he met with President Alfonsín and Foreign Minister Dante Caputo. The principal topic of conversation was the situation in Central America and the efforts of Contadora to deal with it, with Rodríguez insisting that any peace accord must take Nicaragua's security needs into consideration.[10] Later in the year, President Alfonsín journeyed to Cuba for an official visit, during which Cuba's Defense Minister Raúl Castro met with the Chief of Staff of the Argentine Army, General Héctor Ríos Ereñú.[11]

Warmly received by the Cuban government,[12] Alfonsín explained that his trip to Cuba was "part of Argentina's effort to revive Latin American cooperation and integration" and pointed out — as an important point of shared international interests — that both countries were committed, and active, participants in the Non-Aligned Movement.[13] Among the outcomes of the Alfonsín visit were (1) an agreement to increase trade between Cuba and Argentina and (2) a pledge that Cuba would shortly pay $46 million of its outstanding debt to Argentina (which had risen to $200 million), refinancing the balance on better terms than Cuba could obtain from the Paris Club.[14] Other important subjects of the Alfonsín-Castro conversations were (1) the deteriorating situation in Central America, and (2) the case of Chile, of particular concern to Argentina.[15] As further fallout from the visit, in November Argentina and Cuba signed an agreement to cooperate in the use of atomic energy "for peaceful ends."[16]

Restoring diplomatic relations with Brazil, in June 1986, was the most difficult but, at the same time, the most important step in Cuba's re-insertion in the Latin American community. Although Cuba had explored this possibility for some years,[17] it was not able to realize this goal until the new democratic government took office in Brazil. The importance which Havana assigned to this project can be explained by Brazil's obvious positive projections, economic and political, in the region and the world. The importance which Cuba assigned to this project is borne out by the high level of the delegation which Cuba sent to the secret Paris negotiations (which led to the re-establishment of relations), which was headed by the Deputy Minister for Foreign Relations, Raúl Viera Linares, as well as by Cuba's subsequent appointment of another

Deputy Minister, Jorge Bolaños, as its new ambassador to Brasilia.[18]

In reality, ties should have been re-established in 1985. However, among other reasons, delay was due both to the initial resistance of sectors of the Brazilian military, as well as to the shock created in Brazil by the attempt of Cuban Embassy personnel to kidnap a former Cuban official in Madrid — when the final decision was already in the hands of President Sarney.[19] Moreover, bilateral negotiations were quite complex, as Brazil placed restrictions on the movement of Cuban diplomats and insisted that, for the time being at least, Cuba would not send a military attaché to Brasilia. Finally, the Brazilian Ministry demanded an explicit pledge that Cuba would not intervene in internal affairs.[20]

Relations had just been restored when a major incident took place: the Brazilian government denied entry to a Cuban official, René Rodríguez Cruz, due to a photograph displayed in Brazil by Cuban dissident Armando Valladares, in which Rodríguez was shown shooting political prisoners (photograph dated from the 1960s).[21] Moreover, President Sarney received Valladares in his office, while the Ministry studied his application to establish a Brazilian office for Cuban human rights, a move certain to annoy the Cuban government. Nevertheless, Valladares' accusations against Jorge Bolaños, Cuba's ambassador to Brazil, were not well-received.[22]

Aside from these problems, both parties had an interest in strengthening the newly restored ties. Brazil hoped to increase its trade with Cuba from $5 million (before relations were resumed) to $200 million in 1988. Brazilian businessmen had already visited Havana, and Brazil began to study the possibility of granting $150 million in credit to Cuba. In 1986 the Cuban government obtained $10 million in agricultural equipment from Brazil, and Havana hopes, in the years to come, to increase its acquisition of Brazilian technology and goods, thus replacing, at least in part, its imports from developed countries in the West.[23] Finally, both countries can now coordinate their foreign policies more effectively in multilateral fora, as well as in more specific areas. The appointment of Itamaraty's principal specialist in African affairs as new ambassador to Havana reveals Brazil's interest in using Cuba to heighten its presence in Africa. Brazil and Cuba also agreed to hold bilateral meetings to coordinate their actions toward the United States and the European Economic Community (EEC) regarding the sugar market.[24]

With regard to Central America and the Caribbean, the Cuban government reiterated its support for the Sandinista revolution in 1986, as well as its support for a negotiated solution to the conflict in El Salvador.[25] In an important shift in policy, Cuba endorsed the Cerezo government in Guatemala, its foreign policy of neutrality, and Cerezo's proposal to create a Central American parliament. Cuba also lauded initiation of a dialogue between the guerrillas and the Guatemalan government, while the latter's Minister of the Interior confirmed that Cuba had moderated its position toward Guatemala's internal situation.[26] During the same year, the Cuban government supported Panama's General Noriega in his problems with the United States.[27]

Cuba's relations with Mexico are cordial and remain important to Cuba's diplomatic agenda. The Congress of the Cuban Communist Party reported favorably on Mexico's role in the Contadora negotiations, receiving in return an equally favorable response from the Mexican ambassador in Havana. Carlos Rafael Rodríguez visited Mexico in May; which was followed by a visit to Havana by the former Mexican president, Luis Echeverría, at the special invitation of Fidel Castro. In 1986, Mexico granted Cuba a new line of credit for $150 million so that Cuba could purchase Mexican products, and both countries agreed to make efforts to achieve a better balance of trade — which has favored Mexico up to now.[28]

After its reverses in Grenada and the virtual isolation of recent years, Cuba's future in the Caribbean appeared to brighten. In March 1986, the Guyanese Minister visited Havana and signed a new protocol for bilateral cooperation while Desmond Hoyte, Guyana's new president, affirmed that he would not sacrifice relations with Cuba as the price of increased *rapprochement* with the United States.[29] During the same month, Foreign Minister Isidoro Malmierca paid an official visit to the Bahamas, which resulted in the subsequent appointment of a Cuban ambassador to the Bahamas; Cuba also appointed an ambassador to Barbados.[30] The House of Deputies of the Dominican Republic voted unanimously to restore diplomatic relations with Cuba, and, even though one cannot forecast for the short run, both countries have begun to increase trade ties and other low-level contacts.[31] Cuba takes a positive view of the recent changes in Haiti, while in Jamaica the probable future prime minister, Michael Manley, indicated that he would resume relations with Cuba, though on a less close basis than in the past.[32]

Finally, on the multilateral level, in 1986 Cuba joined the *Asociación Latinoamericana de Integracion* (ALADI) as an observer — demonstrating Cuba's interest in expanding its trade relations with Latin America. Cuba continued to support the Contadora peace negotiations, in 1986 in particular: the Caraballeda Declaration (in January) and the new Peace Act presented by the Group, as mediator (in June).[33] The Cuban Government also increased its presence and participation in the *Sistema Económico Latinamericano* (SELA) and the Latin American Parliament. Moreover, Havana succeeded in allying itself more closely with the Latin American group in the Non-Aligned Movement. For example, at the April meeting in New Delhi, this group of 11 countries (Argentina, Bolivia, Colombia, Cuba, Ecuador, Guyana, Jamaica, Nicaragua, Panama, Peru, Trinidad/Tobago, Suriname) issued a statement supporting Cuba in its differences with the United States. Later, at the summit meeting in Harare (September), the Latin American group appointed President Fidel Castro to represent the region in the opening speeches of the conference.[34] However, Cuba has not expressed any interest in joining the interamerican system in the future, despite recent decisions of the Organization of American States (OAS) affirming its commitment to political pluralism and universalism of the interamerican system.[35]

In summary, in 1986 Cuba began to consolidate its re-entry into the Latin American community, which, in terms of recent chronology, began in 1982-83 with the war in the Malvinas/Falklands and the regional redemocratization process. Cuban leaders have always considered that Latin America was the "natural area" of integration and involvement for Cuba. The recent normalization of diplomatic relations with the majority of the Latin American countries represents, above all, a major foreign policy achievement that the Cuban government will seek to consolidate even more in the years to come. The concern which Fidel Castro himself has shown toward this process (supervising personally the *rapprochement* and bilateral relations with some countries), as well as the Cuban leader's increased interest in subjects of great regional impact — such as foreign debt and religious phenomena,[36] demonstrate that Latin America will continue to be a strategic priority in Cuban diplomacy in the years to come.

RELATIONS WITH THE UNITED STATES

RELATIONS BETWEEN THE United States and Cuba suffered a new setback in 1985 after Radio Martí was established and immigration agreements (signed by both countries in December 1984) were terminated.[37] Other events further exacerbated existing differences, bringing Cuban-American relations to their lowest level in recent years: (1) in October 1985, everyone connected with the Cuban government and/or the Communist Party (with the exception of diplomats registered in Washington or with the United Nations) was denied entry to the United States by the Reagan administration;[38] and (2) in December, Secretary of State Shultz accused Cuba of being directly involved in the military action in Nicaragua.[39]

These actions, plus other decisions in 1985 — such as escalation of the war in Nicaragua and annulment of the Clark Amendment (which prohibited assistance to dissidents in Angola) — by Washington and the US Congress, led the Cuban leaders to expect that, during 1986, the Reagan administration would probably intensify its hostilities toward Cuba and other revolutionary governments in the Third World. It was in this context that Fidel Castro proclaimed in February 1986, through the report of the CCP Congress, that "since Reagan came to power, Cuba has been going through the worst and most dangerous era since the October crisis of 1962."[40]

These apprehensions were only reinforced when the Reagan administration requested funds to modernize its base at Guantanamo, termed by Cuban leaders "an unfriendly and provocative act." In April, the US launched an air attack against Libya which Cuba interpreted as further proof of that administration's interventionist "neoglobalism," and which became the subject of the Cuban president's hard words at the 25th anniversary celebrations of the Bay of Pigs, when he described the attack as a "terrorist act," comparing President Reagan to the Nazi leader Adolph Hitler.[41]

Cuba's response to the increase in US pressure was to reaffirm its support for allies harassed by anti-communist guerrillas. In the case of Nicaragua, the Cuban leader promised to match whatever new assistance the Reagan administration sent to the *contras*, while, in the case of Angola, Cuba hardened its position when Fidel Castro indicated that the Cuban military contingent stationed there would remain until *apartheid* was dismantled in South Africa.[42]

On its side, the Cuban leadership declared, at its party congress in February, that Cuba stood ready to discuss and resolve its historical differences with the United States "always, and when, that country would agree to negotiate seriously, in a spirit of equality, reciprocity, and absolute mutual respect."[43] Thus, Cuba repeated its position of the last few years that it remained willing to negotiate pending bilateral affairs directly with the United States and would not exclude dialogue (if not negotiation) with respect to other areas of difference in which the two countries were involved.[44]

In June-July 1986, a step was taken in this direction when US and Cuban officials opened new meetings to explore the possibility of reviving the 1984 immigration accords. Cuba had expressed interest in re-opening discussions on this subject and, taking advantage of the stay in Havana of one of Senator Kennedy's assistants, Cuban authorities gave formal notification, by letter, of their willingness to discuss re-establishment of immigration procedures.[45] In order to renew this discussion, the Cuban government had relaxed some of its original demands, no longer demanding the closing of Radio Martí (whose existence, besides being a *fait accompli*, had not produced the results hoped for by the Reagan administration) but, instead, asking for establishment of equal rights for Cuban transmissions to the United States.[46]

Finally, early in July, meetings between the Cuban and US delegations opened in Mexico City; however discussions broke down when the Reagan Administration refused to grant the transmission rights sought by Cuba as a condition for reviving the immigration agreement suspended when Radio Martí went on the air.[47] Deputy Minister Ricardo Alarcon later stated that re-instating the immigration agreement would be "impossible" absent a resolution of the transmission rights dispute. However, he also indicated, that, despite the breakdown in negotiations, Cuba had benefited politically since it had established, in principle, the right of his country to make transmissions to all US territory.[48]

Following this breakdown, Cuban-US relations entered a period of renewed chill which lasted through the end of 1986. In his speech on the anniversary of July 26th, the Cuban president strongly censured US foreign policy toward the Third World, particularly the Reagan administration's close relationship with South Africa.[49] The United States, for its part, took new steps to increase its economic embargo of Cuba, particularly in limiting the flow of US dollars and goods which Cuba could obtain through third countries.[50] As part of these measures, the Reagan administration suspended virtually all immigration (with the exception of some political prisoners who had served long prison terms and their families) from Cuba to the United States and placed new limits on tourism and the amount of money which could be sent to Cuba.[51]

In conclusion, it seems unlikely that the relations between Cuba and the United States will improve during the remainder of this administration, particularly given the course of this relationship since President Reagan took office, and taking into account that the beginning of the election campaign in 1987 will restrict any possible normalization, even on specific issues, even more (the Republicans cannot appear to be making concessions to Cuba in the middle of a presidential campaign). On the other hand, looking at the long run, Cuba will continue to search for understandings with the United States on bilateral issues and will maintain a disposition for dialogue regarding international matters involving both countries. Full normalization of relations seems far-off, however, so long as US foreign policymakers seek to modify substantive aspects of the Cuban revolution, such as its political system and specific aspects of its international involvement (especially Cuba's Third World presence and its ties to the socialist camp). Normalizing relations with the United States is a major goal of present Cuban foreign policy, but its leadership will not alter their basic political principles as a trade-off for establishing ties with the United States.

RELATIONS WITH THE SOVIET UNION

WITHOUT DOUBT, 1986 was an important year for the future course of Soviet-Cuban relations. In the political arena, relations ostensibly improved under Gorbachev's new leadership, as evidenced by Castro's presence at the meeting of the Congress of the Communist Party of the Soviet Union (PCSU) in February 1986, as well as by the fact that he occupied a place of honor among the foreign visitors. On that occasion, the two leaders met for the first time, producing a "unanimity of viewpoints on all matters discussed:" Castro and Gorbachev condemned the "new globalism" of the United States, especially in the area of regional conflicts, and pledged they would continue "delivering assistance to those peoples who are fighting for liberation."[52]

Several other indications and symbolic acts during February confirmed this new climate of cordiality between Cuba and the Soviet Union. For example, the Soviets sent a high-level delegation, headed by Yegor Ligachev (Politburo second-in-command), to attend the Cuban party congress, who delivered a message from the Soviet leader to the effect that "Soviet-Cuban friendship is indestructible."[53]

Significantly, neither of the two party congresses (Cuban or Soviet) included the traditional reference to "the correlation of world forces favorable to socialism," which would suggest that both countries agree, at least in general, on the need to adopt a more cautious strategy in the face of the "most tense international situation since the beginning of the postwar period" — as the report of the PCC Congress put it.[54] Over and above this, however, and even though Castro and Gorbachev agreed (in their personal meeting) on the need "to consolidate socialist achievements" and to support liberation forces in Third World countries, important differences were manifest with respect to the capability, intensity, and priority which their respective foreign policies assigned to these objectives. This became apparent when Gorbachev omitted (in the PCSU Congress report) all references to "support for movements of national liberation" — the first omission of this type in PCSU congresses in the last 30 years. In response, Fidel Castro used his address to the PCSU Congress to remind the Soviet leadership of the importance of supporting socialist countries in their struggles for national liberation. Moreover, although Castro praised other aspects of Soviet foreign policy, he insisted that the Soviet Union needed to pay more attention to the economic needs and struggles of the Third World.[55] After a trip to North Korea following the PCSU Congress, Castro returned to Moscow for a second meeting with Gorbachev, which could be interpreted as an attempt of both countries to iron out their respective viewpoints on Third World economic matters and differences.[56]

In the economic area, at the end of 1985 the Soviet Union renewed its agreement with Cuba whereby Cuba may resell, in order to obtain convertible foreign exchange all Soviet oil which it does not consume (about 10 million tons are sent by the Soviet Union annually).[57] In April 1986, the Soviet Deputy Minister of Foreign Trade, Iván Arkhipov, met with his Cuban counterpart and signed 4 economic and trade agreements, totalling approximately US$ 3 billion. According to *Granma*, the Soviet Union increased its financial assistance to Cuba by 50% for the 1986-1990 period.[58]

Nevertheless, important differences emerged in the bilateral economic negotiations of 1986 due to the fact that Cuba experienced a serious deterioration in its income from hard currency owing to a drop in the price of petroleum and a falloff in its sugar harvest (as a result of weather problems).[59] According to Castro, although the island stood to lose about US$600 million in convertible foreign currency in 1986, it appeared that the Soviets would not make up those losses. On the contrary, Gorbachev insisted that Cuba should work to increase its level of economic efficiency and productivity as well as to fulfill its agreements with the Council of Mutual Economic Assistance (CMEA), especially in regard to the sugar quota it has pledged to export to the socialist countries. Thus, it would appear that not only is Soviet assistance reaching its limits but, moreover, it may well be increasingly conditioned on the internal "re-ordering" of the Cuban economy and its ability to fulfill its CMEA commitments.[60]

It was within this context that Castro pointed out (in the report of the Cuban party congress) that Cuba's most important economic goal "is strict compliance with agreements to deliver merchandise which we have with the socialist countries." At the end of 1985, Cuba had to spend convertible currency to acquire half a million tons of sugar in order to meet its commitment to the USSR.[61] It is estimated that Cuba spent another $120 million in 1986 to buy sugar on the free market for re-export to the Soviet Union in exchange for oil.[62] This suggests that the Soviet Union is not making any concessions in this area despite Cuba's domestic economic crisis (especially the shortage of exchange currency) — a reversal of past Soviet practice during Cuba's periods of crisis. Furthermore, news reports indicate that Cuba's requests that the price of sugar be maintained and the price of oil reduced have not fared well. On the contrary, in the 1986-1990 period, the Soviets will reduce the price it pays for Cuban sugar from 40-45¢ per pound to only 30-36¢ per pound.[63]

This situation has given rise to tension and major differences. In spite of Castro's "self-criticism" regarding the functioning of the domestic economy, and his subsequent austerity measures, the Soviets have not agreed (at least so far) to grant new facilities by which Cuba could service its debt to the Western countries. On the other hand, Cuba would be conditioning itself for greater integration into CMEA (a long-time Soviet goal) if it accepted additional Soviet assistance for development of new industries which have not been finished, or are not operating at full capacity, due to lack of raw materials, replacement parts, or investment, which the Soviets have refused to deliver.[64] According to some reports, Cuba abstained from sending a sports delegation to the friendship games in Moscow (July 1986) as an indication of its unhappiness over current differences on economic issues.

Nevertheless, both countries have avoided allowing the occasional differences that have arisen to alter the strategic nature of Soviet-Cuban ties. As in the past, these differences will be negotiated discreetly, thus assuring continuity in the existing close relations. The award of the Order of Lenin to the Cuban leader on his 60th birthday (August 1986) and the recent visit of the Soviet Foreign Minister, Edward Shevardnaze, to Havana (in October)[65] testify that, no matter how great the differences, Cuba will remain as the Soviet Union's principal socialist ally in the Third World.

RELATIONS WITH WESTERN EUROPE

RECENTLY, IN 1986, economic issues tended to dominate Cuba's relations with Western Europe. Financial difficulties of the Cuban economy made that country more dependent on trade with Europe, despite the fact that it represents only 13-15% of Cuba's total foreign transactions. This can be explained, in part, by the fact that (1) the socialist countries cannot totally satisfy the needs of the Cuban economy for goods and inputs (technology and goods to maintain plans for domestic industrialization which the socialist countries do not have), as well as by the fact that (2) exporting to the continent allows Cuba to obtain the foreign currency it needs to finance such imports, as well as to service its debt with the Western countries[66] while, at the same time, (3) facilitating renewal of, and access to, new credits from European banks.

It was in view of this situation that, in his report to the Communist party congress, Castro said

> Two things must be given absolute priority in the investment
> program, but understood well, *absolute priority* to all those
> investments which spare us imports from foreign currency
> areas or generate exports in the convertible currency area ...
> between 1985 and 1990 we must diversify exports and in-
> crease them to US$500 million per year.[67]

The Cuban Government had already considered it imperative in 1985 to expand its economic relations with Europe, so, for example, in the 1985-86 economic plan developed by the "Central Group,"[68] one of its priorities was promoting domestic investment which would produce funds exportable to the West.[69]

Even though Cuba obtained some bilateral credits from European countries[70] and reached a major economic agreement with England (designed to increase bilateral trade by US$500 million in the 1986-1990 period),[71] major obstacles and difficulties have impeded significant progress in its trade relations with Western Europe.[72] For example, in the first quarter of 1986, Cuban-Western Europe trade fell off by 16%.[73] Along with limited European interest in investing in Cuba,[74] a major problem in its financial relations with Europe in 1986 has been Cuba's difficulty (due to above-mentioned foreign exchange crisis) in paying the interest and amortization of its debt with Western governments and banks. In April, Cuba postponed negotiations with the Paris Club, having rescheduled a substantial part of its US$3.5 billion debt with the Western countries,[75] and it suspended payments of principal but continued paying the interest.[76] In July, Cuba requested that the Paris Club permit postponement of its US$19 million payment of interest and, in the following weeks, suspended all payments on its debt (short, medium, and long-term) due to a serious shortage of foreign exchange. At the same time, the Cuban government sought a rescheduling of its foreign debt, on more favorable terms, from the Paris Club and then asked for at least US$300 million in new funds, of which the Western bank offered only US$50 million.[77]

During the month of September, Cuba and the Paris Club held a series of meetings, but they were not able to reach any substantive agreement which would regularize Cuba's financial status with the Western banks. Meanwhile, the consequences of not paying on its debt could seriously affect the immediate functioning of the Cuban economy (restricting access to inputs, technology, spare parts, etc.) as well as long-range development plans. Thus, for example, Holland postponed a bilateral economic agreement with Cuba (and England is investigating doing the same) owing to Cuba's current difficulties with its foreign debt.

Politically, high-level contacts were scarce in 1986, while certain differences over world and bilateral issues persisted. For example, the Cuban government recently criticized Spain's entry into the North American Treaty Alliance (NATO), describing this decision as a "short-term policy lacking any historical vision of the future." For Cuba, this step implied that Spain would be distancing itself from Latin America and the Third World and would become more dependent upon the United States.[78] In the same vein, the Cuban leaders explained that the parliamentary triumph of the French Right in the March elections was the result of "a vacillating and mistaken policy by the French Socialist Party" and denounced the anti-communist direction of Mitterrand's foreign policy as well as his domestic economic agenda.[79] During his address to the summit meeting of the Non-Aligned Movement, the Cuban president strongly attacked the trade practices of the European Economic Community (EEC), suggesting that the European Community "flooded the world with subsidized agricultural products in unfair competition with the Third World, revealing a self-centeredness bordering on insanity."[80]

Another source of tension between Cuba and some of the European countries has been the issue of Cuban exiles and dissidents. The Spanish Government, for example, refused extradition of a high Cuban official who sought asylum in Spain in December 1985, after appropriating funds of the Cuban government. To avoid more tension between the two countries, Madrid did not grant him asylum.[81] Subsequently, Ricardo Bofill, one of the more prominent Cuban dissidents and president of the Commission of Human Rights in Cuba, took refuge in the French Embassy in Havana, but, despite intervention by Mitterrand, he has not received authorization to leave the country. In a related incident, the Cuban government expelled reporters from the agencies of France Presse and Reuter's from the country after they interviewed the vice-president of the Commission on Human Rights which Bofill directed.[82] Finally, the establishment of Committees of Human Rights for Cuba in various European capitals, as the result of efforts by another dissident (Armando Valladares), constitutes another source of friction between the Cuban government and some of the European countries.[83]

On the other hand, many exchanges between Cuban and European officials took place (besides meetings in international fora), among which was the European tour of Deputy Foreign Minister Jorge Bolaños in April; the trip to Stockholm of Cuba's Vice-President Carlos Rafael Rodríguez in March to attend the funeral of Swedish leader Olaf Palme (for whom the Cuban government declared 3 days of national mourning as an indication of its friendship with the late Swedish prime minister); and the attendance of Deputy Minister Ricardo Alarcón at a meeting in Spain to discuss Cuba's relations with the Western world.[84]

Concerning visits to the island, the trip scheduled by the president of Cyprus in 1986 never materialized. Without doubt, the most important visit to Cuba from a European was that of President Felipe González of Spain, in October. Spain is Cuba's principal trading partner in Europe,[85] and both countries have maintained flexible relations since Franco's time. González was given a high-level reception in Havana, and Castro bestowed upon him the Order of José Martí. The Spanish president expressed his solidarity with the Cuban people "under all circumstances," announcing that ties between Cuba and Spain go "very deep and will continue so." Among the subjects under discussion were (1) the freeing of Eloy Gutiérrez Menoyo (and others of Spanish origin), which Castro agreed to as a special concession to Felipe González; (2) the Central American crisis, in which both countries expressed "complete agreement" that the Contadora peace proposal was the only viable option; (3) the indemnity pending to Spanish citizens whose properties were expropriated following the Cuban revolution (Cuba agreed to pay US$40 million thus finally solving the problem); (4) Cuba's debt to Spain of 49 million pesetas, as well as (5) the possibilities of increasing the trade between the two countries.[86]

In sum, relations between Cuba and Western Europe in 1986 were characterized by low-profile, but high-level, political exchanges, and by increasingly difficult economic relations, due to Cuba's problems in paying the interest on its debt to Western Europe. Thus, in order for Cuba to normalize its financial-trade nexus with Western Europe in 1987, it would probably have to come to some sort of agreement with the Paris Club; however, this condition must be met at a time when Cuba suffers from a seriously impaired ability to make payments.

RELATIONS WITH THE THIRD WORLD

IN 1986, CUBA CONTINUED to follow a pragmatic course toward the Third World, giving priority to technical assistance and other forms of state-to-state cooperation, as a major adjunct to the military aid which had characterized its assistance in the 1970s. In effect, Cuba has tried to reduce its level of exposure in the Third World, due to the number of conflicts there, and to emphasize issues which lend themselves to South-South cooperation, especially in fora such as the Group of 77 and the Non-Aligned Movement (NAM). However, Cuba remains active in such points of conflict as Angola and Nicaragua, a policy which receives almost unanimous support from the Third World.

In this context, Africa continued to occupy a special place in Cuban diplomatic offensives in 1986. For example, the CCP

Congress reaffirmed its support for national liberation movements in Africa, especially to the African National Congress (ANC), Southwest Africa People's Organization (SWAPO), and the Popular Front for the Liberation of Saguiat al Hamra and Rio de Oro (POLISARIO), as well as to those "frontline states" of the African subcontinent which have united to oppose the policies of South Africa. Jorge Risquet, a member of the Politburo, went to Angola to attend the party congress of the ruling *Movimiento Popular de Libertaçâao de Angola* (MPLA) and to pledge Cuba's unconditional support for its government in Luanda.[87] In February 1986, Castro met with Angolan leader at the PCSU congress in Moscow and also announced that Cuban troops stationed there would not be withdrawn so long as *apartheid* existed in South Africa.[88] Castro met again with the Angolan leader in April, when the two leaders signed a new agreement of cooperation and security.[89] Later that year, at both the NAM meeting in Harare as well as during his visit to Angola in September, Castro renewed his pledge to tie withdrawal of Cuban troops in Angola to withdrawal of *apartheid*.[90]

Cuba has sought to establish state-state relations with other African states, despite the existence of differing ideologies and international aliances. At the end of 1985, diplomatic relations were established with the Ivory Coast, while the Cuban president sent messages to presidents Mabuto of Zaire and Museveni of Uganda, respectively, expressing Cuba's desire to cooperate with both countries.[91] After a visit by Foreign Minister Malmierca to Zimbabwe in January, Cuba and the government of Prime Minister Robert Mugabe agreed definitely to establish a Zimbabwe Embassy in Havana.[92]

While in Moscow in February, the Cuban president met with Mengistu Haile Mariam, the leader of Ethiopia, to affirm Cuban support of the Addis Ababba regime. Later in the year, Giraldo Mazola, Cuba's Deputy Minister for African Affairs, followed up this initiative by travelling to both Ethiopia and Libya for an exchange of views with their leaders.[93] During the same period, Oliver Tambo, president of Guinea-Bissau, and ANC leader Oliver Tambo made a trip to Havana.[94] In the months that followed, Deputy Minister Raúl Roa travelled to several African countries to meet with African leaders, such as Kenneth Kaunda of Zambia, and pledge Cuba's support for national liberation fronts in Africa's southern cone.[95] In September, Fidel Castro himself went to Algeria to cement ties with that country (which has played such an important role in the NAM) and to meet with the leaders of POLISARIO who maintain offices in the capital there.[96]

In the area of technical assistance and trade, Cuba worked to expand its influence in, and ties with, Africa. Along with "no-cost" aid to countries like Benín, Sâo Tomé, and Principe, the Cuban government exported sugar and paper to Ghana, signed a technical assistance agreement with Tanzania (regarding to the sugar industry) as well as trade and other cooperative agreements with Uganda, Zimbabwe, Malí, and Zaire. In addition, Cuba signed a scientific-technology agreement with Zambia for 1986-1988, in which Cuba will supervise various construction projects for the Zambian government. For the NAM meeting, the Cuban government donated 400,000 worth of Cuban pesos for materials and equipment to the Zimbabwe government.[97]

In other areas of the Third World, Cuba refrained from interfering in the internal conflict in South Yemen, though it later offered its cooperation to the new government. Havana also maintained a position of equidistance in the Iran-Iraq conflict; thus, for example, the visit of a Cuban delegation to Iraq was later offset by the Iranian Foreign Minister's visit to Havana in June.[98] The Cuban president, on his part, sent the Cuban Minister of Education to Syria to demonstrate support for that country in the face of US threats. He also sent a message of congratulations and support to the new leader of Afghanistan, with whom he later negotiated an agreement of cooperation when the latter paid a follow-up visit to Havana.[99]

Castro also continued his low-profile approach to the People's Republic of China (PRC).[100] Early in 1986, Cuba rescheduled its debt payments to the Chinese government and signed a new 5-year protocol, which was followed by the visits of two official PRC delegations to Havana. Nevertheless, Cuba maintained its position that Chinese "aggression" toward Vietnam remains an obstacle to improved Cuban-PRC relations countries[101] given Cuba's ongoing support for Vietnam — as demonstrated by the attendance of Vice-President Carlos Rafael Rodríguez at the funeral of Vietnamese leader Le Duan in October.

Finally, Cuba sought to strengthen its position in the NAM, and Castro's attendance at its meeting in Harare in September stands as testimony to the importance which the Cuban government ascribes to this event. To this end, Cuba tightened its relations with key countries in the Movement, such as India, Algeria, and Yugoslavia. The Cuban Foreign Minister attended the NAM planning conference in New Delhi in April, and Deputy Foreign Minister Raúl Roa visited India in May.[102] In mid-1986, Castro himself travelled to Yugoslavia (ending a 10-year absence), describing his visit as an indication of the closer — and growing — interests of the two countries, after a period of strong differences over NAM policies in the 1970s. Following some years of only limited trade, both countries agreed to increase their cooperation in trade matters during the 1986-1990 period.[103]

In sum, Cuba did strengthen its presence in the Third World in 1986, emphasizing interstate relations as its preferred mode of operation. Thus Cuba has adopted a more cautious strategy to deal with the multiplicity of Third World conflicts, with Cuban leaders opting for a more cooperative, amicable role, and focussing attention on those issues of greatest importance to Cuban policymakers in recent years: South Africa, foreign debt, and US "neo-globalism" (the Reagan Doctrine), designed to destabilize such major Cuban allies as Angola and Nicaragua.[104]

CONCLUSION

CUBAN FOREIGN POLICY had only uneven success in 1986. Without a doubt, its greatest success was re-establishing of diplomatic ties with Latin American, ending 20 years of isolation in the region. Also, to a large degree, Cuba helped the Third World to recover from setbacks suffered at the beginning of the 1980s, maintaining its position of leadership in the Non-Aligned Movement and other Third World fora. The strategic character of Cuba's relations with the Soviet Union was re-affirmed in 1986, and Cuba remains the Soviet Union's principal ally in the Third World. Nevertheless, differences over economic affairs and over the policies best suited to deal with regional conflicts created tension in the relationship, but these discrepancies did not appear to threaten their areas of agreement over the long term (the designation of Raúl Castro as possible successor to Fidel testifies to the fact that Cuba will probably consolidate its ties to Moscow in the years to come, since the Soviets view Raúl as more orthodox and pro-Soviet than Fidel).

With the Western world, on the other hand, the relationship ran into new difficulties in 1986. In the case of Western Europe, there were no important political exchanges (despite Cuba's interest, and with the exception of Felipe González' visit to Cuba and Carlos Rafael Rodríguez' visit to Sweden), while the financial relationship entered a period of crisis which will probably make fulfillment of the economic objectives spelled out at the CCP 3rd Congress more difficult. Relations with the United States entered into a new period of deterioration following the break-down of bilateral negotiations in July, and there seems to be no prospect for improvement while the Reagan administration remains in power (in an apparent new setback, the White House recalled the Head of the US Interests Section in Havana and apparently has no plans to name a replacement at the moment.)

Confronted by a difficult, complex international situation (as the report of the 3rd CCP Congress put it), as well as economic difficulties and demands for domestic political reform, Cuba will probably maintain those pragmatic features which its foreign policy developed during the 1980s.[105] This is what the report of the CCP Congress would lead us to believe. After renewing its commitment to the principles and cardinal goals of its foreign policy (anti-imperialism, support for national liberation movements), the other specific international issues which guide Cuban foreign policy interests are: normalizing relations with the United States, emphasizing state-to-state relations as Cuba's preferred operating strategy toward the outside world, fulfilling its economic commitments to the socialist bloc, promoting increased trade with Europe, and strengthening Cuba's role in the NAM through strategies based on consensus and agreement.[106] The extent to which Cuba can attain these objectives will determine its foreign policy profile in the 1980s.

NOTES

1. For the perceptions of Cubans regarding this *acercamiento*, see the interview of Cuban Vice Chancellor Ricardo Alarcón in Cuadernos De Nuestra América (july-december 1985: 317-320).

2. Granma (weekly summary) 4 August 1985: 4; DESCO (Lima) (weekly summary) 28 September 1985: pp. 1-2.

3. ALASEI, AL-RC MEX-499-86 83.

4. Agencia Efe (Madrid), 8 February 1986.

5. Prensa Latina (Havana), 9 October 1986.

6. El Siglo (Bogotá), 15 March 1986.

7. The address of the Cuban Vice President was extremely moderate, emphasizing that Cuba was interested in Latin American integration and was not trying to export its revolution. See La Hora (Montevideo), 30 March 1986.

8. Agencia IPS (Montevideo), 28 May 1986.

9. Prensa Latina (Havana), 28 May 1986.

10. El Mercurio (Santiago), 2 June 1986: A-7.

11. Prensa Latina (Habana), 20 October 1986.

12. The Cuban Government declared a holiday the day Alfonsín arrived. According to comments made by Cuban officials, the reception for Alfonsín "could only be compared to that given Omar Torrijos in 1975" (Somos, 22 October 1986:. 11-12).

13. On the other hand, Alfonsín asked Cuba not to transmit its conflict or bilateral problems with the United States to the region (*Ibid.*: 12).

14. *Ibid.*: 10.

15. Somos, 527 (29 October 1986): 16.

16. El Comercio (Lima), 26 November 1986.

17. Veia, 930 (2 July 1986): 25.

18. *Ibid.*: 27-28.

19. *Ibid.*: 23-24; El Mercurio, 27 June 1986: A-7.

20. El País, 27 June 1986: 6; Informe Latinoamericano, 10 June 1986: 310.

21. Colonel Rodríguez Cruz is the director of the Cuban *Instituto para la Amistad entre los Pueblos* (Veia, 940 [10 September 1986]: 54).

22. *Ibid.*

23. El País (27 June 1986): 6; Prensa Latina, 22 September 1986.

24. Informe Latinoamericano (13 November 1986): 518; Veia, 930 (2 July 1986): 23.

25. Miami Herald (9 February and 22 February 1986). For more details about Cuban politics in Central America, see p. 147 in America Latina y El Caribe: Politicas Exteriores para Sobrevivir, Heraldo Muñoz (ed.) [Buenos Aires: GEL, 1986].

26. Verde Olivo, 3 (23 January 1986); Informe Latinoamericano (25 April 1986): 189.

27. Granma, 9 July 1986.

28. Cuba Update, 1-2 (Winter-Spring 1986): 7; Agencia IPS (Havana), 23 June 1986; Radio Rebelde (Havana), 2 June 1986.

29. Granma, 21 March 1986; El Nacional (Caracas), 23 June 1986.

30. The Tribune (Nassau), 8 May 1986: 1; Granma, 18 July 1986.

31. Agencia Reuters, 17 September 1986; ALASEI (AL-RC MEX-554-86-86).

32. The Daily Gleaner (Kingston), 12 June 1986: 5.

33. Cuba supports Contadora for three basic reasons: (1) the concluding of a peace agreement would serve to limit the US presence in Central America; (2) since it functions outside the inter-Aamerican system, Contadora lays the foundation for a future inter-Aamerican political subsystem; (3) the Contadora agreements guarantee the survival of Nicaragua, Cuba's principal ally in the region (América Latina y El Caribe, edited by Muñoz, *op. cit.*: 147.

34. Prensa Latina, 17 April 1986; FBIS (Latin America) 30 August 1986.

35. La Tercera (Santiago), 9 December 1985: 17; El Mercurio (6 December 1985): A-1.

36. Although Latin America's debtor countries have distanced themselves from Fidel Castro's proposals, regional officials recognize that such suggestions have improved Latin America's ability to negotiate with its creditors (see International Business Week, 4 November 1985: p. 31; and ALASEI, AL-RC-MEX-499-85/36). On Fidel's discovery of religion and its impact on Latin America, see Frei Betto's Fidel y la Religión (Santiago: Ed. Aconcagua, 1986), and the Managua publication Pensamiento Propio (No. 33, June 1986: 42).

37. Muñoz' (ed.) América Latina y El Caribe, *op. cit.*: 156.

38. Excelsior (9 October 1985): 2-A; Miami Herald (6 November 1985): 1-A.

39. Cuba Update 1-2 (Winter-Spring 1986): 24.

40. Nevertheless, the United States has maintained reconnaissance flights over Cuba in spite of protests from Havana (Cuba Socialísta 5 1986: 168; Granma, 16 February 1986: 22).

41. Miami Herald, 21 April 1986.

42. Washington Post, 9 February 1986; Miami Herald, 9 February 1986.

43. A policy of opening towards the United States has not always received universal support within the Cuban PC. One of the factors which resulted in the removal of Antonio Pérez Herrero in 1985 (then responsible for the regime's ideological affairs) was precisely his opposition to the expansion of relations initiated between the two countries in the December 1984/May 1985 period (see p. 120 in Jorge Dominguez' "Cuba in the 1980s," in the Fall 1986 issue of Foreign Affairs).

44. Author interview with Ricardo Alarcón, Vice Chancellor of Cuba, in June 1985.

45. New York Times, 3 July 1986; Miami Herald, 7 July 1986.

46. Miami Herald, 10 July 1986.

47. New York Times, 11 July 1986.

48. In the negotiations, Cuba also demanded that the name of Radio Martí be changed. For Cuba, these conversations were basically of symbolic importance: extracting from the US a recognition of Cuba's right to transmit into US territory as well (Miami Herald, 29 July 1986).

49. Cuba Socialista 5 (October 1986): 134.

50. New York Times, 11 August 1986.

51. Los Angeles Times, 15 August 1986.

52. Agencia TASS (Moscow), 3 February 1986.

53. Problems of Communism (March-April 1986): 45.

54. Cuba Update 1-2 (Winter-Spring 1986): 45.

55. Foreign Broadcast Information-Latin America (FBIS-LAM), 26 February 1986: 1-46; and 27 February 1986: 1-2.

56. On his first visit to North Korea, Fidel Castro signed a major 20-year agreement for cooperation in the areas of defense and security. Korea also extended credit to Cuba to obtain 100,000 automatic rifles and millions of munitions. One of the immediate goals of this Korean-Cuban *rapprochement* was to establish a more effective resistance to the Reagan administration's Third World policy (Agencia TASS, 3 September 1986; Granma, 11 March 1986).

57. Financial Times, 8 January 1986.

58. The Washington Post, 12 April 1986.

59. Cuba Socialista 5 (October 1986): 128-133.

60. Actually Cuba receives about 51% of the total Soviet assistance to the Third World (Problems of Communism, March-April 1986: 51; Juventud Rebelde, 23 September 1986: 1).

61. During 1984 negotiations, the Soviets conveyed to Vice-President Carlos Rafael Rodríguez that "the more Cuba would fulfill its obligations, the better relations would be" between the two countries (Latin American Weekly Report, 31 May 1985: 6; South, July 1985: 22; Cuba Socialista 5, October 1986: 17).

62. Financial Times, 7 May 1986.

63. Foreign Broadcast Information Service-Latin America (FBIS-LAM) 3 September 1986: 1-2; Market Report, 21 August 1986: 1.

64. Juventud Rebelde, 23 September 1986: 1; Granma, 23 September 1986: 3).

65. Miami Herald, 14 August 1986; Los Angeles Times, 6 October 1986.

66. Muñoz (ed.) América Latina y El Caribe, *op. cit.*: 101.

67. Cuba Socialista 5 (October 1986): 14.

68. Muñoz (ed.) América Latina y El Caribe, *op. cit.*: 159.

69. *Ibid.*

70. Austria gave Cuba US$ 6.5 million in trade credits to buy chemical products, and Canada gave another US$13 million for Cuba's tourist industry. A French company invested close to US$30 million for Cuban

port repairs and installations (Financial Times, 10 October 1986; Radio Rebelde [Havana], 15 May and 2 June 1986).

71. Financial Times, 31 January 1986.

72. One of the obstacles to Cuban-European trade is Cuba's membership in COMECON, which prevents Cuba from participating in the Lomé Convention, by which the EEC grants preferential treatment to exports from the Third World. There are also problems regarding EEC products which compete with leading Cuban exports, particularly since the EEC decided, some years ago, to enter the sugar industry and hopes, via subsidized prices, to capture 25% of the world sugar market. Finally, there are political obstacles. For instance, even though Cuba is the largest Caribbean trade partner of the Federal Republic of Germany, Havana's reluctance to sign the so-called "Berlin Clause" (which recognizes West Berlin as part of the German Republic) has at times impeded export financing and insurance necessary for some businesses to send new exports to Cuba at times (Financial Times, 27 June 1985; South, July 1985: 22; Latin American Weekly Report, 19 April 1985: 9).

73. Financial Times, 29 October 1986.

74. See p. 20 of "Cuba's Economy in the 1980s," by Jorge Pérez-López, which appeared in the September-October 1986 issue of Problems of Communism.

75. Miami Herald, 1 May 1986; Wall Street Journal, 7 May 1986.

76. Financial Times, 14 May 1986.

77. Financial Times, 10 July 1986; Wall Street Journal, 22 July 1986.

78. Radio Rebelde, 3 March 1986; Granma, 21 February 1985.

79. Cable Agencia AFP (Paris), 11 May 1986.

80. La Segunda (Santiago), 2 September 1986: 10.

81. Informe Latinoamericano, 20 November 1986: 539.

82. New York Times, 31 August 1986; Miami Herald, 30 August 1986; Granma, 26 September 1986: 3.

83. *Ibid.*

84. Informe Latinoamericano (18 April 1986): 179.

85. See p.55 of "Cronología de las Relaciones entre Europa Occidental y América Latina: 1985," Working Paper 2 of IRELA (Instituto de Relaciones Europeo-Latinoamericans, Madrid), 1986.

86. El País (17 November 1986): 1, 11.

87. A number of African leaders visited Havana in 1985, including the presidents of Sri Lanka, Zambia, and Tanzania (Excelsior, 20 October 1985: 2-A; Cuba Update 1-2, Winter-Spring 1986: 24).

88. This announcement is less flexible than others made by Fidel Castro in 1985, when the main rationale for withdrawing troops appeared to center on the independence of Namibia (see Excelsior, 22 November 1985: 2-A; Washington Post, 9 February 1986).

89. Granma, 10 April 1986.

90. Miami Herald, 3 September 1986.

91. Radio Habana, 17 January and 10 February 1986.

92. The Prime Minister of Zimbabwe, Robert Mugabe, visited Havana in October 1985 (Miami Herald, 23 October 1985; Prensa Latina, 24 January 1986).

93. Radio Habana, 1 and 26 February 1986.

94. Granma (16 February 1986): 22.

95. Foreign Broadcast Information Service (FBIS-SSA), 15 July 1986.

96. Miami Herald, 11 September 1986.

97. Granma (13 June 1986): 5; FBIS-SSA (15 July 1986); FBIS-LAM (25 August 1986): 2.

98. Granma, 6 March 1986; Prensa Latina, 28 May and 24 June 1986.

99. Granma, 9 May 1986.

100. Radio Rebelde, 1 March 1986.

101. Radio Rebelde, 4 February 1986.

102. The Prime Minister of India visited Cuba in 1985 where he was given a high-level reception (Excelsior, 22 November 1985: 2-A; Informe Latinoamericano, 22 November 1985: 543; Granma, 16 April 1986; Miami Herald, 3 September 1986).

103. Cable Agencia Tanjug, 19 March 1986; Miami Herald, 3 September 1986.

104. The outcome of the Harare summit meeting was not particularly auspicious from the Cuban standpoint: Nicaragua was not chosen as site of the 1990 NAM meeting, nor were the more radical proposals for dealing with foreign debt adopted (FBIS-LAM, 2 September 1986).

105. On Cuban domestic reforms and their impact on foreign policy, see pp. 143-66 in Munoz (ed.) America Latina y El Caribe, *op. cit.*; and pp. 118-35 in the article by Jorge Domínguez in the Fall 1986 issue of *Foreign Affairs*.

106. Radio Rebelde (Havana), 4 and 7 February 1986; Cuba Socialista 5 (October 1986): 4-18.